The Rationality of Science

W. H. Newton-Smith

Balliol College, Oxford

London and New York

0292938

First published in 1981
by Routledge & Kegan Paul Ltd
Reprinted in 1983 and 1986

Reprinted 1990, 1991, 1994, 1996
by Routledge
11 New Fetter Lane, London EC4P 4EE
29 West 35th Street, New York NY 10001

© W. H. Newton-Smith 1981
Set in Press Roman by
Hope Services, Abingdon, Oxfordshire
and printed in Great Britain by
Redwood Books, Trowbridge, Wiltshire

British Library Cataloguing in Publication Data
A catalogue record for this book is available from the British Library

Library of Congress Cataloguing in Publication Data
A catalogue record for this book is available from the Library of Congress

ISBN 0–415–05877–5

For
Apple Casey Newton-Smith

CONTENTS

Contents

Contents

ACKNOWLEDGMENTS

This book began life as a series of lectures given at Oxford. Subsequent versions evolved through lectures given at the universities of Aarhus, Malaysia, Nijmegen, Oslo and the Inter-University Centre for Post-graduate Studies in Dubrovnik. I am thankful for the constructive criticism of those who attended these lectures. I would like to have been able to benefit from the comments of my Czechoslovakian colleagues on Chapter I, and hope that this will one day be possible. In the meantime my thoughts are with those colleagues whose work on Philosophy in most difficult circumstances is an inspiration. Without the opportunity of having sabbatical leave in Hilary Term 1980 I would not have been able to produce the final version and I am grateful to the Master and Fellows of Balliol College for having made that possible. During this time I was a visitor at the Institute of Philosophy, Nijmegen University, and I wish to thank the members of the Institute for their hospitality, particularly Professor A. A. Derksen, whose careful and penetrating criticisms saved me from many an error.

In the course of this book Popper, Kuhn, Feyerabend and Lakatos are severely criticized. No one should assume that I wish to belittle their achievements. I have learned more from their work about the nature of science than from any other source, with the exception of Hilary Putnam's writings. We are fortunate to have (and, in Lakatos, sadly to have had) such lively, forceful and provocative articulations of varying perspectives on the scientific enterprise. Their writings have given form to the most important contemporary questions about science.

Sections of the book have appeared in *Social Sciences Information*, *Critique* and *Grazer Philosophische Studien* and I am grateful to the publishers and editors for permission to reproduce these. For the production of the typescript I am thankful to Mrs Mary Bugge and my secretary, Miss Jane Long. Mrs Bugge and Mr Peter Lipton generously gave invaluable help with the proofs, as did Mr Eckart Förster with the index. To them and to my editor, Mr David Godwin, whose suggestion it was that I write this book, I am most grateful.

Square brackets have been used in quoted passages to indicate my interpolations.

I

THE RATIONAL IMAGE

1 THE SCIENTIFIC IMAGE

The image that the scientific community likes to project of itself, and indeed the image that most of us accept of that community, is that of rationality par excellence. The scientific community sees itself as the very paradigm of institutionalized rationality. It is taken to be in possession of something, the scientific method, which generates a 'logic of justification'. That is, it provides a technique for the objective appraisal of the merits of scientific theories. In addition it has even been claimed by some that the scientific method includes a 'logic of discovery', which is to say that it provides devices to assist the scientist in the discovery of new theories. And in the noble (or perhaps it is Nobel) pursuit of some worthy aim (variously characterized as truth, knowledge, explanation, etc.) the members of the community dispassionately and disinterestedly apply their tools, the scientific method, each application of which takes us a further step on the royal road to the much esteemed goal.

By and large philosophers of science in the twentieth century have accepted this image and have expended considerable effort in analysing the theories and methods of science on the assumption that the realities of the situation at least approximate to the image. If a slightly more modest view of science is occasionally advanced, this is usually because an even more modest view is taken of other forms of human activity. Thus Popper writes:[1]

> The history of science, like the history of all human ideas, is a history of irresponsible dreams, of obstinacy, or error. But science is

one of the very few human activities – perhaps the only one – in which errors are systematically criticized and fairly often, in time, corrected. . . in other fields there is change but rarely progress.

The overwhelming popularity of this image of science arises in part at least from the great successes of recent science, particularly physics. How else are the successes of 'hard' science to be explained except on the assumption that there is some privileged method and a community that disinterestedly applies that method? That is, it is assumed that there must be something special about the method and the community in order to account for the superior achievements of science. Indeed philosophers and others who stumble on without reaching community-wide consensus on obviously successful theories are often seen as perversely and wilfully spurning this epistemologist's stone. If only the philosopher and his compatriots in the Kingdom of Darkness would emulate the scientist he would acquire the capacity 'to solve those problems that in earlier times have been the subject of guesswork only'.[2] In the *Rise of Scientific Philosophy*, Reichenbach, from whom this quote is taken, claimed:[3]

> Those who do not see the errors of traditional philosophy do not want to renounce its methods or results and prefer to go along a path which scientific philosophy has abandoned. They reserve the name of philosophy for their fallacious attempts at a superscientific knowledge and refuse to accept as philosophical a method of analysis designed after the pattern of scientific enquiry.

Recently this image of science has come under attack from various historians, sociologists and philosophers of science. Feyerabend, for instance, regards the beliefs implicit in this image as not merely unjustified but as positively pernicious. Towards the end of *Against Method* he urges us to 'free society from the strangling hold of an ideologically petrified science just as our ancestors freed *us* from the strangle hold of the One True Religion!'[4] For Feyerabend, Kuhn and others, not only does scientific practice not live up to the image the community projects, it could not do so. For that image, it is said, embodies untenable assumptions concerning the objectivity of truth, the role of evidence and the invariance of meanings. Consequently the image is not even capable of serving as an ideal which the practice of science ought to aspire to realize. Further, for Feyerabend at least, the pretensions of the community that it does approximate to the image represent a distorting ideology which is propounded to serve the interests of the scientific community.

If one wishes to consider the extent to which the scientific community's image of itself corresponds to the realities of the situation, a fruitful starting point is to investigate the phenomenon of scientific change. For viewed *sub specie eternitatis* scientists (even physical scientists) are a fickle lot. The history of science is a tale of multifarious shiftings of allegiance from theory to theory. Newtonian mechanics had its hour of flourishing with virtual universal allegiance. Then, following a dramatic and brief period of turbulence, relativistic mechanics came to the fore and is espoused with the same universal allegiance and firm commitment on the part of the community. Much scientific activity consists in accounting for or explaining change. This shifting of allegiances from theory to theory which will be referred to as *scientific change* is itself a type of change that requires explanation. But what sort of explanation? In regard to this question we face what Kuhn would describe as a pre-paradigmatic situation. Unlike the situation in contemporary physical sciences where for many areas of investigation the community of investigators are generally agreed on the form or type of explanation to be sought, we find that when we take science itself as the subject of our investigation there is no such agreement. In this case detailed putative explanations are few and far between. Instead we find only radically divergent types of explanatory sketch. The differences between the proponents of these sketches go as deep as intellectual divergences ever go, involving in this case differences concerning the objectivity of truth, the possibility of rational discourse, the nature of values, language and meaning and explanation, among others. It will be fruitful to begin by dividing models for the explanation of scientific change into two classes, one to be called *rational models* of scientific change, the other to be called *nonrational models*. For as we shall see, we shall only be justified in regarding scientific practice as the very paradigm of rationality if we can justify the claim that scientific change is rationally explicable. At this stage the division must be regarded as a tentative one drawn to assist us in focusing on the central issues in this area. In the course of this book the division will be seen to be of more than organizational significance.

2 RATIONAL MODELS OF SCIENTIFIC CHANGE

A rational model involves two ingredients. First, one specifies something as the goal of science. That is, scientists are taken as aiming at the production of theories of some particular kind. For example, it might be said as Popper would say that the goal of science is the production of true explanatory theories. Or it might be held that the goal is the production of theories that are useful for making predictions (never mind about truth). It is taken that one can justify the claim that science ought to have this goal or that science is constituted as the enterprise of pursuing the goal. Second, some principle or set of principles are specified for comparing rival theories against a given evidential background. Such principles (frequently referred to as a methodology) rate the extent to which theories actually achieve or are likely to achieve the goal in question. Rationalists, among whom I include Popper, Lakatos and Laudan, differ greatly in the specification they offered both of the goals of science and of the principles of comparison.

Given a particular shift in the allegiance of the scientific community, say the shift from Lorentz ether drift theories to Einstein's Special Theory of Relativity at the turn of this century, this shift will be held to have been explained in terms of the rational model if the following conditions obtain:

1 The scientific community had as its goal the goal posited by the model.
2 On the evidence then available, the new theory T_2 was superior to the old theory T_1 (relative to the principle of comparison specified by the model).
3 The scientific community perceived the superiority of T_2 over T_1.
4 This perception motivated the members of the community to abandon T_1 in favour of T_2.

That is, the explanation of the shift of allegiance from T_1 to T_2 is simply that the community saw that T_2 was a better theory. I will describe such an explanation of a particular scientific change as one which explains the change in terms of *internal factors*. The qualification 'internal' means that the factors cited relate only to features of the theories in question and to features concerning the relation between the theories and the available evidence. By contrast, psychological or sociological factors relating not to the theories and the evidence but to the

4

proponents themselves (i.e., their propagandizing abilities, the social climate of the time, etc.) will be called *external factors*. In so far as a particular scientific change is amenable to a rational explanation, that explanation makes no reference to such factors.

To this juncture I have referred only to the explanation of change. While it is change that we most frequently wish to see explained, there are occasions on which it is not change but its absence that needs explaining. There have been, for instance, cases where the scientific community was particularly slow in shifting its allegiance from one theory to another where in retrospect the latter theory is held to be and to have been greatly superior to the former theory. If this absence of change is to be explicable on a rational model, it will have to be shown that at the time, appearances notwithstanding, the new theory was not superior to the old theory. If this absence of change can only be explained by reference to the facts that the proponents of the earlier theory used, say, control of the journals and of academic appointments to suppress the efforts of the proponents of the rival theory, then it is not in this sense rationally explicable. While for ease of exposition I will in general talk only of scientific change, it is to be taken that the same considerations apply in the context of an absence of change.

To give a little further concrete content to this notion of a rational account of the scientific enterprise, consider briefly a particular example, in this case an example of the absence of change. In the early 1800s Young articulated a wave theory of light. At the time the prevailing opinion favoured corpuscularian theories of light of the type advocated by Newton. Eventually, however, everyone came to favour wave theories of light. Indeed, it seems to many so obvious that wave theories are right, and could be seen to be better in the early 1800s, that attempts have been made to explain this absence of change by reference to external factors. It is said that Young was simply ignored because of the hero-worship of Newton (if Newton said it, it had to have something going for it). Reference is also made to Young's alleged unfortunate manner of presentation and to an anonymous character assassination of Young published in the *Edinburgh Review*.[5] Those who take it that this failure of the community to shift its allegiance can be rationally explained endeavour to show that Young's theory, as it stood at the time, was, relative to the evidence then available, objectively inferior to the Newtonian corpuscularian theories. They will have to show also that this inferiority was perceived. One cannot credit the Newtonians with rational action if they did not perceive the alleged inferiority.

Even those who opt for a rational model of scientific change are not so rash as to assume that all aspects of all scientific changes are rationally explicable. In general it is conceded that there are or may be shifts of allegiance that can be explained only by reference to external factors and, further, that in any particular change that can basically be accounted for on the rational model there will be aspects of that change the explanation of which requires reference to external factors. For a clear example of the contrast between explanation in terms of internal factors and explanation in terms of external factors one can compare Zahar's study of the development of the Special Theory of Relativity[6] with Feuer's account.[7] As Feuer tells the story, questions of the relative merits of the theory were not important. The social climate of the times made the situation ripe for the acceptance of a new theory regardless of merit, and in the revolutionary atmosphere of Zurich one was almost bound to be propounded. In Zahar's account of the matter one learns nothing of the sociological conditions of the time. The entire explanatory role is carried by gradual realization of the relative superiority of Einstein's theory.

The presupposition made by rationalists is that psychological and sociological explanation is appropriate only when the persons whose behaviour is under consideration deviate from the norms implicit in the rational model. An analogy will serve to bring out this point. In Newtonian mechanics we have a framework for explaining change in a state of motion. However, that bodies at rest or in uniform motion continue to be at rest or in uniform motion is not explicable within that theory. Uniform motion is a sort of natural state, deviations from which are explained. This situation is not uncommon in scientific theories. There is some notion of natural states which are left unexplained; explanations are provided only to account for deviations from natural states. What is a natural state in one particular theory might itself be explained through the medium of another theory. The rationalist takes it that behaviour which is in keeping with the norms implicit in the rational model constitutes a natural state for any cognitive sociology of science. That is, sociological explanation of shifting allegiances from theory to theory is appropriate only when there are deviations from the rational model. How much is to be accounted for sociologically, then, depends on how rich the theory of rationality in question is. To see this, consider the fact that some rationalists in this century have construed the scope of evidence as being no wider than empirical evidence. That is, the only factors deemed to be relevant are those relating to the fit of theories with the outcome of observations and experiments. This leads Reichenbach in his discussion of Newton to explain Newton's allegiance to absolute space in external terms. However, one might have a richer theory of rational choice in which relevant evidence is taken to include not only fit with empirical data but also compatibility with metaphysical or philosophical theories. Once the scope is widened the tables might be reversed and absolute space held to be the best bet on the evidence then available. In this case Newton's behaviour might be explicable internally. I do not wish to take sides here. My point is only to draw attention to a question that will concern us throughout much of this work: namely, how wide is the scope of factors that it is rational to take into account in deciding between scientific theories. On the analogy deployed above, the wider the scope the less room there will be for sociological explanation. In addition we shall have to inquire about the aptness of the analogy. Is it really the case that the only role for the sociologist is to pick up the unsavoury rejects from the rationalist's table? While the proponents of rational models make the concession that not all shifts of allegiance can be rationally explained and that not all aspects of a more or less rationally explicable change are rationally explicable, it remains true that they assume that by and large change can be rationally explained and that external factors play only a minimal role. Indeed those (i.e. Lakatos) who adopt a rational model and work in the history of science tend to take as research projects the task of showing that particular changes the explanation of which initially appears to require reference to external factors do not in fact require such an appeal. The residue for the sociologist is taken to be minimal.

To this juncture very little has been said about non-rationalist models for the explanation of scientific change, a non-rationalist model being one in which change is explained exclusively by reference to external factors. It has, for example, been held that the best explanation of the behaviour of science is to be achieved through a game-theoretic model in which scientists are seen as endeavouring to maximize their prestige within the scientific community. Others have sought to explain major changes in science as the causal effects of changes in the organization of the modes of production in society. *Prima facie* such accounts are implausible, for they appear to give no role to the deliverances of the application of the methods of science in the scientific community's decisions. In view of this our first task must be to display what non-rationalists see as the deficiencies in the rationalist programme. Most

7

but not all non-rationalists have been motivated by a conviction that the rationalist programme fails to surmount certain major hurdles to be outlined below. Anyone who holds that the rationalist has failed at one of these crucial points will be inclined to opt for a non-rationalist model, the particular character of which will depend on which of the rationalist's presuppositions are held to fail. My sketch in this chapter of the hurdles facing a rationalist will be somewhat cursory. My intention at this stage is only to give a flavour of the challenges that will be followed up in greater detail throughout the course of this work.

3 THE RATIONALIST HURDLES

As we shall see, one might seek to challenge a particular rational model by showing that it simply does not fit the history of science. That is, a particular model might require one to construe virtually all change as non-rational. If one was courageous one might regard this as showing how poorly the scientific community has fared in attempting to live up to the ideal. However, rationalists are not courageous in this way. For rationalists have tended to argue as follows:

Mature science (i.e. twentieth-century physics) is basically successful. This success is only explicable or intelligible on the assumption that some rational model is applicable.

Thus if a particular model is seen not to be applicable, this argument requires that that model be jettisoned in favour of another rational model. As the commitment of the rationalist is to a research programme designed to vindicate some model or other and not to a particular model, the most serious challenge advanced to the rationalist is the claim that there are presuppositions implicit in any rational model which cannot be satisfied. That is, the most interesting counter to the rationalist position is not that a particular model fails, but that any rationalist model whatsoever involves implicitly untenable presuppositions.

In view of the above it will be convenient to distinguish between two sorts of attack on the rationalist position, one of which will be referred to as *boring attacks*, the other as *exciting attacks*. The boring attack is waged by someone who accepts the rational model as a defensible ideal. He is, however, pessimistic about actual scientific practice in that he may not be particularly impressed by the rate at which science has progressed and, more significantly, he regards scientific change as much more influenced by non-rational factors than would be acknowledged by the scientific community. An exciting attack is, on the other hand, an attack on the very possibility of rational change. As such this attack will be based on the claim that the presuppositions of any rational model of science are untenable. No rational model can even serve as a defensible ideal to which actual scientific practice might be compared. It is with exciting attacks that I shall be primarily concerned. A word of caution is in order here, for it is not always entirely clear whether exciting or boring attacks are being mounted. At times, for instance, Kuhn writes as if his attack was intended to be exciting. However, under criticism he tends to construe his own attack in a boring way. Feyerabend, on the other hand, wages an exciting campaign and relishes the fact.

It should be noted that the use of the labels 'rational' and 'non-rational' without qualification can be misleading. Consider a highly esteemed scientist whose reputation depends crucially on his discovery and defence of some theory. Suppose that, in the face of anomalies, the scientist advances a sequence of hypotheses which he himself believes to be unacceptably *ad hoc* with the hope that he can preserve his reputation for a time (since others may not detect the sleight of hand). This is the sort of situation which in my terminology is to be given a non-rational explanation. However, this is not to be taken as implying that the scientist is not acting rationally. Given his goal and his beliefs this may well be a rational strategy for realizing that goal. The label 'non-rational' applied in this context indicates only that his actions are not rational relative to his goal *qua* scientist. A final answer to our question about the rationality of science requires a general theoretical account of rationality which is given in Chapter X.

4 THE INCOMMENSURABILITY OF THEORIES

The rationalist is committed to articulating a set of principles which provide for the objective assessment of the relative merits of rival theories against any given background of evidence. Clearly this enterprise cannot get off the ground unless theories can be compared. What is characteristic of the position of non-rationalists such as Kuhn and Feyerabend is the claim that this cannot be done; theories are incommensurable. Kuhn's favourite example of incommensurability would be represented by an encounter between a proponent of Newtonian mechanics and a proponent of relativistic mechanics. Even though both may express their theories in English and to a large extent use the same words it does not follow that they mean the same thing by these words. According to Kuhn there has been a shift in meaning so extreme that the concepts of one theory cannot be expressed in terms of the concepts of the other theory. He concludes that the theories simply cannot be compared. If this were the case one would have to say that while the two theoreticians in question appeared to say incompatible things about, say, mass, space, time and so on, they were in fact merely equivocating. Their assertions simply pass one another by without conflicting. Feyerabend seems somewhat more restrained than the early Kuhn in his view of the extent of actual incommensurability. For him it is only in certain conditions (only vaguely specified) that incommensurability arises.[8] However, on his own interpretation of these conditions the particular theory change from Newtonian mechanics to relativistic mechanics counts as a case of incommensurability.

Kuhn, who rejects the standard view that Newtonian mechanics can be derived as a limiting case (for velocities much less than c) from relativistic mechanics because of incommensurability, holds that this 'illustrates with particular clarity the scientific revolution as a displacement of the conceptual network through which scientists view the world'.[9] He goes on: 'the Einsteinian scientific tradition that emerges from this scientific revolution is not only incompatible but actually incommensurable with what has gone before'. It should be noted that there is a major problem here: if they are non-comparable can they be incompatible? Both Kuhn and Feyerabend pass from the thesis of incommensurability to a thesis of the relativism of truth. Kuhn says that the most fundamental feature of incommensurability is: 'In a sense I am unable to explicate further (that) the proponents of competing paradigms (i.e. incommensurable theories) practise their trades in different worlds'.[10] Feyerabend[11] holds that the proponents of incommensurable theories differently constitute the facts. For him there are no facts which are independent of our theories concerning them.

There are a number of sources for this doctrine of incommensurability. In order to bring into focus the nature of this challenge to the rationalist I will consider briefly the chief source (see Chapter VII for a fuller account). To see this, we need to recall the positivist doctrine of the meaning of theoretical terms in science according to which the meaning of a theoretical term in a given theory is a function of the role that term plays in the theory. The role is revealed through two sets of postulates involving the term. In one the term is linked to other theoretical terms in the theory; in the other set the term is linked to observational terms.[12] For instance, an example of the former would be the postulate: electrons have negative charge. An example of the latter would be: magnetic fields in certain circumstances produce a deflection of a compass needle. These postulates are said to define implicitly or to define partially the meaning of the theoretical term. This has the consequence that any change in this postulate set *ipso facto* produces a change in the meaning of the theoretical term. Initially these meaning postulates were taken to be analytic truths. That is, they were held to be true in virtue of the meanings of the words in them. As scepticism grew about the possibility of identifying which postulates of a given theory were in fact analytic truths, and as a more extreme scepticism about the very notion of analyticity developed, and as a realization that plausible candidates for being meaning postulates could not be construed as being entirely free of empirical content, the meaning postulate approach was replaced by a holistic conception of the meaning of theoretical terms. The meaning of a theoretical term was said to be determined by the entire set of sentences within the theory containing the term. Consequently any change in the postulates containing a given theoretical term was claimed to bring a change in the meaning of that term. Thus, if Einstein and Newton discourse about mass, force and all that, they fail to disagree. And this is not because they agree – they fail equally to agree. They are simply equivocating. On this account of the matter the assertion by the Newtonian 'Mass is invariant' and the assertion by the Einsteinian 'Mass is not invariant' are not logically incompatible, as the meaning of 'mass' is not constant across the theories.

For the positivist and neo-positivist, the meaning-postulate approach and the holistic approach were taken to be applicable only to theoretical terms. Observational terms were thought to be directly applicable to experience; their meaning was specified in terms of the verification and falsification conditions given by reference to possible experience. It was taken that while theory change meant change in the meaning of theoretical terms, the meaning of observational terms was invariant under theory change. Hence, the observational vocabulary constituted a theory-neutral observational language. That is, Einstein and Newton could get into genuine agreement and disagreement if they discoursed at the observational level. This would mean that the respective theories could be objectively compared by recourse to the observational level. Thus is Einstein's theory entailed an observation sentence *O* and Newton's entailed the negation of *O* the theories were in genuine conflict. The principles of theory comparison presupposed by the rational model would operate on the observational level with the result, for instance, that one theory might be held to be better than another if its observational consequences tended to be true, whereas the observational consequences of the other tended to be false.

In the post-positivist era an ironic development took place. The critics of positivism (both rationalists, such as Popper and Putnam, and non-rationalists, such as Kuhn and Feyerabend) attacked the conception of a dichotomy between theory and observation. The rallying cry became: all observation is theory-laden. That is, there is no such thing as a theory-neutral observation language. The irony of this development is that the non-rationalists who are militantly anti-positivistic abandoned the observation-theory distinction but retained the basically positivistic doctrine of the meaning of theoretical terms and simply extended it to all terms.[13] Consequently, both so-called theoretical terms and so-called observational terms are treated as being implicitly defined by the theory in which they occur. In this event Newton and Einstein cannot even communicate about the observational consequences of their theories! Not only do they mean something different by 'mass'; they also mean something different by 'The needle points at 4', 'Look, it's turned green', and so on. Thus the non-rationalist rejection of positivism is superficial. A basic assumption of positivism is extended to produce highly counter-intuitive results. Given this thesis that in theory change the meanings of all terms change (hereinafter cited as the *radical meaning variance* thesis or *RMV*) all theories will be incommensurable and there will be no possibility of making rationally grounded theory choice.

Non-rationalists not infrequently represent themselves, in contrast with rationalists, as taking science seriously. That is, it is said that their position is infused with insights derived from a careful examination of the history of science and the actual practice of scientists. It is ironic, then, that the non-rationalists should be led to embrace the doctrine of incommensurability due to *RMV*. For scientists certainly take it that theories drawn from rival 'paradigms' are commensurable. The practising Einsteinian certainly takes his assertion that simultaneity is not an invariant to be logically incompatible with the assertion of the Newtonian that simultaneity is an invariant. This is, of course, merely an ironic

12

feature of the position of the non-rationalists and not an argument against *RMV*. For it may be that scientists are under a truly massive misconception of the nature of their own discourse! While that may be so, the consequences of the *RMV* are so extreme and so counter-intuitive that one has reason to refuse to accept *RMV* unless it is backed by particularly forceful argumentation. Admittedly, if one restricts attention to highly theoretical terms the thesis, as applied to those terms, may seem to be plausible. For some may be inclined to think that in cases in which there is a great change in the set of sentences containing a given term, the term has shifted in meaning. However, the thesis has no initial plausibility whatsoever if it is applied to the terms in such sentences as 'The needle points at 4'.

In so far as one finds in the writings of non-rationalists an argument for *RMV*, it is the argument outlined above which derives from a holistic conception of the meaning of scientific terms together with an attack on the putative observation-theory dichotomy. If one turns to the question of what grounds this preference for a holistic conception of meaning one finds that it is a case of *faute de mieux*. But this is simply not good enough. Consequently, one should regard the non-rationalist case for incommensurability as displaying the need to explore rival conceptions of meaning and not as vindicating incommensurability. Unless it can be established that there is no viable conception of meaning that avoids *RMV*, one should reject the thesis of incommensurability. The chief merit of non-rationalist writings on incommensurability is that they display that an initially plausible conception of meaning is not in fact plausible since it has such unpalatable consequences. The challenge to produce an alternative will be met in Chapter VII.

5 THE GOAL OF THE SCIENTIFIC ENTERPRISE

The rationalist programme cannot even get off the ground unless the problem of incommensurability is solved. If that problem can be solved, the rationalist has to vindicate his claims about the goal of the scientific enterprise and to provide a rational justification for the claim that the principles of comparison relate to the goal. This involves showing that the employment of these principles will tend to increase the chances of attaining the goal. Rationalists have tended to be realists, and part of the realist view of science is the claim (1) that theories are true or false

13

in virtue of how the world is, and (2) that the point of the scientific enterprise is to discover explanatory truths about the world. One's initial reaction when this is made explicit is to regard it as so obvious so as not to need justification. However, a second glance reveals so much that is problematic about this assumption that some have been inclined to conclude that no rationalist model which takes a realist view of science can be tenable.

Some of the problems will manifest themselves if we reflect on the fact that all physical theories in the past have had their heyday and have eventually been rejected as false. Indeed, there is inductive support for a *pessimistic induction*: any theory will be discovered to be false within, say 200 years of being propounded. We may think of some of our current theories as being true. But modesty requires us to assume that they are not so. For what is so special about the present? We have good inductive grounds for concluding that current theories — even our most favourite ones — will come to be seen to be false. Indeed the evidence might even be held to support the conclusion that no theory that will ever be discovered by the human race is strictly speaking true. So how can it be rational to pursue that which we have evidence for thinking can never be reached? Is it rational to try and get to the moon by flapping one's arms if one has evidence that it will not work? The rationalist (who is a realist) is likely to respond by positing an interim goal for the scientific enterprise. This is the goal of getting nearer the truth. In this case the inductive argument outlined above is accepted but its sting is removed. For accepting that argument is compatible with maintaining that current theories, while strictly speaking false, are getting nearer the truth.

This move of re-interpreting the goal of science as increasing the degree to which theories are approximating the truth is viable only if this notion of approximation to the truth is intelligible. Popper's attempt to explicate such a notion (which he calls 'verisimilitude') is, as we will see in Chapter III, an utter failure. And the failure of more recent attempts to provide an account of this notion has warmed the hearts of non-rationalists. Indeed, the failure has been of such a magnitude that in a defensive move some rationalists such as Laudan have sought to develop models which posit a goal other than either truth or approximation to the truth.[14]

This nest of problems will be discussed in Chapter VIII. The two most crucial ones are:

1 What reasons are there for taking the goal to be truth or approximation to the truth? Can one render the scientific enterprise intelligible by assuming some other goal?

2 If no account other than one making the goal approximation to the truth is acceptable, can we provide a satisfactory explication of this notion?

6 PRINCIPLES OF COMPARISON AND THE ACTUAL HISTORY OF SCIENCE

Given that the rationalist succeeds in establishing his claims about the goal of the scientific enterprise, the next step is to provide a rational justification of the particular set of principles of comparison involved in the model. For example, Popper's principles are roughly:

T_2 is better than T_1 if and only if:
1 T_2 has greater empirical content than T_1
2 T_2 can account for the successes of T_1
3 T_2 is not yet falsified, T_1 is falsified.

To justify these principles rationally would be to show that they relate to the specified goal in the appropriate way. That is, to show that if these conditions are fulfilled it is reasonable to believe that T_2 has (or likely has) more verisimilitude than T_1. This is no trivial task. As will be argued, Popper's attempt is a dismal failure. For all his *ex cathedra* pronouncements, it will be established in Chapter II that there is no reason to assume that selecting theories on the basis of these principles will maximize the verisimilitude of our theories.

There is a more general problem involved with regard to the justification of the principles of comparison. It is not simply that Popper's has failed. This general problem concerns the nature of the justification. Some, notably Popper, have attempted to vindicate their favourite principles in an almost, if not entirely, philosophical or *a priori* fashion. Most philosophers of science, including Popper's own followers, have been reluctant to follow him in this. For, unlike Popper, most philosophers of science have a due degree of modesty. Being mindful of the notorious failures of philosophers to tell the physicist how the world has to be (i.e., Kant on the Euclidean character of space) they are mindful of the dangers attendant on telling physicists how they ought

15

to proceed in the task of comparing the merits of theories. They would be disturbed to find their principles giving results at odds with the judgment of the scientific elite (i.e., that astrology is better than Quantum Mechanics or that Aristotle's theory of motion is better than the General Theory of Relativity). One wants to allow the judgment of the scientific elite to have a relevance which it would not have if the Popperian approach to the justification of the principles was correct.

At the same time, no one wants to maintain that the principles are such that every judgment of the scientific community would be in accord with them. There would be no hope of articulating a consistent set of principles given this constraint. For it amounts to assuming that the scientific community is never mistaken in its judgments! The standard ploy used by rationalists at this juncture is to maintain that we can expect to reach general agreement on certain particular dramatic success stories in science. That is, we can expect agreement that Newton's account of motion was better than his predecessors' and that Einstein was better than Lorentz. Given these assumptions we can hope to vindicate our principles of comparison by showing that they give the correct answer in these cases. The principles thus vindicated can be appealed to in making normative assessments of the relative merits of other scientific theories.

It is easy to see that there are seeds here of another source of non-rationalism. For instance, Feyerabend accuses those who attempt to justify principles of comparison in this way of elitism. For Feyerabend, there is no justification for the assumption that modern science is better than magic. Hence any selection of the 'good guys' versus the 'bad guys' (Lakatos's phrases) for the purposes of vindicating a particular principle or set of principles amounts to an ideological judgment for which no rational justification can be given. That is, even though theories may be comparable, there is no possibility of identifying objective principles to be used in assessing the relative merits of the rival theories.

There is a final task facing the rationalist which relates closely to this previous task. For once he has opted for a principle or set of principles, he has the task of looking at the actual history of science to see how well it can be fitted into a rationalistic reconstruction. The rationalist could very well run into problems at this point. If he has made an *a priori* case for his principles and finds that science never proceeds rationally (given those principles) his rational model becomes uninteresting. And if it fits no better with the history of science on a revision of these principles, the notion of a rational model loses utility in just the way that the notion of absolute simultaneity lost utility (i.e., there is no point in talking about it since it never applies). If, like Lakatos, he has attempted to vindicate his principles with regard to a selection of paradigm cases and it turns out that no other scientific changes are rational under those principles, his position begins to look *ad hoc*. Unlike the other three problems for the rationalist, this one is specific to a particular model. It amounts to a general problem only if no rational model fits history.

In summary, then, the following four tasks face the would-be defender of a rational model: first, to defeat the incommensurability argument by showing that theories are comparable; second, to justify the goal; third, to articulate a set of rationally justifiable principles for comparing the relative merits of rival theories; fourth, to investigate the extent to which actual scientific change approximates to the ideal rational model. Non-rationalists base their position on claims that the rationalists fail to fulfil the first three tasks. They also hold that the fourth step fails. This is not generally used, however, as a separate argument *contra* the rationalist. For the failure to clear this fourth hurdle is explained by the non-rationalist via the failure of the first three. That is, if theories cannot be rationally assessed in the required manner it would not be surprising that the history of science fails to approximate to a rational model. Where the rationalist sees progress (or the possibility of progress) judged in relation to his standards, the non-rationalist sees mere change which is to be explained sociologically and/ or psychologically. Theories simply supplant one another. The explanation of these mere changes lies in the external factors and not in the internal factors specified by a rational model.

The notion of a rationalist model introduced in this chapter involves a host of contentious presuppositions and simplifying assumptions. In the course of the following chapters these will be exposed and evaluated. In the end that model as characterized will have to be jettisoned. However, it will be shown that none the less the appropriate perspective from which to view that scientific enterprise is, broadly speaking, a rationalist one.

My aim in this book is to decide between a rationalist and non-rationalist perspective on the scientific enterprise. The notion of a rational model as introduced in this chapter will serve to provide a convenient framework within which to organize the discussion. The positive account that will emerge is a temperate form of rationalism. As we shall see, this requires a vindication of a realist construal of theories. The first steps towards such a vindication will be taken in the next chapter, where a preliminary defence of realism will emerge from a consideration of the nature of observation and theory. In Chapter III I critically examine the theory of science of the most influential rationalist, Popper. This will serve to heighten our appreciation of the difficulties facing any would-be rationalist. For it will be seen that in spite of himself Popper has developed an account which makes science non-rational if not positively irrational. Lakatos, as we shall see in Chapter IV, has a more viable grasp of the actual practice of science than Popper. However, he has inherited sufficient of the deficiencies in the Popperian framework to preclude his vindicating his own particular form of rationalism.

Having found Popper and Lakatos wanting, I turn in Chapters V and VI to discuss Kuhn and Feyerabend, respectively. While neither has made out a compelling case against the rationalist, both have provided challenges (some of which have been indicated in this chapter) which need answering. I show in Chapter VII that the challenge of incommensurability can be met once it is realized that in comparing theories the notions of truth and reference are more important than that of meaning. Having established that theories are comparable, I argue (Chapter VIII) that we have good reason to believe that science is making progress towards the truth and that this in turn provides us with reason to believe, contrary to Feyerabend, in the existence of scientific method. Just how to characterize that method is a complex and controversial matter which will occupy us in Chapter IX. It will be seen that in this area rationalists such as Popper and Lakatos have much to learn from the perceptions of Kuhn and Feyerabend. Having answered the main challenges to rationalism I turn in the penultimate chapter to a discussion of rational explanation. The particular issue concerns the relation between rational explanation and sociological explanation. It turns out that the rationalist's unduly simplistic conception of what it is to explain a transition in science erroneously leads him to assume that the proper province for sociology is exclusively the explanation of transitions that fail to fit his rational model. The final chapter provides a summary of the temperate rationalist position which emerges in the course of the previous chapters.

II

OBSERVATION, THEORY AND TRUTH

1 OBSERVING AND THEORIZING

My central aim in this work is to vindicate a rationalist account of the scientific enterprise based on a realist construal of scientific theories. It will prove fruitful to introduce in this chapter the central ideas and issues concerning realism prior to considering in Chapters III to VI the views, respectively, of Popper, Lakatos, Kuhn and Feyerabend. In these chapters we shall see how difficult it is to combine realism and rationalism and it will require the balance of the book to meet the challenges that emerge. In this chapter a characterization of realism is developed and it is shown that realism is more promising than either of its primary rivals, instrumentalism and relativism. We begin with a discussion of the relation between observation and theory, since it will emerge that the primary difficulty in an instrumentalistic construal of theories is that it presupposes an untenable view of the relation between theory and observation.

Positivist and neo-positivist philosophers of science held that expressions used in science were either observational or theoretical. The class of observational, or O-terms, was held to include such expressions as: '... is warm', '... is yellow', '... sinks', '... points to five'. Theoretical or T-terms included: '... is a field', '... is a quark', '... has spin ½'. The distinction between O-terms and T-terms was supposed to represent a difference in kind and not merely a difference in degree. For it was held that O-terms and T-terms functioned in science in significantly different ways. In our discussion of this view it will be useful to have available the following terminology. By an *observational sentence* I shall mean a singular sentence containing only *O*-terms such as 'The pointer is at five'. The term *theoretical sentence* will be employed to cover any sentence containing only *T*-terms such as 'Electrons have zero rest mass' or sentences containing both *T* and *O*-terms such as 'Electrons passing through a cloud chamber in certain conditions will produce a track recorded on a photographic plate'. By *observational language* I shall mean *O*-sentences used in reporting the outcome of observations. In the next section of this chapter we shall consider the reasons why it was assumed that there was a dichotomy between *O*- and *T*-terms. It will be seen that the assumption in question is mistaken and that no such distinction can be drawn.

The putative distinction (hereafter referred to as the *O*/*T* distinction) is between types of expressions used in scientific language. As such it need not be confused with the viable distinction between the two types of scientific activity; namely, theorizing and observing. Einstein's development of the General Theory of Relativity can serve as a paradigm example of the former. An example of the latter is found in the activities of Eddington and Cottingham when they photographed the field of stars in the Hyades group during the solar eclipse of 1919 in an attempt to test the General Theory. The salient difference between these activities is the following. In the case of the latter one is seeking to produce a true description of the state of a particular physical system at some moment of time. In the former case one is hoping to articulate an interesting generalization or body of generalizations covering the behaviour of all systems of some type. This is usually marked linguistically by the fact that theorizing leads to general statements and observing to singular statements. Of course, these different types of activity may go on more or less simultaneously. A scientist in the course of observing the outcome of experiments may come up with both a singular statement reporting the outcome and a general hypothesis about all systems of that type.

This distinction does not generate any dichotomy between *O*-terms and *T*-terms. For observational reports as standardly given in science frequently involve the use of terms which would be deemed theoretical. For instance, a scientist observing the deflection of a pith-ball in the presence of a van der Graaff generator may report that an electromagnetic field is present. Or, on seeing a track on a photographic plate exposed in a cloud chamber, he may report that an electron was present. This fact points to one reason (others are given in the next section) why the question of the existence of an *O*/*T* dichotomy has seemed of crucial importance. For in theorizing we are indulging in a risky activity in that we produce generalizations going well beyond the evidence. The scientist who makes observational reports of the sort cited above is presupposing extensive theories about fields and particles. Suppose for the sake of argument that there is no O/T dichotomy and that this means that all observation reports presuppose some theory. Under this assumption our naive view that observation provides the primary control on the acceptability of theories seems to generate an impasse. If any observation report presupposes some theory, how do we ever get evidence on the basis of observation for a theory? Surely, one might argue, there must be some privileged class of terms, the O-terms, which can be used in a theory-neutral way in describing the outcome of observation. For unless there is such a language we can never obtain evidence for any theory on the basis of observation without presupposing some theory and consequently we would seem to be caught trying to pull ourselves up with our own theoretical boot-straps. This is but one of the problems we shall have to resolve as a consequence of the arguments to be given in the next section against the possibility of drawing the putative O/T distinction. I have introduced the problem to indicate one of the reasons why the issue of the existence of this distinction is of importance and also to present my own terminological distinction between the activities of observing and theorizing. In future by an *observation report* I shall mean any singular statement reporting the state of a system whether or not that statement involves putative T-terms or putative O-terms and whether or not the report was arrived at with the aid of instruments. Any generalization which goes beyond the available evidence will be counted as a piece of theory whether or not it contains T-terms exclusively, O-terms exclusively, or a mixture of these terms.

Following the critique of the putative O/T distinction I consider in Section 3 the minimal common factor among all realists: namely, the claim that the sentences of scientific theories are true or false as the case may be in virtue of how the world is independently of ourselves. The negative results concerning the O/T distinction are deployed to refute the position of the instrumentalist according to whom only O-sentences are capable of being true or false. After displaying further deficiencies in instrumentalism I consider in Section 4 another rival to realism, relativism. For the relativist, unlike the instrumentalist, the notions of truth and falsity are applicable to all sentences. However, truth is made relative to theory and is construed not as a matter of a relation between a theory and an independent reality. As will be shown, this position is incoherent. Until that juncture I shall have employed a very minimal form of realism. The balance of the chapter will be concerned with the development of a stronger and more interesting form of realism. In Section 5 we consider what ontological claims to add to realism. By supplementing this with an epistemological thesis about the possibilities of discovering which of a pair of rival theories is more likely to be the best approximation to the truth we arrive in Section 6 at the basic form of realism to be defended in this work.

This basic form of realism, however, may require qualification. For, as we shall see in the final section of the chapter, the possibility that there might be two rival theories having exactly the same observational consequences generates a dilemma for the realist. Consequently I outline two alternative responses a realist could make giving reasons for preferring a response which will introduce a limited degree of instrumentalism. However, this limited instrumentalism will be seen to be relatively harmless, unlike the blanket instrumentalism which will have been rejected.

2 THE DISTINCTION BETWEEN THEORETICAL AND OBSERVATIONAL TERMS

Prima facie it looks as though there is an important difference between such putative *O*-terms as '. . . is warm' and such putative *T*-terms as '. . . is an electron'. One can grasp the meaning of '. . . is warm' without having to learn any scientific theory and one can apply the term on the basis of one's perceptual experience with a high degree of justified confidence. By contrast, to learn what is meant by 'electron' one has to have at least a partial mastery of a complex scientific theory. And, furthermore, one does not sense the presence of electrons in the way that one senses that something is warm. One has to use sophisticated equipment to detect the presence of electrons and one's judgment that one has detected electrons is risky in that it presupposes a host of theoretical assumptions. This intuitive characterization of the alleged difference has both a semantical and an epistemological aspect. On the one hand it seems that the meaning of an *O*-term can be conveyed to someone through its direct connection with experience. We teach a child the meaning of '. . . is warm' through an ostensive training procedure in which warm things and things that are not warm are presented.

Eventually he is able to make the requisite discrimination himself. Since no such ostensive teaching procedure is available in the case of *T*-terms their meaning seems relatively problematic. I refer to this aspect of the characterization by speaking of *O*-terms as being *semantically privileged*. On the other hand, *O*-terms might be described as *epistemologically privileged* since we can apply them more easily and can have more confidence in the judgments we form using them.

Corresponding to the semantical and epistemological aspects of the intuitive characterization were two motives some had for wishing to defend an *O/T* dichotomy. If *O*-terms are semantically privileged in the sense that their meaning could be conveyed through their connection with experience, it was thought that their meaning would remain constant through theory change. The meaning of *T*-terms, which can at best (for the positivist) be partially specified by showing their connection both with *O*-terms and with other *T*-terms, changes as these connections alter through theory change. As we noted in Chapter I, even if there is a change in meaning of, say, 'mass' from Newtonian mechanics to relativistic mechanics of such a character that the Newtonian's assertion that mass is an invariant and the Einsteinian's assertion that mass is not an invariant represents an equivocation and not a genuine disagreement, we can none the less regard these theories as being in genuine conflict if one entails an *O*-sentence, '*p*', and the other entails the *O*-sentence, 'not-*p*'. For '*p*', in virtue of being an *O*-sentence, will have constant meaning across this theory change.

If *O*-terms are epistemologically privileged in the sense that we can determine whether or not they apply without making any theoretical assumptions, we can avoid the dilemma articulated in Section 1 of this chapter. For by describing the results of our observations in *O*-sentences we can gain evidence for theories without having to make theoretical assumptions. The proponents of radically different theories whose differing theoretical assumptions might lead them to make different observational reports in the same situation may be able to make progress in resolving their conflict by formulating their observational reports in theory-neutral *O*-sentences.

Those who have defended an *O/T* distinction have sought to defend it as representing a difference in kind and not a difference in degree. For if the semantical aspect was a matter of degree we would have no guarantee that the observational vocabulary is constant in meaning across all theory change. And if we cannot find a class of *O*-terms the application of which is free of all theoretical assumptions, we shall not find the hard bedrock in terms of which the proponents of competing theories can describe their observations without having to rely on theoretical assumptions about which they may disagree. In what follows we first establish that no distinction in kind can be drawn between *O*- and *T*-terms. None the less, a rough pragmatic distinction of degree can be established and that, it turns out, is all we need.

How were the intuitive feelings of a distinction to be cashed out in hard terms? Carnap stipulated that an *O*-term corresponded to an observable quality whose presence or absence could be established by an observer in a relatively short time and with a high degree of confirmation.[1] For Hempel, *O*-terms are those occurring in *O*-statements where such statements:[2]

> Purport to describe readings of measuring instruments, changes in colour or odour accompanying a chemical reaction, verbal or other kinds of overt behaviour by a given subject under specified observable conditions – this all illustrates the use of intersubjectively applicable observational terms.

This characterization is entirely unenlightening unless it is supplemented by an account of what it is that makes a quality an observable one. My strategy will be to take the three most reasonable construals of this notion and show that none of them gives a definition which will sort out terms in the way that Hempel and Carnap assume. First, an observable quality might be taken to be one whose presence or absence can be detected by using our actual perceptual faculties unaided by instruments. 'Force' is a putative *T*-term the application of which can sometimes be ascertained in this way. We actually feel the force of the wind on our faces and we feel a force when we accelerate rapidly in a car. Admittedly we cannot always detect forces in this way. However, if we were to require of observable qualities that they can *always* be detected in this way, even colour predicates would cease to count as *O*-terms, for we cannot detect the colour of small pieces of matter without the use of instruments. It may be objected that we do not sense the force, we only sense its effects and infer its presence by appeal to a scientific theory. This is unconvincing for two reasons. First, we could easily teach a child to apply the term 'force' in certain contexts on the basis of his experience without first introducing him to a background scientific theory about forces. Second, the distinction between directly sensing the presence of something and inferring it on the basis of its effects is problematic. If one assumes that it can be appealed to in the case of 'force', it can with equal justice be employed to derive the conclusion that 'yellow' is not an observable quality on the ground that what I am directly aware of is only a sensation and that I infer the existence of something yellow producing that sensation in me. Thus, a paradigm *O*-term 'yellow' would turn out to be a *T*-term.

A further difficulty with this characterization of observability emerges if we consider the following typical development in the history of science. At one stage genes were posited in order to explain observed phenomena. At that time no one had in any sense observed or detected the existence of genes. However, with the development of sophisticated microscopes scientists came to describe themselves as seeing genes. Presumably, the defender of the *O/T* distinction would now wish to count '... is a gene' as an *O*-term. For we can ostensively display examples of genes and we can be highly confident in our judgment that they have been observed. This suggests a second construal of the notion of observability in terms of which *O*-terms would be those whose application could be decided on the basis of perception with or without the aid of instruments. But this would be to open a flood-gate through which probably all *T*-terms would flow into the *O*-pool. For there are instruments that enable us to detect the presence of forces, fields, electrons, etc. Indeed, it is hard to think of any property which cannot be observed if we count detecting it with the aid of instrument as observing its presence.

It may be objected that while in detecting both fields and genes we use instruments, we actually *see* the gene but not the field. For fields lack colour and anything we can see must have colour. However, this approach is not going to give an *O/T* distinction which makes the use of *O*-terms theory-neutral. For in correctly describing ourselves as seeing a gene we are making theoretical presuppositions about both microscopes and genes. For instance, we are making the assumption that microscopes are reliable and we are assuming that a certain visual appearance is characteristic of a gene. The mere fact that we make a report on the basis of visual experience does not mean that the acceptability of that report presupposes no theory.

If a residual unease is felt at this point it is likely to arise from the following. In describing ourselves as seeing a gene through a microscope we are implicitly presupposing a host of theoretical assumptions. However, if our eyes were much better than they are, we could see the gene without the aid of a microscope. We could then describe what we see without implicitly relying on theory. But suppose we allow something to count as observable on the grounds that it could be detected by beings with superior perceptual faculties without their first having to develop the theory we rely on in describing ourselves as seeing a gene. But on this third construal of 'observable' putative *T*-terms turn out to be *O*-terms. For one can imagine acquiring a perceptual faculty which would enable us to detect the presence of, say, fields without the aid of instruments or theory. Unless some other analysis of the notion of an observable is forthcoming, we should conclude that that notion is not capable of generating a partition of all qualities of the sort assumed by the defenders of the *O/T* distinction.

Carnap's characterization also made reference to the ease with which *O*-terms can be applied and the degree of confidence we can have in their application. To the extent that this aspect of the characterization is stressed, it becomes explicitly a difference of degree and not of kind. In fact, the only way in which one could obtain a difference of kind would be to count as *O*-sentences only those reports of inner experience which are incorrigible. For example, such sentences as 'It seems to me now as if I see a red patch' or 'I am having a blue after-image' are bound to express a truth if sincerely asserted by someone who understands them. To make this move is to construe the *O*-language as a sense-data language. Certainly for some positivists this is what the *O*-language was supposed to be. However, such a position raises a host of well-canvassed philosophical problems which happily need not detain us here. For the object of our investigation is the actual practice of science and such statements reporting merely on inner sensory experience and not making any claims whatsoever about the external world play no role whatsoever in the practice of, say, physics or chemistry.

My dismissal of the alleged *O/T* dichotomy has been brisk. Obviously much more discussion would be needed to make it conclusive. For this the interested reader is referred to Achinstein (1968), Churchland (1979), Hesse (1974), and Suppe (1977). However, enough has been said to indicate the problematic character of the claims of the proponents of the distinction. It remains to be shown that the problems which lead them to articulate the distinction can be solved without it. This is not to say that we need not make any differentiation whatsoever. For the features alleged to identify a special class of *O*-terms do serve to provide a rough and ready pragmatic differentiation between the more observational and the more theoretical which we shall find it convenient to employ. Thus in future when I speak of an *O*-term, I mean a term towards the end of a rough spectrum of terms determined by the following principles:

1 The more observational a term is, the easier it is to decide with confidence whether or not it applies.
2 The more observational a term is, the less will be the reliance on instruments in determining its application.
3 The more observational a term is, the easier it is to grasp its meaning without having to grasp a scientific theory.

It is to be emphasized that characterization is being employed for terminological convenience. It is not an attempt to re-introduce the objectionable dichotomy. To re-inforce this point I will display the sense in which terms from the *O*-end of this spectrum are theory-laden in both the semantic and epistemological sense.

An *O*-term such as '. . . is yellow' was supposed to be semantically privileged in that its meaning was to be specified by giving the experiential conditions in which it was applicable and those in which it was not. To grasp the meaning of '. . . is a field', on the other hand, one has to learn a host of generalizations (a theory) in which the term functions. But if we accept this assumption about 'field' (an assumption which needs qualification, as we shall see in Chapter VII), we have equally to accept it in the case of '. . . is yellow'. For a full grasp of that concept involves coming to accept as true bits of theory: that is, generalizations involving the term 'yellow'. One has to learn that anything which is yellow is coloured. One has to learn that yellow things retain their colour when unperceived and that yellow things tend to look the same colour in standard conditions to different persons. To see that these last two generalizations are essential, imagine someone who has failed to grasp them. As a result he applies the term yellow only when he has the visual experience associated with seeing something yellow and refuses to apply the term to yellow objects when the lights go out. In this case he has failed to grasp that 'yellow' is a name for a quality of an object and not a name for a sensation. Of course there remains a difference of degree between 'yellow' and 'field' in that in the former case the generalizations required are small in number and humble in content. Conceding that the difference in meaning between *O*- and *T*-terms is one of degree and not kind is not going to lead us to incommensurability due to radical meaning variance. For we shall see in Chapter VII that this problem can be solved none the less.

O-terms are also theory-laden in the sense that any *O*-sentence, no matter how well-corroborated by different observers, may be revised by appeal to theory. For instance, prior to the development of modern astronomy, anyone would have said that the stars were yellow and, indeed, anyone not versed in science would still say the same. But on the basis of a highly successful theory of colour and on the basis of an instrument-aided study of stars we reject those observation reports. However, we must not make the fallacious inference that, as *any* observation report no matter how well-corroborated may be rejected by appeal to theory, *all* observation reports might be rejected by appeal to theory. For we can reject particular reports involving O-terms only if we have strong evidence (which will rely on other observational reports) for a theory and if we can find through that theory, or some other, an explanation as to why we were inclined to make mistaken observational reports.

Even this may seem unsettling. If any low-level observation report (i.e., a report of an observation framed using O-predicates) may be revised, how do I know that the particular reports which I rely on in making my theory choices now will not in fact need revising? To this the reply can only be that while we cannot have absolute faith in any particular reports or a particular range of reports, we are entitled to have general faith in the low-level O-reports we are inclined to make. Our success in coping with the world gives us grounds for this general confidence. If such judgments were not by and large reliable, we should not be still here to make judgments. This justification is good enough. Our reasonable general confidence in low-level O-judgments is enough to pull ourselves up slowly. We can gain evidence for theories which may in turn lead to the revision of some of the low-level O-judgments and which will issue in the development of new concepts which we use in making observational reports of the more risky sort, i.e. those involving T-terms. Thus we do not need to seek the epistemological bed-rock sought by some proponents of the O/T distinction.

3 REALISM VERSUS INSTRUMENTALISM

Our conclusions concerning the relation between theory and observation will play an important role in our preliminary defence of a realist construal of theories. For, as we shall see in this section, those conclusions are incompatible with instrumentalism which is the most influential alternative to realism. 'Realism' has been used to cover a multitude of positions in the philosophy of science, all of which, however, involve the assumption that scientific propositions are true or false where truth is understood in terms of a cleaned-up version of the correspondence theory of truth.[3] By this latter qualification I mean that we are assuming that to be true (false) is to be true (false) in virtue of how the world is independently of ourselves. The notion of correspondence is not to be understood as, say, propositions picturing or mirroring the world *à la* early Wittgenstein.

Realism need not be an all-or-nothing matter. Someone might be a realist with regard to some theories and not with regard to others, or someone might be a realist with regard to some but not all the assertions of a given theory. For this reason we need to speak of a realist construal of a class of sentences. One who gives a realist construal of all scientific sentences will be called a *global realist.* As we will be building up a stronger form of realism, we need a label for this minimal aspect of realism. For reasons that will become clear later, the label *the ontological ingredient in realism* will be appropriate. I will describe the position of one who accepts the ontological ingredient in realism with regard to a given class of sentences as a minimal realist with regard to that class of sentences.

Minimal realism has been attacked from at least two directions. Some, the instrumentalists, deny the appropriateness of evaluating theories with the categories of truth and falsehood. Others, the relativists, deny the viability of the particulate 'correspondence' notion of truth employed by the minimal realist. In this section minimal realism is defended from the attacks of instrumentalists and in the next section from the attacks of the relativists. Osiander, writing in the preface to Copernicus's *The Revolutions of the Heavenly Spheres* gave what is sometimes described as an instrumentalist construal of the Copernican theory:[4]

> It is the duty of an astronomer to compose the history of the celestial motions through careful and skilful observation. Then turning to the causes of these motions or hypotheses about them, he must conceive and devise, since he cannot in any way attain to the true causes, such hypotheses as, being assumed, enable the motions to be calculated correctly from the principles of geometry, for the future as well as the past. The present author Copernicus has performed both these duties excellently. For these hypotheses need not be true nor even probable; if they provide a calculus consistent with the observations that alone is sufficient.

I cite this passage to make clear what I am not for the moment considering. Osiander indicates that the theories can be evaluated in the categories of truth and falsehood but is suggesting that that fact is irrelevant. It is enough that they work. The suggestion that theories are true or false but that that fact plays no role in our understanding of the nature of theories or the growth of science, which will be called *epistemological instrumentalism*, will be explored in Chapter VII, where I discuss a defence of this view by Laudan. For the moment I am interested in the view that theories are not even to be thought of as true or false. This position, to be called *semantical instrumentalism*, argued for by Mach among others, is more discussed than believed. Consequently the clearest formulations of it tend to be found in the writings of realists. Hesse, for instance, writes:[5]

> Instrumentalists assume that theories have the status of instruments, tools, or calculating devices in relation to observation statements. In this view it is assumed that theories can be used to relate and systematize observation statements and to derive some sets of observation statements (predictions) from other sets (data); but no question of the truth or reference of the theories themselves arise.

No question of truth or reference arises because T-terms have no meaning. The postulates of a theory which are either T-sentences, or sentences containing both T- and O-terms, function only as devices for enabling us to make predictions. This position has a certain attractiveness. First, the problem of specifying the meaning of T-terms does not arise. And, second, since there is general agreement that science today places us in a better position to make predictions than it did in the past, there is no problem for an instrumentalist in justifying the claim that there is scientific progress. The pessimistic induction does not worry him for, he says, he was not aiming at anything more than an increase in predictive power in the first place.

Instrumentalism is not, however, at all plausible as a claim about how we do in fact regard theories. For we aim in science at more than mere prediction. That this is so is easily seen if we imagine achieving what the instrumentalist takes to be the goal of science. Suppose we have a black box into which we can feed an observational characterization of the state of any physical system at any moment of time and which correctly predicts the state of that system at any specified future moment and retrodicts the state at any past moment. If the instrumentalist were correct in his claim about the aim of science, this would represent the completion of the scientific enterprise. Having achieved perfect observational predictive power, there would be no point in developing physical theories. But the scientific enterprise would continue in the face of this awesome achievement. No doubt some would abandon science and no doubt society would lessen its monetary contributions to science, but science would not end. For we do not wish merely to predict, we also want to explain. We are not satisfied merely to know, say, when a freely falling body dropped from some height at some time will strike the earth's surface, we want to know why it falls at the rate it does. We do not want to know merely that sodium placed in a flame turns it yellow, we want to know what it is about sodium and flames that brings this about. There is no doubt that rightly or wrongly we want not only to be able to predict, we want to be able to explain.

On an instrumentalistic construal of theories, theories cannot explain. For to explain why a system passes from one observable state to another, we need to know something about that system. That is, we must discover some truths or some approximate truths about the system if we are to understand why the transitions that are observed do in fact obtain. In some cases a limited understanding of system may come through discovering generalizations linking observables which the instrumentalist can allow to be true. However, it simply is a brute fact that in seeking deeper understanding of systems we have been led to introduce theories involving T-terms. In regarding these theories as giving us a degree of understanding we are regarding them as theories for which we have some evidence of truth or approximation to the truth. If we regard theories as devoid of meaning and hence as incapable of being either true or false, we cannot regard them as explanatory devices. We can make this point without even claiming that we have any theories at present which we have good reasons to think to be true or approximately true. The point is simply that we are aiming at explanation. It remains possible for an instrumentalist to offer his construal of theories as a reformative programme. He can maintain that in aiming at explanation over and above prediction we are aiming at what cannot be had.

It is at this juncture that our negative conclusion concerning the possibility of drawing an O/T distinction becomes relevant. The instrumentalist regards singular O-sentences and generalizations involving only O-terms as being true or false. T-terms are devoid of meaning, and consequently no sentence containing a T-term is capable of being true or false. That is, the very articulation of his position presupposes that a dichotomy can be drawn which would license a different semantical treatment of *O*-terms and *T*-terms. In the face of the failure of the instrumentalist to provide this we have to reject his position even as a reformative one. An instrumentalist might endeavour to utilize the sort of pragmatic distinction I offered, simply claiming that he intends to regard any *T*-term as meaningless. But why should we accept his advice to do this? Historically speaking, semantic instrumentalists have relied on some form of verificationism. If one held that a sentence is meaningful if and only if it can be conclusively verified on the basis of direct sensory experience, one would be committed to regarding theoretical postulates as being meaningless. However, in order to obtain the instrumentalist conclusion one has to begin with an implausibly strong form of verificationism. For instance, such a form of verificationism would rule out as meaningless the ascription of psychological states to other persons. For there is no possibility of conclusively verifying on the basis of my experience that someone else is in pain. It is compatible with all my experience that he should look like he is in pain and not be in pain. But it would be absurd to deny the intelligibility of ascriptions of pain to others. If we respond by liberalizing our principle of significance so that a statement is meaningful if and only if something would count as some evidence for its truth and something would count as some evidence against its truth, we will not be able to rule out theoretical assertions as meaningless. For such assertions, as the instrumentalist allows, do entail observational consequences when taken with a specification of observable data. That is it is possible to have evidence for and evidence against a theoretical postulate.

In discussion of instrumentalism, the question of the existence of theoretical entities has played a major role. For it is sometimes said that 'since sentences containing the names of theoretical entities do not so refer, they are not really statements at all but are linguistic devices of calculation or prediction.'[6] If this is to be an argument for semantic instrumentalism, the claim that theoretical terms do not refer will have to rest on a proof that they cannot refer on the grounds that they are devoid of meaning. We have already seen that this is an implausible move. It may, however, be based on the claim that we have no reason to think that theoretical entities exist. That is, we have inductive grounds for thinking that no entity postulated by any theory exists; in which case all theories are false. This produces not semantical but epistemological instrumentalism, the refutation of which will not be possible until we have in Chapters VII and VIII developed a theory of reference and shown that we do indeed have good reasons to believe in the existence of theoretical entities.

The final aspect of instrumentalism to be discussed concerns logic, which is a crucial tool for the instrumentalist since it is to be employed in deriving observable predictions from theoretical sentences together with observational sentences specifying initial conditions. These derivations must be valid. One way of determining whether a derivation is valid is to see if it can be constructed using truth-preserving rules of inference (this is not the only way but my argument would be unaffected if some other legitimate procedure was followed). One such rule licenses the inference from any sentence of the form '*A* and *B*' to the sentence '*A*'. We see that such a rule is truth-preserving because we see that any interpretation we can give to '*A*' and to '*B*' which makes '*A* and *B*' true also makes '*A*' true. Theoretical sentences are, for the instrumentalist, incapable of being true or false. *Prima facie* at least, it is difficult to see what sense can be attached to the notion of controlling derivations by truth-preserving rules of inference if those derivations are based on premises that are incapable of being true or false. The question then is: what entitlement has a semantic instrumentalist to use standard logic based on the notion of truth-preserving rules of inference?

There is no puzzle in the instrumentalist's employment of standard logic in carrying out derivations involving only *O*-sentences. One imagines that he will claim that he is simply extending by analogy the use of truth-preserving rules of inference from a sphere (*O*-sentences) where truth is at stake to a sphere (*T*-sentences) where truth is not at stake. In addition he might rely on the fact that rules of inference are justified as truth-preserving by establishing the truth of such conditions: If '*A* and *B*' is true, then '*A*' is true. These conditionals, he might argue, are vacuously true when '*A*' and '*B*' are replaced by theoretical sentences. We may well wish to ask him why we should assume that what is acceptable when truth is at stake is still acceptable when truth is not at stake. Even if we accept his entitlement to use classical logic his position is incoherent. For it is a theorem of classical logic that '*A* or not-*A*'. If classical logic can be applied at the theoretical level, we are asserting that any theoretical sentence, '*A*', is either true or false. But instrumentalism just is the doctrine that theoretical sentences lack truth-value. Suppose he were to reply that 'or' and 'not' have different meaning when applied to theoretical sentences and hence that we cannot construe the sentence '*A* or not-*A*' where '*A*' is a theoretical sentence as asserting that either '*A*' is true or '*A*' is false. In that case he cannot argue for his entitlement to use classical logic in the theoretical sphere by analogical extension. For the logical constants 'or' and 'not' have been given a different sense in the domain of theoretical sentences.

The moral to be drawn from the above considerations is not that instrumentalism is unavoidably incoherent. My intention is to suggest that the most plausible form of instrumentalism is one based on intuitionistic logic rather than classical logic. For our purposes the salient difference between these logics is that the most contested of all classical laws of logic, the Law of Excluded Middle, '*A* or not-*A*', holds in classical logic but not in intuitionist logic. Intuitionistic logic was developed by intuitionistic mathematicians who held that one is not entitled to assert '*A* or not-*A*' unless one can decide, in principle at least, whether '*A*' is true or whether it is 'not-A' that is true. There are considerable affinities between their motivations and those of the instrumentalists. Classically instrumentalists were motivated by a belief in a strong form of verificationism. It was because they could not conclusively verify the truth of theoretical sentences that they conceived of these sentences as not being capable of being either true or false. That is, they were only willing to assert '*A* or not-*A*' if it was possible to decide which it was. As this cannot be done in regard to *T*-sentences they were taken as lacking a truth-value. If the instrumentalist opts for the intuitionistic logic, he is saved from the embarrassment of the inconsistency that otherwise arises from the fact that we can derive '*A* or not-*A*' for any theoretical sentence '*A*' in classical logic. Given his view that an *O*-sentence is such that its truth-value can be ascertained he will be able to assert '*O* or not-*O*' for any *O*-sentence, '*O*'. His verificationism provides him with a rationale for not accepting a logic that allows the derivation of '*T* or not-*T*' for all theoretical sentences *T*.

4 RELATIVISM

Where the instrumentalist challenges the application of the notions of truth or falsity to theories, the relativist allows for their application but disputes the construal of these notions standardly provided by the realist. The picture of the minimal realist involves the thought that theories are true or false in virtue of how the world is independently of ourselves. On the relativist picture, what is true depends in part or entirely on something like the social perspective of the agent who entertains the hypothesis or on the theory of the agent. On this picture,

34

as one passes from age to age, or from society to society, or from theory to theory, what is true changes and not merely what is taken to be true. The challenge of the relativist must be met, for both Kuhn and Feyerabend articulate relativistic positions.

The problem with this picture is initially one of formulation. For it is not easy to formulate the idea so as to make it non-trivial without making it incoherent. For instance, suppose we formulate it in terms of sentences:

It is possible that sentence '*S*' is true in Θ and false in Ψ,

where 'Ψ' and 'Θ' are to be replaced by specifications of whatever it is that truth is supposed to be relative to; say, a particular social group or a particular theory. In this formulation the thesis is trivial and completely devoid of interest. For it reveals only the commonplace and humble fact that the same sentence can be ascribed different meanings and, hence, ascribed under those different meanings different truth-values. We will call this thesis of relativity *trivial semantical relativism* or *TSR*.

If we are to have a non-trivial version of relativism we will have to focus not on sentences but on what is expressed by a sentence. Let us use the term 'proposition' for what is expressed or meant by sentences. Let p be the proposition expressed by sentence 'S_1' in Ψ and by sentence 'S_2' in Θ. Could it be the case that p is true in Ψ and false in Θ? No, for it is a necessary condition for the sentence 'S_1' to express the same proposition as the sentence 'S_2' that the sentences have the same truth-conditions. To specify the truth-conditions of a sentence is to specify what would make it true and to specify what would make it false. If in fact 'S_1' and 'S_2' differ in truth-value, their truth-conditions must be different. If their truth-conditions differ they say different things — they say that different conditions obtain — and hence they do not express the same proposition. Thus if we focus on propositions we cannot find a proposition expressed by a sentence 'S_1' in Θ and by a sentence 'S_2' in Ψ which is true in the one case and false in the other.

The preceding point can be put in terms of translation as follows. If I am able to find a sentence 'S_1' in my language which translates a sentence 'S_2' of another language, I cannot accept it as logically possible that these sentences should differ as to truth-value. If I find myself attributing different truth-values to the sentences I have to revise my view that one is a translation of the other. Thus this attempt to have a thesis of relativity more interesting than *TSR* fails because it is incoherent. Nor can we generate any interesting thesis if we focus on the possibility that there might be sentences that cannot be rendered in a meaning equivalent fashion within our own language. For in this case we have failed to find something which might be true in Ψ but false in Θ.

In view of the fact that it does not seem possible to find an intelligible and non-trivial thesis of relativity, the question must arise as to why many have thought to the contrary. There are at least two reasons. The least respectable of these stems from an elementary confusion of epistemological and semantic issues. One can certainly find a situation in which what appears to be a good translation scheme takes a sentence 'S' of Ψ into a sentence 'S_2' of Θ (our language) where we are absolutely certain that 'S_2' is true and the speakers of Ψ are absolutely convinced that 'S' is false. Given that the translation is correct, we have to conclude either that they are mistaken or that we are mistaken. We cannot conclude under this assumption that what is false for them is true for us. We can only say that we differ as to what is true. Of course, if this situation is widespread and involves many of what we would regard as low-level empirical beliefs about the world of medium-sized everyday objects, it will be reasonable to query the assumption that the translation schema is acceptable. If we query the translation, we have not found something which is true for them and false for us. Clearly the stock of things believed to be true varies from culture to culture, from age to age and from theory to theory. That in itself takes us no way towards an interesting thesis of relativity. Indeed, as we have noted, the assumption that we can identify such diversity in beliefs presupposes that we can identify sameness of meaning in sentences across these differing perspectives; and as that presupposes sameness of truth-conditions of sentences drawn from these differing perspectives the acknowledgment of this plurality of diverse beliefs systems presupposes the invariance of truth across the perspectives. If we were to make the radical assumption that we cannot recognize diversity in beliefs systems (that is, that we cannot tell whether their beliefs are the same as ours or not), we cannot even formulate a non-trivial thesis of relativism.

There is something of interest and importance that does vary from perspective to perspective, and this is the stock of available concepts. There is no fixed set of immutable concepts utilized by those in all perspectives. To take a trivial example, the stock of contemporary scientific concepts allows us to formulate hypotheses that simply were not available to primitive men. But that does not mean that things have become true for us that were not true for him. It means only that we can formulate truths that he could not have formulated. So once again we fail to satisfy the scheme in a non-trivial but intelligible manner.

5 REALISM AND ONTOLOGY

The version of realism that we have defended from the attacks of the instrumentalist and the relativist is very weak. In discussion in philosophy of science one more frequently encounters an apparently stronger form of realism which is explicated as the doctrine that a theory can only be given a realist construal if the theory provides or has an associated model which models the subject matter of the theory in terms of familiar objects of everyday experience. This aspect of realism usually displays itself in a negative fashion when realists remark that instrumentalism gains support from the existence of theories that do not satisfy this condition. Thus, Pap writes:[7]

> It is a natural tendency of the human mind to think of physical reality as something that can be pictured, on the analogy of the objects of common-sense experience. As a result, physical theories are intuitively satisfactory only if they gain pictorial content through *models*. Where such models are lacking, as in the relativistic theory of geodesics in 'curved' space and the quantum theory of probability waves, the feeling may arise that useful conceptual, mathematical constructions have replaced descriptions of physical reality.

And Mary Hesse comments:[8]

> Instrumentalism is also supported by the extreme difficulty in modern physics of finding self-consistent interpretations of the formal calculi of quantum theories and by the fact that different and conflicting interpretations may be used for different parts of a theory, or for one theory under different circumstances (as with quantum particle and wave models).

There is no reason to think that good scientific theories concerned with unfamiliar subject matters like the curvature of space must involve an analogy with familiar objects. For there is no reason to think *a priori* that the unfamiliar must be like the familiar. Items at the sub-atomic level may be *sui generis*. If one builds into one's characterization of realism a clause concerning the generation of an analogy, it will not be

37

appropriate to give a realist construal to, say quantum mechanics or general relativity. Certainly theories that have this property are nice. It makes them easier to teach to students. The greater mathematical complexity of quantum mechanics is not the only reason why it is more difficult to teach than the theory of ideal gases. An available analogy makes it easier to acquire an intuitive sense about what is going on. Such an analogy may be productive of conjectures to be tested on the domain of the theory. Nice as it may be, there is no reason to assume that it is possible to have such theories in all domains of investigations.

A minimal realist with regard to a class of sentences, holds that each sentence in that class is true or false in virtue of how the world is. A minimal realist who holds that he has evidence for the truth or approximate truth of the sentences certainly does take on ontological commitments. For he will be committed to the existence of whatever has to exist in order for those sentences to be true. However, there is no reason *a priori* to assume that the items needed in an explanatory theory will be like the entities of which we have experience. Consequently, we ought not to build any analogical requirement into the specification of a viable form of realism. In building a stronger form of realism we will add the claim that evidence for the truth (or approximate truth) is evidence for the existence of whatever has to exist for the theory to be true (or approximately true). This will be called the *causal ingredient in realism.* For the commitment to theoretical entities most commonly arises when we adopt theoretical hypotheses in giving causal accounts of observable phenomena. For instance, Thomson's theory of the electron was introduced in an attempt to explain observed scintillations in a cathode ray tube. Just what ontological commitments one takes on in believing a theory will not be obvious. If I hold it to be true that the average man has 2.3 children I do not thereby commit myself to the existence of someone (missed out in the last census) with 2.3 children. An analysis of that sentence reveals that I am only committed to the existence of some number of children equal to 2.3 times the number of families. In examining scientific theories for ontological commitment, it will not usually be such a trivial matter. For instance, it remains as controversial today as it was at the time of Leibniz and Newton whether theories of time carry a commitment to the existence of moments of time over and above collections of events.[9]

6 REALISM AND EPISTEMOLOGY

For a minimal realist, theories are true or false. To obtain a more exciting form of realism we must add some epistemological claim about the possibilities of discovering whether a theory is in fact true or false. Simply to add an epistemological claim to the effect that with regard to any theory it is possible either to have good reasons to think it is true or good reasons to think it is false will not be satisfactory in view of the pessimistic induction. For exercising this epistemological power will merely issue in a negative judgment about the truth of any theory whatsoever. Consequently we will add the following weaker but still substantial claim (to be called the *epistemological ingredient in realism*): it is in principle possible to have good reasons for thinking that one of a pair of rival theories is more likely to be more approximately true than the other. This does not mean that given any pair of rival theories at a particular moment of time we can then and there decide reasonably which theory is more likely to be more approximately true. It may be that the appropriate epistemological stance is one of agnosticism between the theories pending the discovery of further relevant data. The claim is only that this sort of reasoned choice is in principle open to us, a claim which, as we shall see in the next section, may none the less be too strong.

The realist tradition in the philosophy of science is an optimistic one. Realists do not think merely that we have in principle the power specified in the epistemological ingredient. They take it that we have been able to exercise that power successfully so as to achieve progress in science. Consequently our final strengthening of realism involves adding what I call the *thesis of verisimilitude* (hereafter cited as *TV*): the historically generated sequence of theories of a mature science is a sequence of theories which are improving in regard to how approximately true they are. *TV* raises questions of interpretation (what is meant by 'more approximately true') and justification (how do we decide that one theory is more likely to be more approximately true than another) which will be dealt with in Chapters VIII and IX. My strategy will be to vindicate *TV* and to argue from the fact that *TV* holds to the satisfaction of the epistemological ingredient. To this stage my aim has been only to articulate the form of realism which will serve as the basis of my rationalist account of the scientific enterprise and to defend realism from the direct attack of the instrumentalist and the relativist. However, before we can even reasonably embark on this ambitious enterprise we must consider an interesting and serious threat posed to even minimal realism by the thesis of the under-determination of theory by data.

It is common in science to find ourselves faced with a pair of incompatible theories which we cannot decide between on the basis of the available data. In such cases we seek further evidence, hoping that it will tilt the balance one way or the other. Until such evidence becomes available the appropriate attitude for the realist is, as we noted, one of agnosticism. Of course he may opt for one of the theories, gambling on the conjecture that it and not the rival will win out. Until further evidence is in, he cannot ground his preference for one theory over the other. This situation in which the choice between theories is under-determined by the actually available data is no threat to the realist so long as there is some possible observation or experiment the outcome of which could give reasons for choosing the one theory over the other as being more likely to be a better approximation to the truth. However, a serious theoretical problem arises for the realist if the following situation is possible. Let T_1 and T_2 be rival theories. Suppose that T_1 and T_2 are *empirically equivalent* in the sense that each has precisely the same observational consequences. Suppose further that T_1 and T_2 fare equally well under any principle other than fit with the data that is indicative of truth or approximate truth. For instance, it is sometimes supposed that simplicity is a guide to the truth. Under this latter supposition we would be assuming that T_1 and T_2 are equally simple. If a pair of rival, observationally equivalent theories fare equally well on any justifiable principles of evidence I shall say that they are *evidentially equivalent.*

The thesis of *under-determination by data*, hereafter cited as *UTD*, in its strong form, is the claim that for any theory for a given subject matter there is an incompatible rival theory which is evidentially equivalent. In its weak form it is the thesis that there can be such theories. Even in its weak form the thesis is highly controversial. For if T_1 and T_2 are evidentially equivalent, it may be that they are not genuinely incompatible. It could be that T_1 and T_2 are mere notional variants of the same theory. Many would argue that whenever T_1 and T_2 are evidentially equivalent, even if they appear to be incompatible, they must in fact be notional variants of the same theory. I have argued elsewhere[10] in favour of the weak thesis by constructing examples of evidentially equivalent but incompatible theories for specific subjects. One difficulty in trying to establish the weak *UTD* in this way is that

40

one cannot definitely rule out the possibility that only one of the two theories can be integrated into a total theory of nature. I concede that if we have a unique total theory which integrates all theories for all subject matters which is compatible with only one of my pairs of rival theories for specific subject matters we would have evidential reasons for selecting that theory. However, there is no *a priori* guarantee that there is such a unique total theory of nature. We have to entertain the thought that there might be massive *UDT*, by which I mean that there could be a pair of incompatible evidentially equivalent total theories of nature.

It cannot be too strongly stressed that we are dealing with a mere theoretical possibility in entertaining the idea that there might be two evidential incompatible rival total theories of nature. The point of considering this hypothetical situation is to reveal an aspect of realism which might otherwise go unnoticed. To bring this out, we need to relax the pessimistic induction in the following sense. Having reached the stage of having two total theories of nature, which as far as we can tell work perfectly, and having ruled out all other theories, we regard these theories as candidates for being the true theory of the world. That is, we no longer simply assign each theory the truth-value false by appeal to the pessimistic induction. The realist faces the following dilemma. He cannot simultaneously satisfy the ontological and the epistemological ingredients in his position. *Ex hypothesi* nothing will give a reason for thinking that one theory rather than the other is true. If he maintains the ontological ingredient he cannot satisfy the epistemological ingredient. This response, which I call the *ignorance response*, involves asserting that one or other of the theories is true but we shall never know which it is. This means embracing the existence of inaccessible facts. That is, something about the world, some matter of fact, makes one theory true and the other false; but that matter of fact is something beyond our power to discover.

In our story the two theories can have a great deal in common. However, in virtue of being incompatible there will be some assertion *p* which is contained in one theory the negation of which is contained in the other theory. In view of our inability to decide which theory is the true one, *p* will be empirically undecidable. On the ignorance response we assume that there is a matter of fact at stake with regard to *p*. However, there is nothing observable that is explained by the supposition that there is a matter of fact at stake. For *ex hypothesi* all observations are explained equally well on the theory containing *p*

41

and on the theory containing the negation of *p*. Thus to posit a fact making *p* true or false is to admit the existence of an inaccessible, gratuitous fact the presence or absence of which could never be discovered. Why, we might ask, should we bother to assume that there is a matter of fact at stake at all? Why assume that the world is determinate with respect to *p*? To move in this direction is to make what I call the *arrogance response* to under-determination. On this response we drop the assumption that there is a matter of fact at stake with regard to any undecidable empirical proposition. We relax the ontological ingredient in realism by restricting from the set of sentences to be given a realist construal any undecidable sentence. What in this case we regard as being the truth about the world would be the common part of the two theories.

The attractiveness of the arrogance response is that it does not posit inaccessible matters of fact. If we cannot discover whether it is a fact that *p* or not, we do not assume that there is a matter of fact at stake. The unattractive aspect of the response derives from the fact that it requires that we abandon classical logic. In classical logic the Law of Bivalence asserts that any proposition must have at least one of the truth-values, true or false. And given that the negation of a proposition is true if and only if that proposition is false, this amounts to the Law of the Excluded Middle, hereafter cited as *LEM*. The defender of the ignorance response will argue by appeal to *LEM* that either *p* is true or the negation of *p* is true. Given that to be true is to be true in virtue of how the world is, the appeal to *LEM* leads to the posit of an inaccessible matter of fact. However, one inclined to arrogance can avail himself of intuitionistic logic in which *LEM* does not hold. If this case is made out, the proponent of ignorance is deprived of the only grounds on which he can argue for his response. However, the proponent of arrogance cannot prove that there is no matter of fact at stake. That is, he cannot assert that it is not the case that ⌜*p* or not-*p*⌝. For it is a theorem of intuitionistic logic that ⌜not-not(*p* or not-*p*)⌝. He simply declines to assert ⌜*p* or not-*p*⌝ for empirically undecidable *p*.

My concern has been only to display the consequences of the theoretical possibility of *UTD* for realism. I favour the arrogance response on the grounds that the proponent of ignorance has to rest his case on *LEM*, the most disputed of all classical laws of logic. It is hard to see how he can develop a non-question-begging argument in the context of the current debate. For the possibility of the *UTD* gives rise to queries about the law. In addition, arrogance has the attractiveness of being the result of applying Occam's razor to matters of fact, in that we do not posit that there is a matter of fact when the posit would be idle. In any event, massive *UTD* is not a phenomenon we in fact face and, as a theoretical possibility, either response will preserve the core of realism to the extent that there is an overlap in the content of the underdetermined theories. If there were nothing in common except the observational consequences, realism on either response would be implausible. For there would be no point in being a realist if no theoretical proposition could be decided (ignorance), and there would be nothing to be a realist about except the observational consequences on the arrogance response.[11]

Finally, by way of summary I give below the form of realism we have developed. The scope of realism would need to be restricted in one or other of the ways outlined above should we face *UTD*:

1 *The ontological ingredient*
   The sentences of scientific theories are true or false as the case
   may be in virtue of how the world is independently of ourselves.
2 *The causal ingredient*
   Evidence that a theory is true or is approximately true is evidence
   for the existence of whatever entities have to exist in order for
   the theory to be true or approximately true.
3 *The epistemological ingredient*
   It is possible in principle to have good reasons for thinking
   which of a pair of rival theories is more likely to be more
   approximately true.
4 *The thesis of verisimilitude*
   The historically generated sequence of theories of a nature
   science is a sequence of theories being ever more approximately
   true.

III

POPPER — THE IRRATIONAL RATIONALIST

1 THE POPPERIAN TABLEAU

According to Popper, truth is the aim of science. But the scientific condition is one of ignorance. For, as we shall see in the next section of this chapter, we are never entitled to claim to know the truth of a scientific theory or hypothesis. In view of the pessimistic induction this might not seem a rash position. Popper goes further and denies that we can ever know the truth of even the most low-level observation report. Naively one might think that one could at least have good reasons on occasion for thinking that one hypothesis or observation report is more likely to be true than false. Not so, says Popper. In Section 3 I outline his reasons for this very strong claim, which amounts to the rejection of all inductive argumentation. That is, Popper denies the legitimacy of any argument in which the premises purport to support the conclusion without entailing it. A scientist who has shown that when 1000 randomly selected samples of sodium were placed in a flame it turned yellow has, according to Popper, no reason to say that the hypothesis that sodium turns a flame yellow is probably true. However, if one piece of sodium were to fail to turn a flame yellow we should be entitled to reject the hypothesis. For the premise 'This piece of sodium did not turn the flame yellow' entails the conclusion 'Not all pieces of sodium turn yellow when placed in a flame'. Since only deductive arguments are legitimate, the method of science is not evidence gathering but conjecture and refutation. The best we can hope for is the refutation of hypotheses.

44

Popper's thesis of the utter inaccessibility of truth leads him to reconstrue the goal of science as that of achieving a better approximation to the truth, or as he calls it, a higher degree of verisimilitude. We see in Section 4 that his analysis of verisimilitude is untenable. His hope that refuting false theories may take us nearer the truth is unfounded for a number of reasons. It will be established in Section 4 that having rejected all inductive arguments he cannot justify the rejection of any theory. For it will emerge that he can give no reasons for accepting observation reports that would refute a theory. Even if this problem is set aside Popper cannot forge the link a rationalist requires between the goal of science and the methods of science. Through the arguments of Sections 6, 7 and 8 we prove that Popper can have no reasons for thinking that the method of conjecture and refutation will tend to produce theories having greater verisimilitude. This means that on his own terms Popper has to regard science as an irrational activity. In giving this very negative critique of the Popperian position it might seem that we are not doing justice to his insight into the importance in science of refutation or falsification. Consequently, I discuss in the final section of the chapter his account of the mechanism of falsification. It turns out that this involves a grave distortion of actual scientific practice.

My treatment of the Popperian system is selective, focusing on those general views of his which are relevant to our concern with the question of the rationality of science, and neglecting many of his varied and interesting discussions of other topics in the philosophy of science. Readers wishing an introduction to these are advised to consult Ackermann (1976) and O'Hear (1980).

It is crucially important to remember in what follows that for Popper one can never cite the outcome of an experiment as positive evidence favouring a hypothesis. If things turn out as the hypothesis predicts, the hypothesis has not been refuted. That is all. One cannot say: Now I have some evidence in its favour. This must be remembered, for what makes Popper seem plausible to many is that they do not take him seriously. They do not think within the constraints of his system. And, indeed, it is extremly difficult if not impossible actually to do what we are required: namely, to set aside all inductive argumentation. By implicitly bringing in at various points what is *verboten*, positive evidence, his position can appear plausible.

45

2 POPPER ON THE AIM OF SCIENCE

Popper is very much the rationalist, and in terms of my schema for a rational model this means that he has to specify an aim for scientific activity and to specify principles of comparison (which he calls methodological principles) to be used in assessing the relative merits of competing theories. It was said that rationalists tend to be realists who construe the aim of science as the production of true explanatory theories. Popper is no exception. In *Objective Knowledge* he writes: 'Our main concern in science and in philosophy is, or ought to be, the search for truth.'[1] 'there are excellent reasons for saying that what we attempt in science is to describe and (so far as possible) explain reality'.[2] Popper, in taking the goal to be the discovery of explanatory truths[3], subscribes to what I called the ontological ingredient in realism. This is the thesis that theories are strictly speaking either true or false, and which a given theory is, it is so in virtue of how the world is independently of ourselves. Popper also holds what I called the causal ingredient in realism. This is the claim that some at least of the theoretical terms of a theory denote real theoretical entities which are causally responsible for the observable phenomenon that prompts us to posit their existence. In addition we shall see that he is firmly committed to the thesis of verisimilitude or *TV*, according to which the history of a mature science is constituted by a sequence of theories which are getting nearer and nearer to the truth. What about the epistemological ingredients? This is the claim that we can in principle at least have rationally grounded reasons for believing that one theory is more likely to be more approximately true than another theory. We shall see that in view of his falsificationist methodology Popper's version of the epistemological ingredient in realism is exceedingly weak (if not of zero force).

The aim then of scientific activity is the production of explanatory truths. But while truth is the aim, ignorance is the game. Popper repeatedly declares that there is no criterion of truth:[4]

> By a criterion of truth is meant a kind of decision method: a method
> that leads either generally, or at least in a certain class of cases,
> through a finite sequence of steps (for example, of tests) to the
> decision whether or not the statement in question is true. Thus in
> the absence of a general criterion of truth it may easily happen that
> we possess true theories, and yet are unable to show, to our satis-
> faction, that they are true. What can also happen is that we are able to

establish some statements as true, by a sort of lucky coincidence rather than an application of a criterion of truth (which may not exist in the case in question).

By this he means that there is no class of statements whose truth-value we can ascertain with certainty and from which we could derive the truth of any scientific theory. Or, more generally, there is no finitary procedure which we could follow that would provide us with certain knowledge of the truth of any given scientific theory. To reiterate this point: if we were to possess a criterion of truth we should have an algorithm allowing us to decide definitely the truth-value of any statement. If there were to be such an algorithm for empirical statements, there would have to be a privileged class of statements, observation statements, or O-statements, satisfying the following two conditions:

1 The truth-value of all O-statements could be ascertained by us with certainity.
2 Any non-O empirical statement would be such that its truth-value could be determined mechanically in finite time from a specification of the truth-values of the class of O-statements.

Popper has two arguments (one given explicitly, one given implicitly) against the possibility of a criterion of truth. The first argument turns on the uncontentious claim that scientific theories contain universal propositions. That is, they involve quantification over large and possibly infinite domains. For instance, Newton's First Law that bodies that are not acted on by forces continue in a state of rest or uniform motion is, if asserted, asserted as holding of any one of the possibly infinite set of bodies, at any time and at any location. In real time we cannot fix the truth-value of more than a finite number of basic statements drawn from observations of our own provincial region of spacetime. We cannot derive from such information the truth of even the humblest of generalizations which range over a larger and possibly even infinite domain. For example, fixing the truth-value of any number of statements of the form 'This is a swan and is white' leaves open the possibility of unexamined black swans and hence such information does not license us to infer deductively that all swans are white.

The implicit argument against the possibility of a criterion of truth derives from Popper's attack on the observational-theoretical dichotomy. For Popper in fact denies that one can ever have reasons to believe in the truth of any statement of the type that positivists would deem observational. Consider what Popper says about such observational statements:[5]

> 'Here is a glass of water' cannot be verified by any observational experience. The reason is that the *universal terms* which occur in this statement ('glass', 'water') are dispositional: they 'denote physical bodies which exhibit a certain *law-like behaviour*'.

Popper's point is that for it to be true that this is a glass of water it has to be true that this is a glass, and the truth of this claim in turn presupposes the truth of some subjunctive conditional of the form: If this were dropped on a concrete floor from a certain height it would break. Popper quite reasonably expects us to agree that the truth or falsity of subjunctive conditionals is not something that can be ascertained by mere observation and, further, that the justification of the claim that this object would break if subjected to certain conditions will involve an appeal to theory. For instance, if pressed one would appeal to the fact that it had a certain constitution (say, being composed of molecules in such and such a state) and to theories about the effects of jolts on such substances. Even if you say that the justification for the claim is much more humble, namely, that other things looking like that thing have broken when dropped, you are appealing to a humble bit of theory: things having a certain look behave in certain ways. Even the humblest of descriptions such as 'this is a glass of water' are true only if certain subjunctive conditionals are true. Thus, according to Popper, to justify the claim that the subjunctive conditionals in question are true we shall have to appeal to the truth of certain bits of theory. Thus the 'observation statement' in question does not have a privileged position *vis-à-vis* the related theoretical statements. In other words, for Popper, in accepting even the humblest of observation statements we are implicitly assuming some theory and can be no more justified in believing the observation sentence than we can be in believing the relevant theoretical sentences. That is, we begin with general conjectures which are implicitly assumed in describing the results of observing.

We have seen that Popper, in keeping with the non-rationalist, denies the positivist doctrine of an epistemologically privileged class of observational statements. None the less, there is a class which has a special role to play within the Popperian account of scientific methodology. Such statements, which he calls *basic statements*, are characterized not epistemologically but in terms of their form and their role. The form of a basic statement is that of a singular existential statement where this means that they are existential assertions about some definite spatio-temporal region. To use Popper's favourite example: 'There is a raven in spatio-temporal region k'. In addition, any conjunction of such statements constitutes a basic statement. Negations, disjunctions and conditionals formed from basic statements are not basic statements. As I have stressed, the role of basic statements is not to provide any epistemological bed-rock: 'Thus our "basic statements" are anything but "basic" in the sense of "final"; they are "basic" only in the sense that they belong to that class of statements which are used in testing our theories.'[6] For a theory to be scientific, there must be a basic statement which is ruled out by the theory. That is, if the theory has empirical content it must forbid something expressible in a basic statement. For instance, the theory that all swans are white is incompatible with the basic statement 'Lo, a black swan'. Such a basic statement constitutes what Popper calls a *potential falsifier* for the theory.

3 THE METHOD OF SCIENCE: DEDUCTIVISM

One is likely to feel in the face of Popper's claim that there is no criterion of truth much as Austin is reported to have felt when someone explained to him that Gödel had shown there were truths of arithmetic which could not be derived from Peano's axioms: 'Who ever thought otherwise?'. This point has been dealt with at some length since what makes Popper's account of the scientific enterprise unique is his particular reaction to this truism. The natural reaction to the situation is to say: 'True, observations do not entail the truth of the generalizations with which they are compatible, but they can serve in appropriate circumstances to provide some positive evidence for the generalization'. Not so, says Popper. No set of observations, no matter how selected, can increase the probability of a generalization which entails them. Popper argues for this conclusion on the grounds that the prior probability of any law is zero. That is, the probability we should assign to any universal generalization over an infinite domain before we have gathered any evidence is zero. To support this contention Popper considers the universal statement 'If there is an A at location x at time t it will be a B'.[7] This generalization entails an infinite number of instances of the form: at x at t either there is no A or there is an A which is a B. Suppose in the absence of any other information we set the probability of each particular statement of this form being true as ½. The probability of any two of them being true will then be ½.½ = ¼. The probability of any n of them being true will be $(½)^n$. The limit of $(½)^n$ as n goes to infinity is zero. Thus the probability that they are all true is zero and the prior probability of the generalizations being true is consequently zero. This argument is not affected if we assign any probability other than ½ to each instance so long as we do not assign the value 1. Clearly we would not wish to do that, as this would imply certain knowledge in the absence of any information of the truth of each instance of the generalization.

If with Popper and others (i.e. Mary Hesse)[8] we set the prior probability of universal generalizations as zero, and if we use standard probability theory, no amount of evidence will raise the probability of the generalizations. To illustrate this, consider Bayes's theorem which is standardly used to assess the extent to which new evidence raises the probability of a generalization h. Writing $p(h/e)$ for the probability of h given evidence e and $p(e/h)$ for the probability of e given h, one form of Bayes's theorem states:

$$p(h/e) = \frac{p(h) \cdot p(e/h)}{p(e)}.$$

Given that the evidence is an instance of the generalization, $p(e/h)$ is 1 and assuming we are absolutely confident in the truth of e, $p(e)$=1. However, given $p(h)$=0, $p(h/e)$=0. Thus no matter how many instances of the generalization we observe, the probability of the generalization will remain where it started, namely at zero. This is a genuine problem which has received much attention in the literature on probability and confirmation. Some have argued with Hesse that universal generalizations do indeed have a prior probability of zero, and that in order to learn from experience we should utilize generalizations which by being restricted to have only a finite scope can be assigned a non-zero prior probability.[9] Others have sought to find principles justifying a non-zero probability to universal generalizations in the absence of all evidence notwithstanding the above argument.[10] I am not going to explore this issue nor will I evaluate the cogency of Popper's argument for assigning universal generalizations a prior probability of zero. My intention has been only to explain why it is that Popper does not recognize instances of generalizations as providing positive evidence for those generalizations. My strategy will be to develop the consequences of Popper's response to this assumption, which is to adopt a purely deductivist methodology.

We shall see that it faces him with the following destructive dilemma: either the scientific enterprise is completely irrational (on his own terms) or inductive arguments of the style he rejects must be deployed in science.

We have noted Popper's correct rejection of the view that observation could provide a criterion of truth and we have outlined one of his reasons for rejecting the view that observation could provide evidence for the probable truths of generalizations. Indeed, Popper's central thesis is his assumption that Hume has shown that no inductive argumentation is ever acceptable. His response is to develop a deductivist methodology in the face of what he calls the logical problem of induction which:[11]

> arises from (a) Hume's discovery . . . that it is impossible to justify a law by observation or experiment, since it 'transcends experience'; (b) the fact that science proposes and uses laws 'everywhere and all the time'. . . . To this we have to add (c) *the principle of empiricism* which asserts that in science, only observation and experiment may decide upon the *acceptance or rejection* of scientific statement., including laws and theories.

But, according to Popper:[12]

> In fact the principles (a) to (c) do not clash. We can see this the moment we realize that the acceptance by science of a law or a theory is *tentative only*; which is to say that all laws and theories are conjectures, or tentative hypotheses . . .; and that we may reject a law or theory on the basis of new evidence, without necessarily discarding the old evidence which originally led us to accept it.
>
> The principle of empiricism (c) can be fully preserved, since the fate of a theory, its acceptance or rejection, is decided by observation and experiment – by the result of tests. So long as a theory stands up to the severest tests we can design, it is accepted; if it does not, it is rejected. But it is never inferred, in any sense, from the empirical evidence. There is neither a psychological nor a logical induction. *Only the falsity of the theory can be inferred from empirical evidence, and this inference is a purely deductive one.*

We can encapsulate the central aspect of the Popperian position in the thesis that only deductively valid arguments are admissible in science. That is, the only arguments which should be employed are those in

51

which the premises entail the conclusion. No argument in which the premises can be true but the conclusion false is admissible. To advance premises for a conclusion which they do not entail but which one would be inclined to regard (pre-Popperianly) as providing some reasons to believe the conclusion is to indulge in 'pernicious inductivism'.

Popper's wholesale dismissal of all inductive argumentation would seem to place him in the camp of the traditional sceptic. Consequently, it might seem appropriate at this juncture to consider the many and varied attempts to turn the argument against the sceptic concerning induction. While I would argue that the sceptical position is untenable, to do so would take us far from our central concern. Consequently, my strategy will involve simply suspending for the sake of argument the use of induction with a view to exploring the consequences of abandoning it. We shall see that if Popper genuinely abandons induction, there is no way in which he can justify the claims that there is growth of scientific knowledge and that science is a rational activity. Popper himself takes it that his falsificationist methodology saves him from simple scepticism. We shall see that this is not so. Even if one thinks that scepticism concerning inductive argumentation can be easily disposed of, one ought not to set Popper aside without further ado. It is often of great interest in philosophy to explore the consequence of jettisoning a concept which seems deeply entrenched in our conceptual system. If one can reconstruct things without that concept one learns something of interest. If on the other hand the enterprise fails, one comes to have a clear appreciation of the importance of that concept. Some would argue that this latter result arises in the context of Quine's attempts to jettison the notion of the analytic. And I will argue that the failure of Popper's endeavours clearly establishes the indispensability of inductive argumentation in science.

4 VERISIMILITUDE

If all inductive argumentation is precluded, what is the method of science? It is simply that of 'bold conjectures and by the critical search for what is false in our various competing theories'.[13] We are to give free creative rein to our imagination in devising theories which we then endeavour to destroy. This does sound strange, for as Lakatos once rhetorically remarked: 'You know a scientist who wants to falsify his theory?' Popper's hope is, of course, that by weeding out bad theories, better theories will be left in the field. The crucial question to which we turn in the next section is: given a methodology that entirely rejects the use of inductive arguments and operates only with a negative notion of evidence against, can there be any way of ascertaining which of a pair of rival theories is the better to adopt? But first some discussion of the qualification 'bold' is required. As we noted, for a theory to be scientific for Popper it must be falsifiable. It must rule out something expressible by a basic statement. The more it rules out the greater its content. Compare a theory that says that all swans are black or pink or white or green with a theory that says that all swans are black. Intuitively we want to say that the latter has greater content. It rules out, for instance, all that the former rules out and in addition precludes white swans, pink swans and green swans. We can agree with Popper that all things being equal we prefer theories of greater content, for they say more things about the world. Whether we can go beyond intuition and give some content to this notion of content is a question which will concern us below. The greater the content of a theory, the more risky it is, for in saying more about the world it runs the greater risk of falsification. In advising us to be bold Popper is giving us the sensible advice to seek theories of high content.

If we abandon induction we can never have a reason to believe in the truth of any contingent statement. That being so, one might well ask what content the concept of truth can have within the constraints of the Popperian system. To see this, consider an analogy. Suppose I tell you that I am very interested in herns. I claim that some things are herns and other things are not. Unfortunately, I add, there is no criterion of hernness. That is, there is no definite test for establishing if something is a hern. No doubt you will inquire if perhaps there is not some symptom, some fallible sign that provides some evidence for the presence of a hern. There is not, I reply. That is why hern hunting is so challenging. To put things politely, you may well doubt that I have given any content to the notion of a hern. Similarly, one may well doubt whether Popper can give any content to the notion of truth as applied to empirical assertions given that not only is there no criterion for truth, there is nothing that can provide even reasonable grounds in ideal circumstances for saying that some empirical proposition is more likely to be true than not. Some would argue that a concept lacking recognizable conditions of applying and lacking any recognizable conditions of not applying is necessarily vacuous. Even if one does not take this hard line, if a concept suffers from this defect the onus is on the user of the concept to defend the claim that it is non-vacuous. That is, if we cannot display its meaning in part at least by giving its conditions of application and non-application, the very question of its meaningfulness must be at least open, unless some other account is offered of its meaning. It was probably a sensitivity to this line of criticism that led Popper to say very little indeed about truth in *The Logic of Scientific Discovery*. Later Popper encountered the work of Tarski, which he has embraced with something approaching total relief. In spite of the inaccessibility of empirical truth, the concept has content. One may well still query the assumption that Tarski's theory shows the concept of truth to have content within the context of an epistemology such as Popper's where it remains something we can never have any reason to think we possess even in the case of the simplest empirical proposition. However, I will not press this line of argument further, for Popper's attempt to vindicate the rationality of science within a deductivist framework faces intractable problems even if we grant him the use of the concept of truth.

The goal is truth, but that there is neither a criterion of truth nor any symptoms of truth. One might well ask, how could it be rational to pursue a goal whose realization cannot be recognized? To use an analogy, imagine Red Adair and Boots Hanson sitting on the oil-rig Echo Bravo and throwing pennies into the North Sea. The winner takes all, and the winner is the one whose coin is the first to hit the ocean floor. This would be all right if there was a criterion, some detecting device on the sea bed. It would also work as a game if there was a symptom given by a theory: first to pass fifty fathoms will be first to the ocean floor, and a device for detecting this. In the absence of either this is not a game (or, given Wittgenstein reminders about the family resemblance character of games we should perhaps say it is a game albeit a pointless game). Popper is aware of the dilemma generated by a conception of science in which there is neither a criterion nor a symptom of progress, and much of his writings consist in attempts to come to grips with it.

The dilemma is generated by a characterization of science as a rational activity the goal of which is truth, where the possession of truth is not recognizable. In the face of this Popper's first move is to revise his account of the goal. That is, we are given instead what he repeatedly calls a more modest and more realistic goal. The goal is not truth itself but increasing verisimilitude. By this he means that, given a pair of rival theories, we ought to adopt the one that is nearer the truth than the other. While there is some truth in Newton and some falsehood, and while Einstein's theory is no doubt false and certainly not known to be true, it is at least more approximately true. If we had a criterion or a symptom for determining whether one theory is nearer the truth than another, it still would be rational to pursue truth. While we shall never know how we have got there we shall at least be able to know that we are getting warmer.

The crucial task is to explicate what is to be meant by verisimilitude. A theory is a set of assertions, and if the number of assertions in a theory were finite we might initially seek to explicate the notion of relative verisimilitude in terms of the number of truths and the number of falsehoods contained within the theories. To illustrate this, suppose that theories T_1 and T_2 for some subject matter each contain ten assertions and that T_1 makes five false and five true claims and that T_2 makes nine true and one false claim. In this case we would say that T_2 is nearer the truth than T_1. Unfortunately, we cannot proceed in this fashion with scientific theories, for such theories contain an infinite number of assertions. A theory contains all the consequences of the postulates and this set, called the deductive closure of the postulates, is infinite in size. This is not just as it were a logical point. Consider applying Newtonian mechanics to an ideal point-particle freely rolling down an inclined plane. The particle traverses an infinite number of spatial points and Newtonian mechanics can be used to derive for each of these points a prediction of the time at which the ball passes the points. If we are dealing with bodies that are moving slowly with respect to the speed of light, within the limits of experimental accuracy, Newtonian mechanics works. Thus it makes an infinite number of true assertions. Since Newtonian mechanics fails for bodies moving with high velocities, it makes an infinite number of false assertions. If we assume that relativistic mechanics works for these cases we have to conclude it makes an infinite number of correct assertions. Given the pessimistic induction, we expect that relativistic mechanics is strictly speaking false and that there are some areas in which it fails and that it therefore generates an infinite number of false assertions. Thus it is reasonable to assume that any theory which has something in it will give rise to the same number of true predictions, an infinite number, and the same number of false predictions, an infinite number. Thus we cannot explicate a useful notion of verisimilitude in terms of the number of truths and the number of falsehoods generated by a theory.

The problem involved in trying to compare theories with regard to verisimilitude by looking at the relative amounts of truth and falsity in the theories points to a more basic problem. We do not have any viable way of comparing theories as to content. That is, if we set aside questions of truth and falsity and look at the deductive closures of theories with regard to seeing which one says the most, we shall find that any interesting scientific theory has the same amount of content. For any such theory will entail an infinite number of empirical assertions. In some cases we compare the size of infinite sets by defining measure functions on those sets. For instance, if we have an interval of a Euclidean straight line where the points have been labelled with the real numbers from 1 to 5, the interval from 1 to 2 and the interval from 2 to 5 contain the same number of points. We can obtain a non-trivial comparison of the lengths by defining a function which gives as the measure of any interval the absolute difference between the numbers labelling the end-points. In this case the first interval is assigned a measure 1 and the second interval a measure 3. However, no one has been able to devise an analogous measure for assigning sizes to infinite sets of sentences. This would be required if we are to have non-trivial comparisons of theories with regard to content. Unless we can develop such a measure we shall not be able to make much use of our intuition articulated by Popper that the increase in content of theories is a good thing.

In the face of this problem it might seem that progress could be made if we made use of the notion of containment as illustrated in the following mathematical example. There is an infinite number of natural numbers 1, 2, 3, . . . The set of even natural numbers 2, 4, 6, . . . has the same size as this set, for we can match the members of these sets one-to-one:

$$1 \; 2 \; 3 \ldots$$
$$\updownarrow \; \updownarrow \; \updownarrow$$
$$2 \; 4 \; 6 \ldots$$

In one sense one wants to say that there are more natural numbers than even natural numbers, for the latter set is contained within the former set but not vice versa. It is this notion of containment that Popper employs in setting up his definition of verisimilitude. This means that he has to restrict attention to the special case of comparing two theories, where one of the theories entails the other. This means that all of the assertions of one of the theories will be contained within the other theory. As we shall see, his approach fails. The task of providing a satisfactory alternative analysis will be taken up later in the book in Chapter VIII.

In explicating Popper's notion of verisimilitude the following definitions will be required:

The content of theory A, $C(A)$, is the set of all statements derivable from the theory.
T = set of all statements that are true.
F = set of all statements that are false.
Truth content of A is the intersection of $C(A)$ and T, which we write as A_T.
The falsity content of A is the intersection of $C(A)$ and F, which we write as A_F.

Popper's definition of notion of relative verisimilitude can be given as follows, assuming A and B comparable:[14]

A has less verisimilitude than B if and only if the truth content of A is less than the truth content of B and the falsity content of B is equal to or less than the falsity content of A; or, the truth content of A is equal to or less than the truth content of B and the falsity content of B is less than the falsity content of A.

Using circles to represent the content of a theory and hatching to represent its truth-content, we illustrate in diagram I a case of a theory, A, having less verisimilitude than a theory, B. Diagram II represents a theory A' which has greater verisimilitude than a theory B'.

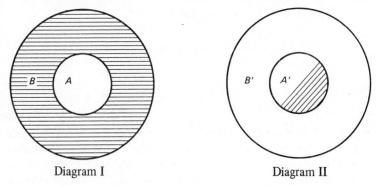

Diagram I   Diagram II

Unfortunately, Popper's account of relative verisimilitude is unacceptable. For the point of introducing the notion was to allow a comparison of two false theories with regard to their relative truth and falsity contents.

However, as Miller[15] and Tichy[16] have shown, for any two distinct false theories A and B, it is false that A has less verisimilitude than B, and it is false that B has less verisimilitude than A. The proof, which a reader uninterested in technicalities can skip, runs as follows:

1 Assume that A and B are false; that A and B are distinct theories; that A and B are comparable, i.e. $C(A) \leqslant C(B)$ or $C(B) \leqslant C(A)$.

2 Writing '—— $<v$ ———' for '——————— has less verisimilitude than ——' we can give Popper's definition of verisimilitude as follows: $A <_v B$ if and only if (i) $A_T < B_T$ and $B_F \leqslant A_F$ or (ii) $A_T \leqslant B_T$ and $B_F < A_F$.

3 Let $p \in A_F$ (i.e. p is false and p is a consequence of A) and let $q \in B_F$. Thus $(p \, v \, q)$ is false and $(p \, v \, q) \in C(A)$ and $(p \, v \, q) \in C(B)$.

4 Assume $A_T < B_T$ and $B_F \leqslant A_F$.
 Let $r \in B_T$ and $r \bar{\in} A_T$.
 Then $r \, \& \, (p \, v \, q) \in B_F$.
 If $r \, \& \, (p \, v \, q) \in A_F$ then $r \in A_F$. But r is true.
 $\therefore r \, \& \, (p \, v \, q) \bar{\in} A_F$.
 $B_F \not\leqslant A_F$ contrary to our assumption that $B_F \leqslant A_F$.

5 Assume $A_T \leqslant B_T$ and $B_F < A_F$.
 Let $s \bar{\in} B_F$ and $s \in A_F$.
 s is false and $-(p \, v \, q)$ is true.
 $\therefore s \, v -(p \, v \, q) \in A_T$
 $\therefore (p \, v \, q) \to s \in A_T$
 If $(p \, v \, q) \to s \in B_T$ then $s \in B_F$. But $s \bar{\in} B_F$
 $\therefore (p \, v \, q) \to s \bar{\in} B_T$
 $\therefore A_T \not\leqslant B_T$ contrary to our assumption that $A_T \leqslant B_T$.

6 Consequently, both possibilities in (2) lead to a contradiction. Thus, $A \not<_v B$. And similarly, $B \not<_v A$.
 Therefore no two false theories are comparable in regard to verisimilitude.

It would be wrong to dismiss the Popperian project without further ado on the grounds that his definition of verisimilitude produces a notion that is not fitted to the role required. For it may be that some other analysis such as the one to be given in Chapter VIII will avoid these problems. For the moment we assume that our intuitive grasp of the notion of being more approximately true can be given a satisfactory philosophical analysis, and proceed to show that Popper fails none the less to display science as a rational activity.

What is the utility of this notion? It is tempting to think as many have that, in view of his claim that verisimilitude constitutes a 'less remote and more applicable notion than truth', relative verisimilitude is something for which we can have either a criterion or a symptom. For if we had that we could at least recognize progress in the general direction of the goal. Clearly we do not have and could not have on Popper's account of the matter any such criterion or symptom. For to recognize that *A* is less in verisimilitude than *B* we have to ascertain the truth and falsity contents of *A* and *B*. But to do this we would have to know all the truths that are expressible in the language in question. For the truth content is just the intersection of the statements of the theory and the set of all truths.

5 CORROBORATION AND THE SWAMP OF BASIC STATEMENTS

What is our rational guide in making judgments of verisimilitude? For Popper we are to be guided by the degree of corroboration of a theory where this notion is understood as:[17]

> a concise report evaluating the state (at a certain time *t*) of the critical discussion of a theory, with respect to the way it solves its problems; its degree of testability; the severity of tests it has undergone; and the way it has stood up to those tests. Corroboration (or degree of corroboration) is thus an evaluation *report of past performance*.

It must be emphasized that for Popper corroboration is not forward-looking:[18]

> To sum up: We can sometimes say of two competing theories, *A* and *B*, that in the light of the state of the critical discussion at the time *t*, and the empirical evidence (test statements) available at the discussion, the theory *A* is preferable to, or better corroborated than, the theory *B*.
>
> Obviously, the degree of corroboration at the time *t* . . . says nothing about the future – for example, about the degree of corroboration at a time later than *t*. It is just a report about the state of discussion at the time *t*, concerning the logical and empirical preferability of the competing theories.

If corroboration is not forward-looking, it is difficult to see how the greater corroboration of a theory A over a theory B should be a reason for preferring theory A to theory B. For in selecting between A and B we want to select on the basis of the available evidence the theory which will provide us with the better explanatory and predictive power in the future. If corroboration carries no future implications it cannot be a guide to theory choice. This point, which has been made by several of Popper's critics, will be pressed further. For our primary interest concerns the questions as to how greater corroboration might indicate greater verisimilitude. How can corroboration help? It is clear that in the first instance Popper thinks that this may help by eliminating a theory. That is, suppose that T_1 and T_2 are theories in the field. A report of a test might reveal that one theory passed the test and the other theory failed the test. If this is the only test to date, we know that one theory is false and the other theory is not yet known to be false. Should we conclude that the falsified theory has less verisimilitude than the non-falsified theory? We shall see that Popper fails to justify a positive answer to this question and that within the Popperian framework corroboration is no indication of verisimilitude.

In certain circumstances, circumstances which do not obtain in science, a deductivist could forge a link between corroboration and verisimilitude. For instance, suppose that there is only a finite number of possible theories, say ten, for a given subject, one of which is true. Eliminating some theories as false would raise the probability that an arbitrarily chosen unfalsified theory was true. By eliminating all but one we could arrive at the true theory. However, in any scientific context we are faced with an infinite number of theories and, hence, the elimination of any finite number of theories does not raise the probability that an arbitrarily chosen unfalsified theory is true.

One important ground, then, for holding that Popper has in fact articulated a non-rationalist if not irrationalist account of the scientific enterprise, is that there is no way of forging the necessary link between corroboration and verisimilitude within a deductivist framework (i.e., the method is not related to the goal). This problem will be explored further below. There are at least two other reasons for regarding Popper as a non-rationalist in spite of his protestations to the contrary. First, the Popperian system rests on basic statements the acceptance of which can never be rationally justified. Second, even if we set aside the problem of the basic statements and take them for granted, the rejection of a theory solely because it is in conflict with the basic statements is neither the actual practice of the scientific community, nor ought it to be its practice. It is not always reasonable to drop a theory when it is in trouble with observation. While Popper himself acknowledges this, he fails to provide an adequate account of the conditions in which a theory in conflict with observation should be retained.

To develop the first line of argument, imagine that we are conducting a test to guide us in choosing between theory T_1 and theory T_2. Let us suppose that T_1 is incompatible with some basic statement A which is not incompatible with T_2 and let us suppose that as a result of doing the experiment we are disposed to accept the basic statement A. The grounds we have for rejecting T_1 can be no stronger than the grounds we have for accepting A. Let our theory be the humble one that all swans are white and let the basic statement be 'Lo, a black swan'. It should be clear that this procedure puts pressure on the status of our judgments concerning a basic statement. But what licenses us to accept a basic statement as true? Remember that for Popper basic statements are neither incorrigible nor can they be supported inductively by positive evidence. We cannot say the character of my experience was such as to make it highly likely that that was a black swan. Popper's account of the matter is:[19]

> From a logical point of view, the testing of a theory depends upon basic statements whose acceptance or rejection, in its turn, depends upon our *decisions*. Thus it is *decisions* which settle the fate of theories. To this extent my answer to the question, 'how do we select a theory?' resembles that given by the conventionalist; and like him I say that this choice is in part determined by considerations of utility. But in spite of this, there is a vast difference between my views and his. For I hold that what characterizes the empirical method is just this: that the convention or decision does not immediately determine our acceptance of *universal* statements but that, on the contrary, it enters into our acceptance of the *singular* statements – that is, the basic statements.

It is misleading for Popper to describe his view of the status of basic statements as conventionalism. For conventionalism in philosophy of science as applied to a set of statements is the thesis that with regard to these statements there is no matter of fact at stake. That is, the statements are not to be thought of as being, strictly speaking, true or false independently of decisions on our part. Popper subscribes to a correspondence theory of truth and regards basic statements as being either true or false depending on what the facts are. In this misleading reference to conventionality Popper is quite candidly drawing attention to the fact that basic statements for him are ungroundable. One simply has to decide whether or not to accept a given basic statement. At any moment of time, the class of basic statements is a class whose membership is determined by ungrounded decision. In *The Logic of Scientific Discovery* he says:[20]

> The empirical basis of objective science has thus nothing 'absolute' about it. Science does not rest upon solid bedrock. The bold structure of its theories rises, as it were, above a swamp. It is like a building erected on piles. The piles are driven down from above into the swamp, but not down to any natural or 'given' base; and if we stop driving the piles deeper, it is not because we have reached firm ground. We simply stop when we are satisfied that the piles are firm enough to carry the structure, at least for the time being.

One cannot over-stress the counter-intuitive character of this position. If I have rejected the theory that swans are white because I have just seen what I take to be a black swan, I assume that I have or could have good reasons for thinking it is true that there is a black swan. Normally one takes it that the character of one's experience constitutes positive evidence for the conclusion 'Lo, a black one'. We may be wrong. We may be hallucinating but none the less as things stand we have reasons to believe that it really is a black one. But to argue thus is to indulge in 'pernicious inductivism'. Certainly it is low-level induction but none the less it is according to Popper *verboten*.

It is my conjecture that the Popperian position seems attractive to many because they do not succeed in thinking themselves into the system. One is inclined to assume that the basic statements which report the results of tests can be grounded on evidence. Given this it would not be implausible to suppose that theories, unlike basic statements, are purely conjectural. That is, we conjecture theories which we can at best reject on the basis of a failure to fit with the observational basis. But this is not the Popperian picture. The official position is that the base level is a matter of ungrounded conjecture. Basic statements are accepted not because they are grounded by the evidence but because we have made a free choice, a choice unconstrained by reason and evidence. This means that it simply will not do for Popper to contrast his position with that of the fully-fledged conventionalist on the grounds that for him convention only enters in at the level of basic statements. If theories are rejected because of conflict with basic judgments and accepted in the absence of such conflict, their acceptance or rejection is a matter of convention just because the basis on which they are accepted or rejected is itself a conventional matter. If from some convenient convention alone we derive results, these results will themselves be conventional in status.

Popper reports himself to be upset by those who take it that the decisions involved are arbitrary decisions. And, indeed, it is an upsetting thought that our faith in theories rests on arbitrary decisions to accept or reject certain judgments about the results of tests. But what can possibly prevent this conclusion? In his 'Replies to Critics' all is revealed. For Popper there tells us why this is not an arbitrary matter though it is a conventional matter. For it is not up to my arbitrary decision: 'The acceptance or rejection of basic statements is a matter for something like a scientific jury – the scientific community (which may or may not come to an agreement).'[21] This is puzzling. If each of us makes an arbitrary decision about the colour of a swan by flipping a coin and if we opt on a democratic basis to add up the results for each side, the resulting decision is as arbitrary as the individual decisions on the basis of which the collective decision is reached. It is no less ungrounded. If we accept Popper's claim that it is reasonable to rely on the scientific jury this is probably because we are thinking of each member of that jury as being in the position of making a grounded non-arbitrary decision and, allowing for individual error, we think that these will tend to cancel out if we average. But for Popper no one has any reason for his decision. Thus there is no reason for the collective decision.

If any further argumentation is needed at this point, let us remember that for Popper there is no observation-theory or O/T dichotomy, and that for him all judgments are on an equal footing in epistemological status. If theories are conjectures, so are the reports of our experiments. If the reports of our experiments represent conventional decisions, so do our judgments to reject a theory. There is no easy way out of this dilemma. It is tempting to think that Popper should allow that we can rationally justify the acceptance of the basic statements. But this would require inductive argumentation. In view of the fact that there is no O/T distinction, we could then argue inductively on behalf of theoretical judgments. This would mean the collapse of the Popperian system. For the only feature that makes his position unique is his refusal to countenance inductive argumentation.

It is exactly at this point that the non-rationalist ought to put the boot in. For the Popperians are fond of accusing Kuhn of reducing the acceptance of scientific theories to a 'matter of mob psychology'. But it is exceedingly hard to see how Popper can resist this description on his own account of what is involved in theory choice. Acceptance or rejection of theories for Popper rests on the ungrounded and ungroundable conventional decisions of the scientific community. That is exactly to make it a matter of mob psychology. As I have remarked, it is in one sense hard to appreciate the force of the point being made. For we are so totally committed to the thesis that the character of our experience provides inductive evidence for the truth of the humblest of our observational claims, that we do not succeed in bracketing this. But bracket it we must. For unless we do we lose what is unique and hence what is interesting about Popper: namely, the complete rejection of inductivism.

6 THE CORROBORATION-VERISIMILITUDE LINK

The problem we are considering is how to justify the claim that one theory has greater verisimilitude than another. If we could have grounds for rejecting one theory and not another, we might have grounds for thinking (conjecturing) that the one had greater verisimilitude than the other. We have seen that the rejection of a theory because of incompatibility with basic judgment is not rationally grounded. Hence judgments about verisimilitude reached in this way will be groundless. Thus we are not making progress towards the vindication of a rational model which is supposed to provide rationally justifiable principles of comparison for selecting one theory over another relative to the posited goal for the scientific enterprise.

Well, let us entertain, for the sake of argument, the non-Popperian assumption that observational statements can be grounded. Perhaps God whispers in our ear 'accept the conjecture that you see a black swan'. Will this help? Unfortunately, no. For consider theories T_1 and T_2. Let us suppose with the help of the Greater Experimenter in the Sky we have been given the definite results of a sequence of tests, all of which are passed by T_1 and most of which are failed by T_2. This result on its own establishes nothing conclusive about the relative verisimilitude of the two theories. For it may well be that the theory which has passed the tests to date has a huge quantity of false content lurking somewhere else. We do know that T_2 has lots of falsity content. We know it has some truth content. We know that T_1 has some truth-content. But T_1 may have greater falsity content than T_2, content which has not been detected so far. That is, T_1 could have a much higher degree of corroboration than T_2 and yet have less verisimilitude. Surely, one may object, it could have less verisimilitude, but it is most reasonable to assume that it does not. Why? How can the Popperian justify the claim that corroboration is an indication of verisimilitude? How, that is, can Popper justify the claim that a theory which passes lots of tests as opposed to a theory which fails lots of tests has greater (or is likely to have greater) verisimilitude, i.e. more truth and less false-hood? Popper has two strategies designed to forge this link. One will be called the *truth-content strategy* and the other will be called the *whiff of inductivism strategy*.

7 THE THEOREM OF TRUTH-CONTENT

As we have already noted, a rationalist must forge a link between his articulated goal and the principles of comparison. In Popper's case this means showing that corroboration can be used to support claims about verisimilitude. In much of his writing Popper restricts his attention, when considering the comparison of theories, to the very special situation of a pair of theories one of which entails the other. Let B be a theory that entails a theory A where A does not entail B. For this situation Popper is able to establish (quite trivially) what he calls the theorem on truth-content,[22] which has the consequence that if B entails A and if the falsity-content of B is either the same as that of A or is contained in that of A, B has greater verisimilitude than A. Popper responds to this result as follows:[23]

> This assertion [that the theory with the greater content will also be the one with the greater verisimilitude unless its falsity-content is also greater], forms the logical basis of the method of science – the method of bold conjectures and of attempted refutations. A theory is the bolder the greater its contents [so if you want to increase verisimilitude you have to go for stronger theories]. It is also riskier: it is the more probable to start with that it will be false. We try to find its weak points, to refute it. If we fail to refute it, or if the refutations we find are at the same time also refutations of the weaker theory which was its predecessor, then we have

reason to suspect, or to conjecture, that the stronger theory has no greater falsity content than its weaker predecessor, and, therefore, that it has the greater degree of verisimilitude.

We can think of the situation as follows. Suppose we have a nice theory and want a better one. Given that a better theory is one with more verisimilitude, we try to get a stronger theory, one that contains the given theory. It will have more truths than the given theory. For it will have all the truths of the first one plus some more. However, we risk generating more falsehoods, for what we add may contain all manner of error. We only increase verisimilitude if the increase in truth-content is not offset by an increase in falsity-content. Thus what we have to do is to check this by submitting the new stronger theory to tests. If we fail to refute it, or if any refutation of it is also a refutation of the weaker theory, we conjecture, says Popper, that the new theory has greater verisimilitude than the older theory. Thus, it is claimed, positive corroboration can provide grounds for asserting one theory to have greater verisimilitude than another. I do not want to dispute the claim that this is the conclusion we would draw. Indeed it would be the reasonable conclusion to draw. What I do challenge is Popper's right to use this argument. For what makes the argument reasonable is the fact that it is good inductive argument. That is, if after some period of time we have conducted, say, 100 appropriately designed tests on B, which it has passed, we infer that it is likely that it will pass other tests and that it does not have a whole mass of falsity-content. The employment of standard inductive techniques (random sampling, etc.) will increase the reasonableness of the argument.

It was shown on pp. 57–9 that no two false theories are comparable with regard to verisimilitude on Popper's analysis of that notion. The result given can be used to show that if B entails A, the only conditions under which the falsity content of B is no greater than that of A is when A and B are both true. This means that the theorem on truth-content is of no help to Popper in his attempt to forge a link between verisimilitude and corroboration. I have none the less critically considered the use he makes of the theorem in order to display the following additional deficiency in his position. No link of the required kind can be established in the manner Popper hopes without the implicit use of inductive argumentation.

This strategy would in any event be of very limited applicability. For it would be appropriate only where we are comparing two theories, A

and *B*, one of which entails the other. And it is hard to think of a single realistic example. For the sorts of case Popper seems to have in mind do not fit the requirement. Consider, for example, relativistic mechanics and classical mechanics. Even if we set aside the Kuhnian doubts about the entailment of classical mechanics by relativistic mechanics and maintain to the contrary that the meaning of the crucial terms of classical mechanics can be expressed in terms of the vocabulary of relativistic mechanics we do not get an entailment between the theories. All we find is that assuming, say, velocities low with regard to the velocity of light then there is no detectable difference in the testable predictions of the two theories. There is simply no derivation of the Newtonian laws from relativistic mechanics on its own. If there were there would be no incompatibility between the theories. Choice in science is generally choice between incompatible theories. Hence even a successful account of theory choice for cases where one of the theories entailed the other would be of very limited value.

8 THE WHIFF OF INDUCTIVISM STRATEGY

This argument appears as a footnote in Popper's replies to his critics in the Schlipp volume. In view of its significance I quote in full:[24]

> Truthlikeness or verisimilitude is very important. For there is a probabilistic though typically noninductivist argument which is invalid if it is used to establish the probability of a theory's being true, but which becomes valid (though essentially non-numerical) if we replace truth by verisimilitude. The argument can be used only by realists who not only assume that there is a real world but also that this world is by and large more similar to the way modern theories describe it than to the way superseded theories describe it. On this basis we can argue that it would be a highly improbable coincidence if a theory like Einstein's could correctly predict very precise measurements not predicted by its predecessors unless there is 'some truth' in it. This must not be interpreted to mean that it is improbable that the theory is not true (and hence probable that it is true). But it can be interpreted to mean that it is probable that the theory has both a high truth content and a high degree of verisimilitude; which means here only 'a higher degree of verisimilitude *than*

those of its competitors which led to predictions that were less successful, and which are thus less well corroborated'.

The argument is typically noninductive because in contradistinction to inductive arguments such as Carnap's the probability that the theory in question has a high degree of verisimilitude is (like the degree of corroboration) inverse to the initial probability of the theory, prior to testing. Moreover, it only establishes a probability of verisimilitude relative to its competitors (and especially to its predecessors). In spite of this, there may be a 'whiff' of inductivism here. It enters with the vague realist assumption that reality, though unknown, is in some respects similar to what science tells us or, in other words, with the assumption that science can progress towards greater verisimilitude.

Popper goes on to claim that in the face of the high degree of corroboration of Einstein's theory it would be most improbable that it should have less verisimilitude than its predecessors. On one meaning of the word 'whiff' a whiff is 'a kind of flatfish', and certainly this argument is kind of fishy. On another construal 'whiff' is a puff of air. But it is just false to say that there is a whiff of inductivism here – there is a full-blown storm.

Note that one of the premises in the argument is what I called the thesis of verisimilitude or *TV* and which Popper calls 'a vague realist assumption' that theories are approximately true and more true than their predecessors. What exactly is the argument? It seems to be the following:

1 Current theories have more verisimilitude than previous theories (the thesis of verisimilitude).
2 Current theories have a greater degree of corroboration than previous theories.
3 Thus, corroboration is a sign of verisimilitude.

But this is an inductive argument twice over. For if this vague realist assumption of *TV* is to be grounded at all it will have to be grounded inductively. That being so, Popper is positing an inductive correlation between verisimilitude and corroboration which is to be appealed to in other contexts to justify the claim that T_2 has greater verisimilitude than T_1 on the grounds that T_2 has greater corroboration than T_1. This amounts to comparing two live competitors for our allegiance on the basis of a principle extrapolated from past success; namely, whenever we have had a theory with greater corroboration than another it has gone into the main corpus of science and, given *TV*, it is a better approximation to the truth than its predecessors.

At an earlier stage Popper used the style of argument considered above to support the weaker conclusion that corroboration is a guide to apparent verisimilitude:[25]

> There is something like verisimilitude, and an accidentally very improbable agreement between a theory and a fact can be interpreted as an indicator that the theory has a (comparatively) high verisimilitude. Generally speaking, a better agreement in improbable points may be interpreted as an indication of greater verisimilitude.
>
> I do not think that much can be said against this argument, even though I should dislike its being developed into yet another theory of induction. But I want to make quite clear that the degree of corroboration of a theory (which is something like a measure of severity of the tests it has passed) cannot be interpreted simply as a measure of its verisimilitude. At best, it is only an *indicator* (as I explained in 1960 and 1963 when I first introduced the idea of verisimilitude; see for example *Conjectures and Refutations*, pp. 234f.) of verisimilitude, as it appears at the time *t*. For the degree to which a theory has been severely tested I have introduced the term 'corroboration'. It is to be used mainly for purposes of comparison: for example *E* is more severely tested than *N*. The degree of corroboration of a theory has always a temporal index: it is the degree to which the theory appears well tested at the time *t*. This cannot be a measure of its verisimilitude, but it can be taken as an indication of how its verisimilitude *appears* at the time *t*, compared with another theory. Thus the degree of corroboration is a guide to the preference between two theories at a certain stage of the discussion with respect to their then apparent approximation to truth. But it only tells us that one of the theories offered *seems – in the light of the discussion –* the one nearer to truth.

As before, the argument is inductive. Moreover the conclusion is devoid of interest. For if it is to be rational to pursue verisimilitude we need a rationally grounded guide (which may of course sometimes lead us astray) to the actual verisimilitude of a theory and not a guide to the apparent verisimilitude.

To draw together the strains of the argument to date:

1 For Popper the goal of science is increasing verisimilitude. The principles of comparison involved are based on corroboration – the more corroborated theory is to be preferred.
2 There is no way within the confines of the Popperian system to ground rationally the claim that corroboration is linked to verisimilitude.
3 Popper's way out involves abandoning what is unique about his system.

For he needs an inductive argument to establish the conclusion that modern science has (by and large) more verisimilitude than previous science, and a second inductive argument to correlate corroboration and verisimilitude. But if we admit these grand high-level inductions we cannot object to all inductive argumentation *per se*. If we concede a role to induction here there is no reason not to admit inductive arguments right from the start. If we do this we lose what was unique and interesting in Popper: namely, the jettisoning of induction. Without using such arguments as considered above Popper has not provided and cannot provide any reason for thinking that the methods of science as he conceives them are a means to what he takes to be a goal of science. Thus he has either illicitly (given his own terms) brought in inductive argumentation or he has failed to vindicate his view of science as a rational activity.

9 *AD HOC* HYPOTHESES

There remains the major problem in the Popperian perspective on the scientific enterprise noted on p. 61. This problem which concerns the conditions under which one should reject a theory, is to a large extent independent of the difficulties explored so far and it will be instructive to develop it for two reasons. First, it shows the problematic nature of Popper's attempt to delimit the sphere of the scientific in terms of what is potentially falsifiable. Second, it introduces us to a major problem in the philosophy of science for which Lakatos and Kuhn have in differing ways attempted to provide a more adequate solution. For Popper a theory is scientific if and only if it is falsifiable. This means that it must entail some basic statement which could turn out to be false, thereby falsifying the theory.

How do theories entail basic statements? The short answer is that they do not. If we think of a theory as the set of postulates such as the laws of Newtonian mechanics together with their deductive consequences, we shall not find among those consequences any basic statements. In order to derive a testable prediction from a theory we need to specify initial conditions together with a host of auxiliary hypotheses. To illustrate, suppose we are considering a theory with the following single law giving the distances that a body falls from rest in time t in the earth's gravitational field:

$$s = \tfrac{1}{2}gt^2.$$

Our initial condition might be that the body is released from point x_o at time $t = 0$. If we are to derive a prediction of its location after a time lapse t we need a value for the gravitational constant g. We are also assuming auxiliary hypotheses to the effect that we have suitable systems for measuring distance and time. Suppose we find ourselves inclined to say that the predicted result did not obtain. Have we thereby falsified the theory? Certainly we have an unhappy situation which we can use Kuhn's notion of an anomaly to describe. But the presence of an anomaly does not, just like that, show the theory to be false. We may have been mistaken in our reading of our instruments, either in the initial readings or in the final readings. It may be that our auxiliary hypotheses are mistaken. Perhaps our ruler is not really rigid or perhaps our clock is at fault. It may be that the value of the gravitational constant is wrong. Or it may be that some extraneous factor intervened (some other object may have collided with the object when falling). All we know is that something went wrong, but we cannot conclude without further ado that our theory is at fault. The fact that we recognize the need to ignore anomalies where some extraneous factors have intervened makes theories particularly resistant to easy falsification. This point is usually expressed by saying that all laws have built-in *ceteris paribus* clauses. That is, our law should be formulated as: All things being equal, $s = \tfrac{1}{2}gt^2$. This qualification is obviously needed since no one would count it against the theory in question if someone had slowed the descent of the object by catching it in his hand, holding it for a moment and then releasing it. But once we admit the need to cushion our theories in this way, the impossibility of specifying in advance all the factors the intervention of which would not lead us to hold the outcome against the theory, we see how difficult it is going to be to falsify a theory that has something going for it.

Popper faces two crucial questions. First, when should an anomaly be taken as showing that there is falsity content in a theory? Second, how much falsity content has to be discovered before it is reasonable to reject a theory? In answer to this latter question it certainly will not do to say that the discovery of any falsity content provides a sufficient reason for rejecting a theory. For as Feyerabend is fond of remarking: all theories are born falsified. No theory has ever been totally free of anomalies. To reject a theory just because it has generated an anomaly will deprive us of any theories whatsoever. If this is going to be our response we might as well close down our laboratories and take up poetry and/or push-pin. As we shall see in the next chapter there is a case for saying that one should never reject a theory that has something going for it no matter how much falsity content has been discovered, unless one has a better theory to put in its place. Blame your tools, hypothesize some factor you know not what which is generating the anomalies, but do not give up your only theory. Popper is obviously not going to accept this line of argument. For he is not only interested in defending the rationality of main-line science, he is determined also to reject what he regards as the pseudo-scientific, i.e. Marxism and psychoanalysis. If one were entitled to stick by a theory in the absence of a better one, the psychoanalyst could concede the presence of many anomalies and yet insist it was rational to retain the theory on the grounds that it is the only theory we have of certain aspects of human behaviour. Thus it is crucial for Popper to provide and justify principles to guide us in answering the two questions articulated above.

The only thing we can reasonably do on Popper's account of science is to reject theories. Even if we set aside for the moment the problem of justifying the acceptance of basic statements, we shall never have reasoned grounds for rejecting theories unless the two crucial questions cited above are satisfactorily answered. Popper deploys two related strategies in this context. One of these, which I call the *anti-ad hoc strategy*, seems designed to deal mainly with the discovery of falsity content; and the other, which I will call the *cards on the table strategy*, seems more designed to answer the question concerning the rejection of theories which have been discovered to have some falsity content.

The first strategy involves forbidding us to make *ad hoc* moves in the face of an anomaly. If we can only preserve our theory by making an *ad hoc* move, out it goes (running foul of the point mentioned previously). When is a move *ad hoc*? It is clear from his examples that the intuitive content of saying that a move is *ad hoc* is that it involves a justification which runs in a circle. To explain the storm at sea by appeal to Neptune's anger is *ad hoc* if the justification for the claim that Neptune is angry is that there is a storm at sea. Take my simple theory that all swans are white. Suppose the scientific elite is inclined to assent to the basic sentence that there is a black swan on the Cherwell. If I defend my theory by claiming that some things that look like swans (identical up to colour) are not in fact swans my move is *ad hoc* if my only justification is the theory that all swans are white. While this seems reasonable in the abstract, attention to actual scientific practice shows that it is not. For instance, consider the apparent anomaly for Newtonian mechanics due to the observed motion of Uranus. The scientific community did not give up Newtonian mechanics. Instead they posited the existence of Neptune. The only justification for making this move at the time was the fact that the theory was pretty good. Popper is aware of this problem and has more recently written:[26]

> On the other hand, I also realized that we must not exclude immunizations, not even all which introduce *ad hoc* auxiliary hypothesis. For example, the observed motion of Uranus might have been regarded as a falsification of Newton's theory. Instead the auxiliary hypothesis of an outer planet was introduced *ad hoc*, thus immunizing the theory. This turned out to be fortunate; for the auxiliary hypothesis was a testable one, even if difficult to test, and it stood up to tests successfully.
>
> All this shows not only that some degree of dogmatism is fruitful, even in science, but also that logically speaking falsifiability or testability cannot be regarded as a very sharp criterion.

The criterion Popper employs to distinguish between good and bad auxiliary hypotheses is that of independent testability. A move is not *ad hoc* if it is independently testable. What is it for an auxiliary to be independently testable? According to Popper it is so if and only if conjoining it to the theory gives a new theory which is greater in content.

This will not do, for the reason given above in section 4: namely, that Popper has no satisfactory way of comparing theories as to content.

In fact, in deciding whether or not to immunize a hypothesis, we are not guided by judgments about increase in content (indeed, we may even decrease content). We look at the positive evidence for the theory. We may have such good reasons for believing in the truth of a theory that those reasons provide a ground for thinking that the immunizing hypothesis is true. That is, the only viable means of distinguishing between good and bad moves in this context is by reference to a positive doctrine of evidence. Popper cannot allow this. For his criterion makes reference only to the character of the theory plus auxiliary hypotheses without reference to evidence at all.

Popper has noted that scientists have sometimes introduced *ad hoc* hypotheses, hypotheses for which they had neither independent evidence nor had any reason to think it would ever be practical to subject them to independent testing. As an example, Popper cites Pauli's introduction of the hypothesis of the existence of neutrinos. Popper responds to this situation by warning us not to 'pronounce too severe an edict against *ad hoc* hypotheses: they may become testable after all'.[27] But if in order to accommodate as legitimate some obviously successful scientific moves we allow that it is sometimes acceptable to save theories by introducing *ad hoc* hypotheses, we need guidance concerning when such moves are legitimate. Without rationally grounded guidance, of greater content than Popper's advice not to retain untestable *ad hoc* hypotheses for too long, one can stick by any theory one likes, making *ad hoc* hypotheses and hoping that in the fullness of time they will become testable.

Someone once remarked that there is nothing more dangerous than a philosopher in the grip of a theory (no move will seem implausible to him), and Popper has this same cynical vision of scientists. What worries him is that immunization could prevent any theory ever being rejected (and that would be the end of the Popperian scheme of things, for what makes theories scientific is their rejectability). Sometimes this worry manifests itself in what I called the *cards on the table strategy*:[28]

> *Criteria of refutation* have to be laid down beforehand: it must be agreed what observable situations if actually observed, mean that the theory is refuted. But what kind of clinical response would refute to the satisfaction of the analyst not merely a particular analytic diagnosis but psychoanalysis itself? And have such criteria ever been discussed or agreed upon by analysts?

Here we are not so much deciding in the face of an anomaly whether or not it is *ad hoc*, we are specifying in advance what are the killing outcomes. For Popper rationality requires us to put our cards on the table in advance. One's first response to this claim is to ask rhetorically whether physicists ever lay down in advance what would lead them to reject either physics itself or a particular physical theory. Even if we set aside the Popperian hostility to pyschoanalysis, do physicists ever lay down in advance what would lead them to give up, say, Quantum Mechanics? Of course not. Has anyone ever encountered a paper in the *Review of Physics* that begins with an explicit statement or an implicit acknowledgment of what anomalies would lead the author to reject his theory? I doubt it. In so far as this is done it should not be done. For to go back to the point made above: the question whether to reject a theory in the face of an anomaly has to be decided on the basis of the availability of a rival theory and on the basis of the positive evidence for the theory in question. In any event, Popper cannot get round the problem by appealing to prior agreement as to which anomalies would constitute grounds for rejection, for that agreement requires rational justification if this is to be part of a rationalist account of scientific activity. In short, there seems to be no way within the confines of a purely deductivist account of science which abandons positive evidence to rationally ground principles guiding us in deciding between immunization and refutations.

It is not clear that the institution of science could survive if all or most members of the community made it their aim to falsify theories in the sense of trying to generate anomalies. For that is too easy, and it also involves neglecting the need for the sympathetic development of *prima facie* plausible theories. Of course this developmental process is likely to issue in the discovery of further tests to be made. However, to stress the goal of attempted refutation as strongly as Popper does is to give a distorted picture of the actual practice of science. If it were accepted as a reformative programme, it would be counter-productive. Progress requires that most scientists get themselves in the grip of a theory which they aim to develop and defend, and without simply trying to dispose of it as fast as possible.

In the end we have to conclude that Popper has failed to deliver a rational model of science. His 'pernicious deductivism' precludes him from establishing what he takes to be the methods of science (falsification) as a means to what he takes to be the end of science (increasing verisimilitude). In fact the situation is worse than this, for his model fails to fit actual scientific practice. This will become clearer in Chapter IV when we discuss some further aspects of his model in the face of Lakatos's critique of Popper. Notwithstanding these failures, Popper's account of science contains the important insight that the goal of science is increasing verisimilitude, an insight that will be retained in my own positive account. We will, however, in Chapter VIII, have to develop an alternative analysis of verisimilitude and to invoke inductive arguments in defending the claim that there has been an increase in the degree of verisimilitude of theories.

IV

IN SEARCH OF THE
METHODOLOGIST'S STONE

---

1 LAKATOS: THE REVISIONARY POPPERIAN[1]

In developing his model of science Lakatos saw himself as correcting the deficiencies in and developing the insights of Popper. His model, which is considerably less simplistic than Popper's, is indeed an improvement. In this section I outline the model. In the following section it will be shown that in spite of its virtues it embodies serious internal tensions and confusions. These preclude, as will be argued in Section 3, the possibility of using the model as Lakatos hoped to distinguish between science and non-science and to give hard advice on how to decide between rival theories. In addition, Lakatos, as a rationalist, wished to use the model in giving rational explanations of scientific changes. In this chapter the manner in which he sought to do this is noted, leaving a detailed evaluation of this aspect of his programme until our general discussion of the explanation of scientific change in Chapter X. Lakatos was not interested in questions of meaning and did not take up the challenge presented to a rationalist by the arguments for incommensurability. He was, however, particularly concerned with the question of how a rationalist could vindicate his principles of comparison (his methodology). His criterion for the selection of a methodology will be outlined and found wanting in Section 4. It will be seen (Section 5) that he is unable to establish that the methodology he takes to be selected by this criterion is a means to what he takes to be the goal of science, increasing verisimilitude. Like Popper he fails to establish the link the rationalist needs between the methods of science and its goal. Until that juncture of the chapter I shall be reading Lakatos as a neo-Popperian. In the final section I consider the embryonic, non-Popperian, neo-Hegelian Lakatos that Hacking claims to have discerned.[2] While one may well doubt that this reading is faithful to Lakatos's intentions, it does present a picture of the scientific enterprise of interest that merits critical evaluation.

Lakatos's primary objection to Popper is that Popper tends to represent the scientific endeavour as a two-cornered fight between a theory and the world in the sense that:[3]

> (1) *a test is – or must be made – a two-cornered fight between theory and experiment so that in the final confrontation only these two face each other*; and (2) *the only interesting outcome of such a confrontation is (conclusive) falsification: 'the only genuine discoveries are refutations of scientific hypotheses.'* However, history of science suggests that (1′) tests are – at least – three-cornered fights between rival theories and experiments and (2′) some of the most interesting experiments result, *prima facie*, in confirmation rather than falsification.

As Lakatos notes, the history of science is not consonant with the Popperian model. For theories have not in fact been jettisoned just because they have led to a prediction which was not borne out. Indeed, as we saw in the last chapter, to abandon a theory simply because it generated an anomaly would be to subvert the entire scientific enterprise. In such two-cornered match victory would go to the world every time. There has been no theory, no matter how successful, that has not generated some anomalies from its inception until its demise. The generation of anomalies is not a sufficient condition for rejecting a theory. For a theory with anomalies is better than no theory at all.

Lakatos's initial proposal is that we should regard the scientific enterprise as a fight between rival theories in which the world acts as referee. Consequently Lakatos suggests that we should regard a theory T as falsified if and only if:[4]

1 another theory T' has excess empirical content over T: that is, it predicts novel facts, that is, facts improbable in the light of, or even forbidden by, T;
2 T' explains the previous success of T, that is, all the unrefuted content of T is included (within the limits of observational error) in the content of T'; and
3 some of the excess content of T' is corroborated.

It should be noted that 'falsified' is used here by Lakatos in a non-standard sense as meaning something like 'ought to be rejected'.[5] Whether or not we should reject (as I will argue we should) Lakatos's account of what it is that makes one theory more acceptable than another, we should certainly agree that no theory having something going for it should be abandoned except in favour of a better theory. Equally, we should accept his point that an assessment of the relative merits of competing theories should be delayed until proponents of the theories have had time to explore modifications in their theories which might make them better able to cope with anomalies. One should not simply reject a theory T for a better and entirely different theory T' without exploring the possibility that some agreeable modification in T would produce a theory better than T or T'. This entirely acceptable suggestion leads Lakatos to the view that the unit of appraisal should not be a single theory but a sequence of theories in which each theory is generated by modifying its predecessor. Such a sequence is called a *scientific research programme* (hereafter cited as *SRP*). Lakatos uses the term 'theory' for a particular system of assertions any alteration in which produces a different theory which may be within the same research programme. Thus, in the sense he uses the term 'theory', theories do not have a history – they do not evolve. *SRP*s on the other hand have a history during which the theories within the programme are replaced by different theories. It is because the unit of appraisal for Lakatos is an historical entity and not a fixed set of sentences (a theory) at a moment of time that he introduces the term '*SRP*'. In the more colloquial use of the term 'theories' (when, for instance, we talk of the wave theory of light or the atomic theory of matter) theories are taken to be constituted by an evolving system of assertions about some common subject matter, and in this colloquial sense of 'theory' theories are not dissimilar to *SRP*s.

If the unit of appraisal is not a theory but a sequence of related theories, some criterion is required for determining which theories constitute a particular *SRP*. Lakatos seeks to individuate research programmes through a specification of their three components: the hard-core, the negative heuristic and the positive heuristic. The hard-core of an *SRP* consists of a family of theoretical assertions and any theory which is part of the *SRP* must share those assumptions. The negative heuristic of the programme is a methodological principle stipulating that the components in the hard-core are not to be abandoned in the face of anomalies. In the case of the Newtonian gravitational theory, the three laws of dynamics and the law of universal gravitation are cited by Lakatos as constituting the hard-core.[6] By appeal to the negative heuristic, anomalies arising in the application of the theory are not taken as refuting these postulates. The tension generated by anomalies is to be eased through the modification of either auxiliary hypotheses, observational hypotheses or hypotheses specifying initial conditions. Guidance on what is to be done in the face of anomalies is provided by the positive heuristic of the programme, which:[7]

> consists of a partially articulated set of suggestions or hints on how to change, develop the 'refutable variants' of the research programme, how to modify, sophisticate, the 'refutable' protective belt.

To see what Lakatos has in mind we need to remember the point made in the last chapter that no theory on its own ever gives rise to predictions of a testable sort. A theory itself is a set of general postulates together with their deductive consequences, and to obtain a testable prediction about a system we need to feed in both statements of the initial conditions of the system and auxiliary hypotheses. This means that what faces the 'tribunal of experience' (in Quine's phrase) is the theory plus what will be called the *theory's auxiliary belt* (hereafter cited as *TAB*). When an entrenched theory, T_1, faces an anomaly, when, that is, the theory plus the auxiliary belt, A_1^1, seems to be falsified by an experiment, the most reasonable thing to do may well be to modify something in the protective belt, changing it to A_2^1. We can represent this dynamical situation as shown in Diagram III.

In the case of the Newtonian *SRP* Lakatos describes the positive heuristic as a plan for developing increasingly sophisticated models of the sun's planetary system.[8] The first in this sequence of models has a fixed, point-like sun and a single point-like planet. This is replaced by a model with the sun and the planet revolving around their common centre of gravity, which is in turn supplanted by one with more than one planet. In the next the sun and the planets are treated not as point-like but as extended symmetrical masses and eventually interplanetary forces are introduced and the planets are allowed to be non-symmetrical. On this reconstruction, Newton is taken as ignoring the anomalies of each model in the sense that he did not take them as constituting evidence against the hard-core (his three laws of dynamics and the law of universal gravitation). This story does not provide a very happy illustration of what is insightful in Lakatos's notion of the

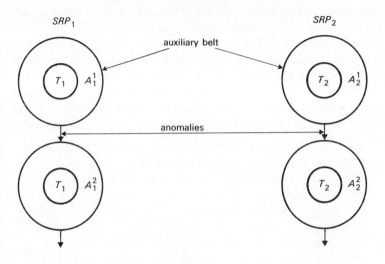

Diagram III

guiding force of a positive heuristic. There is no reason to suppose that Newton seriously posited each model in turn and revised them in the face of observed anomalies. Newton no doubt knew from the start that the initial models would not do. The development of this sequence of models was simply the thought process whereby he arrived at a detailed model worth positing as a theory of planetary motion. Notwithstanding this distortion of history, we can see that Lakatos has discerned two important facets of scientific procedure. First, scientists properly have a sufficient degree of faith in their basic theoretical postulates, the hardcore, that anomalies are explained away. These postulates are not up for the easy falsification in the face of anomalies that Popper presumes. None the less anomalies have to be dealt with and Lakatos's second insightful point is that scientists may have some very general guiding ideas (the positive heuristic) about how one should try to cope.

The positive heuristic, as we shall see in the next section, is, for Lakatos, more than a vague idea giving only very general guidance. It is supposed to be a precise recipe specified in advance and giving quite definite advice for the handling of anomalies. The assumption of the existence of positive heuristics of this character is, as will be shown, dubious. Lakatos's inclination to think to the contrary in part derived from his passionate conviction that 'the central problem in philosophy of science is the normative appraisal of scientific theories; and, in particular, the problem of stating *universal* conditions under which a theory is scientific'.[9] Lakatos seeks a methodologist's stone which would issue precise, definite answers to questions of the relative worth of rival research programmes. Since it is the positive heuristic that makes a programme 'work' it is not surprising to find him building so much hard content into it. The distinction between programmes that work and those that do not is drawn as follows:[10]

> A research programme is said to be *progressing* as long as its
> theoretical growth anticipates its empirical growth, that is, as long
> as it keeps predicting novel facts with some success (*'progressive
> problemshift'*); it is *stagnating* if its theoretical growth lags behind
> its empirical growth, that is, as long as it gives only *post hoc*
> explanations either of chance discoveries or of facts anticipated by,
> and discovered in, a rival programme (*'degenerating problemshift'*).
> If a research programme progressively explains more than a rival,
> it 'supersedes' it, and the rival can be eliminated (or, if you wish,
> 'shelved').

In this characterization of a progressive *SRP* we see on the one hand Popperian-like stresses on the importance of increasing content and of avoiding *ad hoc* moves. On the other hand, it is hoped that corroboration could come to play a positive evidential role so that successful predictions would not merely show that a theory had not been refuted. They would provide a reason for thinking that the *SRP* which has generated them has something in it. As we shall see in Section 5 Lakatos fails to make good this non-Popperian hope.

2 TAKING APART THE MODEL

In individuating *SRP*s the hard-core is the most crucial aspect.[11] However, we are not provided with any explicit principles to guide us in identifying the hard-core within the scientific community's web of belief concerning a given subject matter. Lakatos's examples suggest that the hard-core is what we would normally regard as the basic theoretical postulates or axioms of a theory. The negative heuristic makes this core ' "irrefutable" by the methodological decisions of its proponents'.[12] Elsewhere[13] Lakatos speaks of adopting a convention

82

that these postulates are to be held constant in the face of anomalies. As Lakatos is officially a realist, the suggestion cannot be that the core postulates are made true by convention. The convention must be a convention to treat the hard-core as true and to stick by this decision in the face of anomalies. Lakatos would be hard pressed to show that scientists either individually or collectively do explicitly make such conventional decisions. Consequently it is obfuscating to introduce the notion of convention at all. There is no reason not to say simply that the scientist believes the hard-core to be true or to have some truth in it. Initially this belief may not be well-grounded. It may be a bold conjecture prompted by a hunch. However, if the programme develops and has success, the scientist will come thereby to have reasons for his belief in hard-core.

In applying the notion of convention to the hard-core Lakatos differs from Popper who held that conventions determine the acceptance of the singular; not of the universal statements.[14] Lakatos feels that his extension of the notion of convention to universal statements is needed to explain continuity in science:[15]

> From conventionalism this methodology borrows the licence
> rationally to accept by convention not only spatio-temporally
> singular 'factual statements' but also spatio-temporal universal
> theories: indeed, this becomes the most important clue to the
> continuity of scientific growth.

But the continuity in question can be explained quite simply by the fact cited above. The initial belief of the scientific community in the truth or approximate truth of the hard-core is reinforced by the success of the programme in which it is embedded. Not only is the invocation of conventionality not needed to explain continuity, we shall see also (p. 87) that it seriously misleads Lakatos.

In any event, Lakatos's stress on the fixity of the hard-core is a distortion of actual successful scientific practice. Even when a programme is having great success, the scientist's faith in his basic postulates is not such as to preclude the exploration of the possibility that they may be somewhat mistaken as they stand. To cite but one example, consider the *special theory of relativity*, *STR*, which Lakatos would no doubt count as a progressive *SRP*. It is a basic postulate of the *STR* that all admissible frame-frame transformations are Lorentz invariant. Yet we find physicists working in relativity theory actively exploring variations in this postulate which give relativistic theories that are not empirically distinguishable on the basis of available empirical data from the *STR*.[16] If Lakatos were to counter by saying that in this case the physicists are no longer working in the research programme of *STR* he owes us a clearer criterion for individuating and demarking an *SRP*. In point of fact what should be recognized is that the scientist's faith is a faith that there is something important in the basic theoretical assumptions and not that those assumptions are exactly right as they stand. As we shall see in Chapter VI, on a reasonable individuation of programmes, the constraint that operates is the following weaker one: while progress is being made only those variants on the basic assumptions which preserve the observational successes of the programme should be explored.

The problems involved in identifying the hard-core of an *SRP* pale into insignificance in relation to that of determining the precise content of the positive heuristic. In the case of a powerful programme we are told: 'there is, right at the start, a general outline of how to build the protective belts [the positive heuristic]: this heuristic power generates the *autonomy of theoretical science*.'[17] One cannot discern in the work of Newton, Einstein or others who have launched successful *SRP*s anything like even a 'partial articulation' of the protective responses that are to be made in the case of anomalies. There is no more reason to think that some blue-print existed in advance of the difficulties than there is for thinking, as Popper does, that scientists can specify in advance the circumstances in which they would abandon their theories.

Elsewhere Lakatos says of the positive heuristic that it: 'defines problems, outlines the construction of a belt of auxiliary hypotheses, foresees anomalies and turns them victoriously into examples, all according to a preconceived plan.'[18] It is implausible in the extreme to suppose it to be characteristic of successful theories that they come equipped with this sort of advance warning system. Did the scientific community have some prior ideas as to how to deal with the conceptual anomalies generated for the General Theory of Relativity by De Sitter's discovery of vacuum solutions to the field equations? Presumably not, for the question of how to respond to this discovery remains as controversial today as it was at the time of its discovery half a century ago. Or, to take a hypothetical example, suppose it were to be discovered that the anti-hidden variable theorems in Quantum Mechanics rest on a major mistake. Are we to suppose that the scientific community has some idea now as to how it would then respond? Not at all. Response to anomalies, empirical or conceptual, comes after the fact of their discovery. And so it should be. For it would be a most inefficient use of our intellectual resources to formulate now what our response should be to entirely hypothetical anomalies.

It is, therefore, not surprising to find those students of Lakatos who work in the history of science giving a most minimal construal to the notion of the positive heuristic. For instance, Zahar in his study of Einstein formulates the following two metaphysical principles of great generality which he says correspond to the heuristic prescriptions of Einstein's *SRP*:[19]

I   Science should present us with a coherent, unified, harmonious, simple, organically compact picture of the world.

II Replace any theory which does not explain symmetrical observation situations as the manifestations of deeper symmetries — whether or not descriptions of all known facts can be deduced from the theory.

In virtue of their generality these principles (which have nothing specific to do with the theory in question) do not give anything like the recipe Lakatos sought. Indeed, there is no reason to think that the proponents of the rival Lorentz programme did not subscribe to them. To take another example, in Worrall's study of corpuscularian and wave theories in optics in the early nineteenth century, he accords little to the positive heuristic that is not included in the hard-core. The hard-core is said to include the assumption that light consists of corpuscles emitted from luminous objects and the heuristic is given by the principle that 'the corpuscles of light obey the ordinary (and already known) laws of particle mechanics'.[20] One may well wonder what principle places this assumption in the heuristic rather than in the hard-core. In any event it is, again, far from being a recipe for modifying the *TAB* in the face of anomalies.

If we give this minimal construal to the role of the heuristic, it is hard to see what the song and dance is all about. In the evaluation of theories we are supposed to examine the heuristics of the programme in which they are embedded. However, on the minimal construal there is nothing much to look at over and above the theory itself, which everyone already agrees should be examined. There is some insight in Lakatos's notion of a heuristic on the minimal construal even if it is of no help in the appraisal of a rival *SRP*. For it draws our attention to the fact that there are general principles held by the scientific community which guide theory construction. For instance, consider what I have called elsewhere the principle of the acausality of time,[21] which excludes one from citing either the time of an event as playing a causal role in bringing that event about or the mere passage of time as playing a causal role in bringing about change. Such a principle is not an explicit postulate of any theory nor is it a hypothesis subject to test. None the less it represents a general belief of the scientific community and acts as a constraint on theory construction. We shall miss something important about the scientific enterprise if we do not acknowledge the guiding force of such principles. Talk of a positive heuristic is a device for doing this. However, on this minimal construal of the positive heuristic it will rarely be of value in theory appraisal as it is likely that beliefs of this very general and basic sort will be held in common by the proponents of rival *SRP*s.

Lakatos himself tends to go to the opposite extreme offering what I will call a maximal construal of the role of the positive heuristic. For instance, we are told:[22]

> *two specific theories which being mathematically 'and observationally' equivalent may still be embedded into different rival research programmes, and the power of the positive heuristic of these programmes may well be different.*

The positive heuristic sets out 'research policy'[23] and so, in Lakatos's view, as the above quotation makes clear, we might begin with theories which are mathematically and observationally equivalent and by subjecting them to different programmes of research arrive at theories which differed in their power to generate novel corroborated predictions. This means that for Lakatos, if not for his followers, the positive heuristic must be more than either a vague statement to the effect that one should try to explain things in terms of hard-core, or very general statements which one could expect even the proponents of rival research programmes to accept. The positive heuristic will have to be precise and specific to an *SRP* if different heuristics can generate theories differing in predictive power from a common ancestral theory. This takes us back to the problem of showing that in general scientists have some such specific 'partially articulated' research policies.

If Lakatos construes the notion of a heuristic in this stronger sense he faces embarrassment as a realist. To see this, we must remember that the hard-core contains the primary, basic empirical assertions about the world and that the positive heuristic does not. For it is a policy directive which is specified in non-empirical, irrefutable metaphysical statements.[24] The problem with the methodology of *SRP* for the realist who, *qua* realist, seeks evidence for his substantial empirical hypotheses about the world is that we have no reason to regard the success of an *SRP* as providing evidence for the truth or approximate truth of the hard-core. Why should the success accrue to the hard-core rather than to the heuristic? This is not a problem on the weak construal of the notion of the heuristic. If the heuristic is, for instance, specified by general principles common to rival *SRPs* (as in Zahar's study of Einstein) having different hard-cores it is reasonable to take the greater success of one programme as providing evidence for the great approximation to the truth of its hard-core over the rival hard-core. But, as I have remarked above, the heuristic itself will have no real role to play in the evaluation of rival theories. On the other hand, on the strong construal of the heuristic there is no reason to think that the success of an *SRP* indicates anything more than the power of the heuristic itself to generate successful new predictions. Of course this result would not disturb an instrumentalist who had adopted the methodology of *SRP* since for an instrumentalist predictive success is not to be construed as evidence for the truth of theoretical assumptions. However, Lakatos is a realist and, as I argued in Chapter II and will argue further in Chapters VII and VIII, realism is the only tenable construal of theories.

Perhaps we should not have been surprised that Lakatos faces this problem of how to get the success of an *SRP* to accrue to the hard-core. For, after all, we were told that the hard-core is held to be true as the result of a binding conventional decision.[25] If I really have bound myself to holding it to be true that, say, all Balliol students are clever, there would be little point in my seeking evidence for that assertion. Lakatos's invocation of conventions in this context has blinded him to the fact that the crucial problem is that of obtaining evidence for the approximate truth of theoretical assumptions.

More intractable difficulties emerge if we consider how the methodology of *SRPs* is to be used in deciding between rival theories. According to Lakatos we are to compare theories by examining the track record of the *SRP* within which the theories are embedded in the hope that the past record is indicative of the future success rate. To do this we attempt to discover how successful the rival programmes have been in generating true novel predictions. A preliminary problem is that the explanation of a known fact can be as important in providing evidence for a theory as the generation of true novel predictions. Zahar, in making this point, cites the evidential support given to Einstein's programme by its capacity to explain the previously known anomalous perihelion of Mercury.[26] Lakatos accepts this correction[27] with the proviso that the explanation of a known fact is not to count in favour of an *SRP* if that fact played a role in the design of the theory in question. However, this proviso is too strong. The General Theory of Relativity would have been no less acceptable at the time had Einstein had it in mind to develop a theory with a view to accounting for the anomalous perihelion. If his theory had done this and nothing else, it would not have been terribly impressive. It did have other things in its favour and its value would not have been affected had Einstein had this hypothetical intention. Presumably Lakatos adds the proviso as he does not wish to give positive appraisal to a theory designed *ad hoc* to account for some single known fact. But this can be precluded without having to make our theory appraisal dependent on an evaluation of the intention of the theoretician. For if we are dealing with a theory which depends for its value more on the explanation of known facts than on the corroborated prediction of novel facts, its positive worth will depend on the range and diversity of the facts that it accounts for. Consequently, a theory cooked up to 'explain' a single fact will not be meritorious. If, however, it gives a unified explanation of a diverse range of facts not previously known to be connected, the theory will have merit whether or not the scientist's intention was simply to have a theory which would do just this.

Whether we make reference only to novel predictions or to the explanation of known facts as well, this does not affect the following substantial problem for Lakatos. In explicating what it is for one *SRP* to be better than another, he is making intuitive use of a notion of the relative size of classes of successful predictions and successful explanations of known facts. For the reasons given in the last chapter, any pair of rival *SRP*s each of which generates a novel prediction will generate a class of novel predictions of the same infinite size. Thus we are faced once again with the problem that we do not have any measure for the size of infinite sets of sentences. This objection will not be pressed further here, for my own defence of *TV* to be given in Chapter VIII deploys an approach to this problem that could be invoked by Lakatos in comparing *SRP* as to relative predictive power.

Some readers will no doubt feel that too much is being made of this particular problem. For, it may be objected, it is not the total number of predictions that is important but the significance of certain particular predictions. That is, we may rate one *SRP* over another without regard to the number of successes on the grounds that one has had what we regard as very surprising and very significant corroborated predictions. This move will not suit Lakatos's aim as he seeks to provide a criterion for comparing *SRP*s which is free of such culturally and historically varying factors as judgments of significance. We will take up the question of the role that should be accorded to such factors in our account in Chapter IX of the considerations that ought to govern theory choice. We shall see there that while the generation of novel predictions is an important desideratum, much more is involved. Consequently, we will judge Lakatos's model to be too simplistic. By way of illustration, it might be noted that Lakatos's model accords no role to conceptual evaluation. Consider the debate between the proponents of absolute and relational theories of space and time from the early eighteenth century through to the early twentieth century. It would be a grave misrepresentation of the state of debate to assume that it turned simply on claims about the relative predictive power of these theories. In fact these theories can be developed so as to have the same predictive power. The relationalists urged in favour of their theory that it avoided what they took to be a conceptual fault in the absolutist position: namely, that the absolutist represented as a possibility a totally empty space and/or time and this they held was not intelligible. This debate continues in regard to the General Theory of Relativity. The vacuum solutions of the field equations which give a totally empty spacetime are held by relationalists to show that there is something wrong with the theory, and by the absolutists as vindicating their position. What is at stake in this debate is largely conceptual. Questions of meaning and intelligibility arise and any model of science must leave room for the differential assessment of theories in terms of their power to avoid conceptual difficulties and not just in terms of their power to predict novel facts and explain known facts.

3 THE MODEL AT WORK

Lakatos intended to use his model to achieve three aims:

1 To demark the scientific from the non-scientific.
2 To evaluate competing *SRP*s.
3 To explain scientific change.

In this section it is argued that the first is pointless, and that there is a decisive objection (over and above those already given) to using the model to achieve the second. And I outline how he intends to use the model to achieve the third, leaving the final evaluation of his success until our general discussion of the explanation of scientific change in Chapter X.

Why should it be so important to distinguish between theories that are scientific and those that are not? For Lakatos and Popper, the polemical tone of their discussion reveals that the point is simply to condemn certain forms of activity. As with Popper, the pseudo-scientists who are to be condemned are Freud and Marx: 'Has, for instance, Marxism ever predicted a stunning novel fact successfully? Never!'[28] Referring again to Freud and Marx, Lakatos tells us that 'they do not add up to a genuine research programme and are, on the whole, worthless'.[29] To fail to be scientific is to fail! One does not have to be a Marxist or a Freudian to be uneasy about this equation of worthlessness with non-progressive *SRP*s, an equation which if acted on would have the effect of blinding one to the undoubted insights of these two not uninfluential 'pseudo-scientists'. The question must therefore arise as to why Lakatos (with Popper) feels so passionately the need to distinguish between the scientific and the pseudo-scientific. Lakatos's claim that this distinction is of 'vital social and political relevance'[30] is said to be illustrated by his dubious claim that Copernicus's theory was banned by the Catholic church because it was said to be pseudo-scientific. The claim is dubious because the drawing of this particular distinction is a latter-day development. In any event there is a touching naivety about the substantial claim. Are we to suppose that if the label 'scientific' had been successfully pinned on the theory, the censorship of the authorities would have melted away? Not a bit of it. A theory which appears to be threatening to an authority disposed to repress what it takes to be a threat will appear as threatening under one label as under another. One can well imagine the church retorting that if this is science, so much the worse for science! This enthusiastic manipulation of the rhetoric of science and pseudo-science reveals a failure to appreciate that science is not the only form of activity governable by reason. Scientific inquiry is a particular form of rational inquiry and there is simply no reason to think that it is the only form of inquiry that so qualifies. Consequently there is no reason to condemn some investigation just because it fails to meet some criterion of demarcation. It is trite but true to say that all forms of investigation should be examined on their merits to see what insights they embody and what understanding they provide.

It is in fact pointless to attempt to articulate a principle delimiting the scientific from the non-scientific. What matters is that we have a viable conception of what makes a theory a good one. If we wish merely to label theories that fall below a certain point in our scale of evaluation 'non-scientific' that will not have much point. But if that is all we are doing it will be harmless enough. However, it will not be harmless if we conclude, as Lakatos seems to, that anything which is thereby counted as non-scientific is to be condemned without further investigation as an unworthy activity. For it may be that these activities involve the rational pursuit of some other aim, and it would be as silly to condemn them for not being scientific as it would be to condemn chess or music for being non-scientific.

The methodology of scientific research programmes is not only to be used to delimit the sphere of the scientific, it is to be used also in making action-guiding decisions with regard to theory choice in contemporary science:[31]

> Thus the 'dogmatism' of 'normal science' does not prevent growth as long as we combine it with the Popperian recognition that there is good, progressive normal science and that there is bad, degenerating normal science, and as long as we retain the *determination* to eliminate, under certain objectively defined conditions, some research programmes.
>
> The dogmatic attitude in science – which would explain its stable periods – was described by Kuhn as a prime feature of 'normal science'. But Kuhn's conceptual framework for dealing with continuity in science is socio-psychological: mine is normative.

This normative appraisal is to be used by editors of journals to refuse to publish papers of those working on degenerating programmes and 'research foundations, too, should refuse money'.[32] Even if one held this non-liberal view that the degenerates should go to the wall with the pseudo-scientists, Lakatos has not provided, even on his own terms, a means for identifying them. This is not only because of the problem involved in comparing programmes as to predictive power but also because on his own admission even an *SRP* which turns out in the long run to be spectacularly successful (as judged by the scientific community) may go through degenerating phases. In view of the fact that theories wax and wane in their popularity, any model of science which is to achieve the previously stated aim has to allow for non-linear developments. That is, a successful *SRP* may have its bad patches.

Consequently, the model has to allow it to be rational to stick by an *SRP* during one of its bad patches. Lakatos's response is that it is rational to work on a degenerating programme in the hope of a change in fortune.[33] But once this concession is made, the tough-minded action-guiding force of his methodology dissipates. Hope springs eternal, and even his *bêtes noires* (Freud and Marx) can escape his strictures, working on in the hope that their programmes will be transformed from the degenerating to the progressive. To reiterate the problem: to fit his model to what he regards as successful science, Lakatos has had to concede that an *SRP* may have alternating periods of progression and degeneration. Consequently, he cannot advise that it be used in any tough-minded action-guiding way. As we shall see in our discussion in Chapter VI of Feyerabend, there is a strong rationalist case for not making such use of normative models, a case which Lakatos has in part made in spite of his predilections to the contrary.

The third intended use of the model is in explaining scientific change. Lakatos assumes that by using his model most of scientific change can be accounted for in terms of internal factors. Lakatos's use of his model does not fit that characterization I gave of rational explanation of scientific change. For he takes it that if we can show that *SRP*, P_2, was better than *SRP*, P_1, by reference to the model, that is enough to explain the transition. We do not need to inquire as to whether the scientists who made the transition believed in the principles of comparison articulated in the model or whether they were motivated to achieve the kind of theory the model specifies as the goal of science. As we shall see in Chapter X, any explanation of scientific change must make essential reference to the beliefs of those whose activities we are explaining. It is not enough to show that they acted as if they believed in the model. We would have to show that they did in fact do so.

4 THE METHOD FOR FINDING THE METHOD

In recent years historians and philosophers of science have come to appreciate the extent to which success in their own particular enterprises requires mutual interaction. Unless a philosopher of science takes the courageous *a priori*-tending approach of Popper to methodology, he will want to consider whether the historical development of successful areas of, say, physics, is compatible with his own account of what factors ought to govern theory choice. If it were to turn out that on his model, say, Aristotle's theory of motion is better than Newton's and that Newton's is better than Einstein's, he ought to be disturbed enough to return to the drawing-board. Of course, since the methodologist's task is a normative one (he wishes to uncover those principles which ought to guide theory choice) he need not be dismayed that some actual theory choices are, according to his model, incorrect. However, he must at least concede that investigating the actual evolution of successful science is relevant to the assessment of his model. In addition, the philosopher of science ought to be interested in looking at the history of science to see to what extent, if any, the conceptions with which he is concerned, such as, for example, that of a good explanation, have themselves evolved. There is a strong case for saying that this particular concept has evolved (cf. Chapter IX) and that an awareness of its history will aid our current understanding of its content.

The historian of science has no less need of the philosopher of science. At the very least this is true because the historian must possess some conception of what science is, of what a theory is, of what an explanation is, etc., to use in identifying the subject matter on which he is to expatiate. Whether he likes it or not he will in fact be operating under some grasp of these concepts, and therefore an explicit articulation of these concepts of the sort philosophers of science aspire to provide will not be amiss. More importantly, if he is to illuminate the history of science for us, he must show us how the historical figures in science conceived of the nature of their enterprise, how they thought of the notions of explanation, theory and so on. We want to see how and why they differed (if they did) from us in these regards; and from the philosopher of science the historian can hope to receive an account of our current conceptions with which to make the relevant comparisons.

If the historian of science subscribes as some do to the general thesis that rational transitions are to be given exclusively internal explanations and that non-rational transitions are to be given external explanations, he will have to employ a theory of rationality, the discussion of which is traditionally the province of the philosopher. Even if one does not subscribe to this controversial thesis (to be discussed in Chapter X) that different kinds of transition require different kinds of explanation, which would give philosophy a direct and exceedingly important bearing on the history, the connection between these disciplines is intimate enough for us to accept Lakatos's dictum that 'philosophy of science without history of science is empty; history of science without philosophy of science is blind'.[34] For Lakatos the history of science gives philosophy of science its content through providing the test between rival methodologies:[35]

> All methodologies function as historiographical (or metahistorical) theories (or research programmes) and can be criticized by criticizing the rational historical reconstructions to which they lead.

That is, we compare rival methodologies by comparing the different historical accounts (rational reconstructions) to which their use gives rise. The best methodology is the one which maximizes the role of internal factors and minimizes the role of external facts in the historical reconstructions it generates:[36]

> Progress in the theory of scientific rationality [study of methodology] is marked by discoveries of novel historical facts, by the reconstructuring of a growing bulk of value-impregnated history as rational.

Lakatos argues by appeal to this criterion that the methodologies of inductivism, conventionalism and Popperian falsificationism are less satisfactory than the methodology of *SRP*s in that they are more dependent on appeal to external factors. His critical remarks on these rival methodologies are best ignored since his polemical characterizations of them bear scant relation to the views of those who actually propound these methodologies. To argue, as Lakatos does, that his account of science is superior to those of Kuhn and Feyerabend on the grounds that where they 'see irrational change, I predict that the historian using the methodology of *SRP* will be able to show that there has been rational change',[37] is not an effective move in the context of this particular debate. For Feyerabend, at least, who argues that there are no objective canons of rationality, will no doubt respond that the more a methodology makes the history of science seem rational, the greater the mystification of the methodology. And, more seriously, Lakatos has given us no reason to accept his assumption that the best methodology is the one which minimizes the role of external factors. In fact to use this as a criterion in selecting a methodology is to beg the question under discussion; namely, to what extent have external factors played a role in determining the evolution of science? Someone might well hold that one methodology was better than another even though it left more to be explained externally. Worrall, who is sensitive to the fact that Lakatos's criterion for selecting methodologies is question-begging, has offered the following alternative:[38]

Any such methodology will, given *, be disconfirmed if it claims
that theory A was better than theory B, yet theory B was accepted
historically as better than A, and there is no independent support
for the conjecture that external factors distorted scientists' judgment
at that time. The methodology is confirmed either if its appraisals
and scientists' intuitive appraisals go hand in hand, or if, in the
case of divergence, independent evidence is produced for the
existence of misjudgment-provoking external factors. Such con-
firmations may be particularly significant, if the same historical
cases disconfirm other methodologies.

The assumption * is that:[39]

Other things being equal, working scientists have accepted theory
A as better than theory B if, and only if, A was better than B;
moreover we can tell whether A was better than B by applying
the criterion of scientific merit supplied by the methodology.

Let M_1 and M_2 be methodologies. Imagine that we have determined
relative to each methodology which were the 'right' theory choices. Let
us suppose that M_1 provides a better fit with history of science in the
sense that more of the actual choices made are correct if judged by M_1
than if judged by M_2. On Lakatos's criterion for the choice between
methodologies, M_1 is better than M_2. However, as we have noted, to use
this criterion is to beg the question at hand: namely, how good have
scientists been at making the right choices? Worrall, I take it, hopes to
avoid begging this question by using a criterion for the selection of a
methodology which allows as a theoretical possibility that in our
imagined situation M_2 might in fact be the better methodology. M_2
could be the better methodology for Worrall if there tends to be
independent evidence for the existence of 'misjudgment-provoking
external factors' in those cases where relative to M_2 the scientists made
the wrong choice but not for those cases where relative to M_1 the wrong
choice was made. While Worrall's proposal for testing methodologies
does not beg the question, it is not satisfactory. The reasons why it
fails reveals a serious deficiency in his and in Lakatos's conception of
what it is to give a rational explanation of a transition in science.

Consider first a situation in which theory B is better than theory A
on methodology M to which we subscribe. Suppose theory A is in fact
selected, and there is no independent evidence that 'external factors
distorted the scientists' judgment'. For Worrall such a situation is

disconfirmatory of M. But Worrall has overlooked the possibility that A was selected because the scientific community made its decision on the basis of some other methodology, M'. It may be that there is simply a difference of opinion between us and the scientific community in question as to what makes a good theory a good one. If they were operating under a different methodology we would not expect to find external factors. The fact that they made a choice which we would not make does not count against the normative claims of our methodology. We believe that there has been progress in science. It may be that in part that progress has been achieved through improvements in the methods used by scientists. For that reason we cannot assume that any situation which Worrall would regard as disconfirmatory really is disconfirmatory.

Consider now situations that Worrall would regard as confirmatory of a methodology. In fact, to put my objection clearly and starkly I will suppose that we have articulated a methodology, M, which is invariably confirmed on Worrall's criterion. The vast majority of decisions made would be correct if judged by reference to M. In any case in which the decision is not judged correct there is independent evidence for the existence of external distorting factors. Perhaps in each of these cases the scientific community was trying to please the Vatican by opting for the theory favoured in that quarter. In this situation we would not necessarily have any evidence whatsoever in favour of the methodology. For suppose it turned out that the reasons that the scientists acted on in making their choices were totally different from the reasons specified by the M for preferring one theory over another. That is, let us suppose that they have a system of methodological beliefs, M', which give the same results as M. No doubt Worrall would agree with us that in this case the better methodology is M'. For a methodology is supposed to be an account of the methods that ought to be used by scientists and it must bear some relation to what they in fact regard as the good-making features of theories. This means then that in evaluating a methodology we have to consider not just whether the theory preferences of past scientists correspond to the judgments we would make using M, we have to consider the scientists' reasons for making their judgments. This complexity is entirely missing from both Lakatos's and Worrall's accounts of the evaluation of methodology. In fact, they seemed gripped by the following misleading picture. Scientists make 'intuitive judgments' between theories (Worrall's phrase). We come up with a methodology. It is vindicated if it fits in with their intuitive judgments (or in case of failure there is evidence of external distortion). Scientists are rational when they get the right answer (as we judge it). To show that they got the right answer is to explain their choice. What is misleading about this picture is that there is no room in it for the scientists' own reasons for preferring one theory over another. They do not simply make intuitive judgments, they standardly give reasons for their preferences. We certainly have not explained their decisions unless we make reference to what they believe, which may not be what we believe. And in evaluating the rationality of their decisions there is bound to be a trade-off of a complicated and subtle sort between their standards and our standards. These and related matters will concern us in Chapter IX and X. From the vantage point of our deliberations in these chapters, we shall see that Lakatos and Worrall have proceeded in the wrong direction in attempting to vindicate a methodology. They articulate a methodology and employ it to determine which have been the progressive moves in the history of science. They imagine different methodologies being articulated, and each being used to determine the progressive moves in science. They fail to explain how actual history will give us a reason for selecting one of these methodologies. In fact we need first to establish that there has been progress in science without the use of methodological principles. Having done that, we then carefully examine the history of science to see what principles have actually been operative in bringing about that progress. That is how one vindicates a methodology; that is, by showing that it encapsulates the principles that have in fact been followed in bringing about progress. It is vindicated as a normative model for having judged that there has been progress; we will be committed to saying that following this methodology or improving on it is what scientists ought to do if they wish to continue to make progress.

5 THE POPPERIAN DILEMMA LIVES ON

The strategy suggested above for vindicating a methodology would not be open to Popper. For it requires us first to establish that there has been progress in science and then to examine the record to see what was done that was responsible for this progress. Popper, as I argued, cannot, as a non-inductivist, establish that there has been progress and thus he cannot establish the required link between his methodology and his goal of increasing verisimilitude. Lakatos, who soundly criticizes Popper on just this point, also fails to establish that following his methodology is a means to the aim of science which, with Popper, he takes to be that of increasing verisimilitude. The question Lakatos faces is whether we are entitled to regard the corroboration of the novel predictions of a programme as evidence for the verisimilitude of the theories within the programme. Lakatos's answer is that such corroborations 'only give "support" to the theory on the tentative metaphysical assumption that increasing corroboration is a sign of increasing verisimilitude.'[40] One might have thought that Lakatos, who does not have quite the same horror of induction as Popper, would have endeavoured to argue for this 'metaphysical' assumption. However, it is simply presented as an irrefutable assumption which we may ' "accept," . . . *without believing*'.[41] But if one does not even believe that assumption, one cannot justifiably cite it in support of the claim that the methodology of *SRP*s is a means to the end of science. And, of course, to forge the necessary link one would have not only to believe it but also to support the belief with good reasons. Hence at this crucial juncture Lakatos's attempt to vindicate a rational model collapses for the same reason that Popper's did. No reason is given for thinking that what is taken to be the method of science is a means to what is taken to be the goal. Lakatos at least has the virtue of being candid in simply 'accepting' that there is a link without pretending to argue. But, to paraphrase Russell, the virtue of this move is that of honest theft over dishonest toil. If Lakatos had been able to justify the assumption that there is a correlation between corroboration and verisimilitude, he would have been in a position to offer a reasonable test of rival methodologies. For the best methodology would be the one that best articulated the principles that scientists had been operating under in achieving an increase in verisimilitude.

Before turning to Hacking's incipiet neo-Hegelian Lakatos, I summarize some of the salient differences and similarities between Popper and Lakatos, the neo-Popperian. For both the goal of the scientific enterprise is increasing verisimilitude. For Popper the unit of appraisal is the theory, for Lakatos it is a series of theories, an *SRP*, linked together by a common hard-core, negative heuristic and positive heuristic. Crucial experiments between rival programmes which are all-important for Popper are dropped by Lakatos. For in the face of a conflict between theory and observation it may be more reasonable to modify the protective auxiliary belt than to drop the theory. A theory is to be dropped only if the *SRP* of which it is a part ceases to generate novel predictions which are corroborated. The terms in which rival *SRP*s are compared are fundamentally Popperian, i.e., increase in content and corroboration. And, consequently, Lakatos faces the same problems that Popper does in regard to these notions (i.e., the problem of measuring content). Like Popper, Lakatos hopes that there is a link of the appropriate sort between corroboration and verisimilitude, and like Popper he fails to provide any reason for thinking that there is such a link. Finally, Lakatos's conception of the scientific enterprise is much richer than that of Popper. For Lakatos's notion of a heuristic, in spite of its problems, does direct our attention to important aspects of scientific practice not adequately stressed by Popper.

6 NEO-HEGELIAN METHODOLOGY

Hacking[42] has suggested that just below the Popperian veneer there lurks a shy Hegelian. This neo-Hegelian wants to dispense with the notion of truth as correspondence to the facts by developing a theory of scientific objectivity in which it has no place. The starting point for this enterprise is the assumption that there is growth in knowledge. This is a datum which does not need to be argued for. What is required is an analysis of how it is that this growth has been achieved. For Hacking the methodology of *SRP*s is Lakatos's account of what has been going on in the growth of knowledge. According to Hacking, for this Lakatos the 'objective surrogate for truth [is] to be found in methodology'.[43] Being objective is a matter of keenly and disinterestedly applying this method. The method gives growth (it has after all been abstracted from a study of that growth, or so this Lakatos would claim). Thus the end of science is not increasing verisimilitude but simply that which the methodology of *SRP*s delivers, whatever that may be.

The case for seeing Lakatos as a neo-Hegelian is strengthened if we interpret him as holding a historized conception of method. That is, in contrast to Popper, this Lakatos sees scientific method as evolving through time. Hence his castigation of the hold of the Euclidean model on our thinking as the idea to which all knowledge should conform, and his focus on science in the last two hundred years which, as Hacking has pointed out, is characterized by its introduction of theoretical entities through laws which connect these entities to observable phenomena.

In further support of Hacking's interpretation one might cite Lakatos's claim that the methodology of scientific research programmes does not presuppose a realist construal of science:[44]

Our sophisticated falsificationism combines 'instrumentalism' (or 'conventionalism') with a strong empiricist requirement, which neither medieval 'saviours of phenomena' like Bellarmino, nor pragmatists like Quine and Bergsonians like Le Roy, had appreciated: the Leibniz-Whewell-Popper requirement that *the — well planned — building of pigeon holes must proceed much faster than the recording of facts which are to be housed in them.* As long as this requirement is met, it does not matter whether we stress the 'instrumental' aspect of imaginative research programmes for finding novel facts and for making trustworthy predictions, or whether we stress the putative growing Popperian 'verisimilitude' (that is, the estimated difference between the truth content and falsity content) of their successive versions.

If Lakatos had been toying with the thought that method is to be the surrogate for truth, this would explain his apparently cavalier attitude to the problem of linking corroboration and verisimilitude which was remarked on above. It would relieve the tension between his firm conviction that there has been growth in scientific knowledge and his agnosticism as to whether there has been progress towards greater verisimilitude.

Hacking's Lakatos has his attractions. For if the aim of science is simply to deliver whatever its methods deliver, we do not have the problem which faces, say, a realist of linking the methods and the goal. As we shall see in Chapter VIII, this problem can be solved, and moreover its solution will allow us to explain some aspects of science that would remain mysterious for Hacking's Lakatos. In any event, attractive as he may be, he is not Lakatos, as the following passage makes clear:[45]

> One needs to posit some extra-methodological inductive principle to relate — even if tenuously — the scientific gambit of pragmatic acceptances and rejections to verisimilitude. Only such an 'inductive principle' can turn science from a mere game into an epistemologically rational exercise; from a set of light-hearted sceptical gambits pursued for intellectual fun into a — more serious — fallibilist venture of approximating the Truth about the Universe.

There can be no serious doubt that for Lakatos the methodology of scientific research programmes is supposed to be a route to the truth. In the face of his failure (and of Popper's) to forge the link between the goal of science construed realistically and what they take to be the methods of science, we ought to take seriously the possibility that this aspect of the rationalist programme is radically mistaken. Consequently I turn in the next two chapters to consider the accounts of science given by Kuhn and Feyerabend, which are both non-realist and non-rational.

V

T. S. KUHN:
FROM REVOLUTIONARY
TO SOCIAL DEMOCRAT

---

1 KUHN AND THE IMAGE OF SCIENCE

T. S. Kuhn's *The Structure of Scientific Revolutions* begins with the observation that our image of science might well undergo a complete transformation if we took a dispassionate look at the actual history of science. The image he has in mind is the one characterized in Chapter I in which the scientific community is pictured as the very paradigm of institutionalized rationality. On this picture the scientist disinterestedly applies his special tool, the scientific method, and each application takes him further on the road to truth. In making this observation Kuhn is not simply looking forward to his own conclusion that between the ideology of science and the realities of scientific practice there falls a vast shadow. Rather he is suggesting that mere reflection on the source of our image of science is likely to prompt the conjecture that the image is gravely distorted. For the vast majority of us acquire our image either through contemporary scientific textbooks or through popular accounts of science the authors of which in turn derive their image from the standard texts. Such texts are designed to present contemporary scientific beliefs and techniques. In so far as we learn thereby anything about the history of science, it is through cleaned-up versions of past scientific triumphs. We learn nothing of the failures. We glean nothing about the state of science during its barren periods. And our grasp of the struggles that preceded the great moments of science derives more often than not from what the makers of these moments themselves said about the struggle.

If this is the source of one's image of science one ought to worry about its viability, just as one should be worried about one's image of the political process if that image was derived solely from, say, reading the memoirs of Wilson and Brezhnev. As we noted in Chapter I, two sorts of attack have been made on this image. The weak or boring attack is launched by one who accepts both that there is some special method and some ideal mode of applying it but who thinks that the actual practice of the scientific community falls short to a greater or lesser extent from what could be achieved. The strong or exciting attack, on the other hand, is waged by those who deny that there is any such defensible ideal with which actual practice can be compared. The investigations into the history of science, which Kuhn advises, lead him, initially at least, to embrace the exciting attack. However, in response to criticism Kuhn has so modified and altered or re-interpreted the position advanced in the first edition of *The Structure of Scientific Revolutions* that it is no longer clear whether a rationalist is committed to denying anything that Kuhn asserts. To begin with I shall be concerned with the earlier strong Kuhnian position, which deserves to be taken seriously (more seriously than Kuhn himself now appears to take it). For it articulates the most basic challenge to the rationalist perspective, a challenge which has yet to be met in full.

The model of science which Kuhn sees as emerging from a study of the history of science is to be explicated in terms of his notion of a paradigm. In his original essay Kuhn played fast and loose with this notion to the extent that one critic claimed to be able to discern twenty-two different senses in which the term was used.[1] Indeed, several critics have maintained that this free and easy manipulation of the notion nullifies the value of his work. For instance, Shapere writes:[2]

> Rather, I have tried to show, such relativism, while it may seem to be suggested by a half-century of deeper study of discarded theories, is a *logical* outgrowth of conceptual confusions, in Kuhn's case owing primarily to the use of a blanket term (i.e. paradigm). For his view is made to appear convincing only by inflating the definition of 'paradigm' until that term becomes so vague and ambiguous that it cannot easily be applied, so mysterious that it cannot help explain, and so misleading that it is a positive hindrance to the understanding of some central aspects of science; and then finally, these excesses must be counterbalanced by qualifications that simply contradict them.

Things are not quite as bad as that. For we can discern a way in which the term is used which makes it sufficiently precise to be potentially illuminating. This is what Kuhn now refers to as a disciplinary matrix. If we identify a scientific community in terms of, say, the subject of its investigations, the behaviour of bees or the evolution of the large-scale features of the universe, we should expect to find a considerable number of things held in common by the members of the community. Kuhn's talk of a paradigm is meant to direct our attention to those common factors, reference to which is required in explaining the behaviour of the scientists: 'What do its members share that accounts for the relative fulness of their professional communication and relative unanimity of their professional judgments?'[3]

The particular things that Kunn wishes to isolate through the notion of a paradigm include the following:[4]

(i) Shared symbolic generalizations

This is meant to cover the basic theoretical assumptions held in common which are 'deployed without question'.[5] For instance, cosmologists may agree in accepting the field equation of the General Theory of Relativity. This aspect of a paradigm is comparable to Lakatos's notion of the 'hard-core' of a *SRP*. Unhappily, Kuhn goes on to suggest that 'these symbols and expressions formed by compounding them are uninterpreted, still empty of empirical meaning or application'.[6] While there may be problems involved in specifying what such generalizations actually mean, for reasons given in our discussion of instrumentalism, we cannot regard them as ever being uninterpreted.

(ii) Models

Agreement on models may be agreement either that a particular analogy, say, between electric circuits and steady-state hydrodynamical systems, provides a fruitful heuristic to guide research, or that certain connections should be treated as identities (i.e., the identification of heat with molecular motion).

(iii) Values

Kuhn takes it that the members of the scientific community will agree that theories ought so far as possible to be accurate, consistent, wide in scope, simple and fruitful. While the label 'value' is perhaps unfortunate, it must be agreed that these features are standardly regarded as good-making qualities of theories and that this agreement is important in determining the particular theory choices made by the scientific community.

(iv) Metaphysical principles

A scientific community will agree on certain untestable assumptions which play an important role in determining the direction of research.[7] As an example one might cite a preference for field theories over particle theories. Such principles would have affinities with Lakatos's notion of a positive heuristic on its minimal construal.

(v) Exemplars or concrete problem situations

What Kuhn has in mind is the agreement one finds within a scientific community on what constitutes the nice problems in the field and on what constitutes their solution. Among the ways such agreement is displayed is in the questions set out at the end of chapters in standard texts. It is also meant to include the consensus on what are the significant unsolved problems, as indicated in the research projects set for graduate students and in the agreement as to what constitutes a worthwhile thesis.

This latter notion of a paradigm as a shared example was the genesis of Kuhn's full notion of a paradigm, or as he now prefers to call it 'a disciplinary matrix'.[8] The notion of a shared example derives from his observation that we cannot give a rule specifying necessary and sufficient conditions for the applications of even simple, observational predicates such as ' . . . is a swan'. Often we acquire a grasp of the sense of a predicate through the realization that certain objects constitute paradigm cases of the instantiation of the predicate. We acquire the ability to recognize other objects as being like the paradigm objects in the appropriate respect and apply the predicate to them.

Epistemologically the exemplars of the predicates are prior to any rules for their application. For we can certainly apply predicates without being able to articulate the rules governing their application. In fact, it may not be possible, even having acquired the use of a predicate, to specify its sense in this way. This point about the application of predicates is both familiar and not particularly contentious. Kuhn seeks to extend the general idea to more sophisticated predicates than ' . . . is a swan'. For instance, the notions of a successful scientific practice or a significant problem or a successful solution to such a problem are taken to be notions the application of which is grasped through exemplars or paradigms without prior or even post specification of rules giving the necessary and sufficient conditions of, say, solutions being successful. These 'shared examples can serve cognitive functions commonly attributed to shared rules'.[9] Kuhn is right in maintaining that there are no such rules available for these sorts of notion. However, there is a danger in assuming too easily that this is the case. For an endeavour to search for rules may reveal some necessary and some sufficient conditions, and the articulation of these may be of considerable interest even though we cannot produce rules which specify conditions which are jointly necessary and sufficient. His point remains that an explicit grasp of these partial rules is not a precondition of the application of the predicate. In the end it is not clear just how much light this casts on the nature of the scientific enterprise since it has nothing particular to do with the science. As we noted, Kuhn was led to introduce the particular term 'paradigm' in the context of considering the application of predicates. It was, therefore, misleading (as he now acknowledges) to extend that term to cover the other four ingredients noted above. Kuhn also employs the notion of an exemplar in giving his account of the meaning of scientific terms: 'The process of matching exemplars to expressions is initially a way of learning to interpret the expressions.'[10] Through the positive account of the meaning of scientific terms to be given in Chapter VII we shall see that this will not do as the basis of a satisfactory theory of meaning.

The positive and salutary virtue of Kuhn's use of his notion of a paradigm is to remind us that in looking at the scientific enterprise it is important to focus on more than the theories (in the narrow sense of the term) advocated within a given community. The danger in using the notion is that we may be led to view the history of science as a sequence of discrete, clearly demarked, paradigms. The notion is far too vague and imprecise for this. Given his own characterization it simply will not do to say that 'despite occasional ambiguities, the paradigms of a mature scientific community can be determined with relative ease'.[11] Notwithstanding this danger, it remains a useful term. For, in general, it directs our attention to the fact that in understanding the scientific enterprise we must look not only at theories proper but also at a wider range of beliefs, attitudes, procedures and techniques of the scientific community. In particular it reminds us that in explaining the replacement of one theory by another it is essential to look at this wider nexus and its evolution. However, as noted above, in view of the absence of any associated criterion of individuation we cannot think of the term as identifying any delimited class of particular items. This severely limits its utility as a term of art within the history and sociology of science. It is too vague a term to allow us to ask questions as to why one particular paradigm gives way to another or to seek to devise laws or general theories about paradigms. Kuhn unfortunately writes as if it were a technical term capable of utilization in this way. Interestingly, he himself finds no need to use the term in his recent historical study of the origins of Quantum Mechanics[12]. And, more seriously, as we shall see, Kuhn holds a number of untenable theses about this only vaguely delimited phenomenon of paradigm change.

2 REVOLUTIONS

Kuhn characterizes a period of time during which a particular scientific community shares a paradigm as a period of normal science. During such a period the energies of the members of the community are given over to solving puzzles defined by the paradigm, which is itself based on some significant scientific achievement. Of course, given the vagueness of the notion of a paradigm, we cannot suppose that there are clearly defined periods of normal science. However, it remains true that there are periods in which there is a high degree of agreement, both on theoretical assumptions and on the problems to be solved within the framework provided by those assumptions. During such times the faith in the underlying theory is such that anomalies are not treated as refuting the theory but are treated as puzzles to be solved. In time there may be a growing number of unsolved puzzles and anomalies, as a result of which the community's confidence in its theory is eroded. This crisis of confidence means that the agreement which constitutes the sharing of the paradigm begins to break up and attempts are made to articulate alternative theoretical structures.

At this juncture Kuhn introduces the notion of scientific revolutions making an explicit analogy to political revolutions. Kuhn sees a situation as revolutionary in a political sense if an ever-increasing number of persons feel sufficiently estranged from the political process itself to wish to change that process as currently institutionalized. Similarly, a growing set of anomalies generates an awareness of the constraining character of the paradigm and this leads some to articulate a new paradigm to put in place of the old. In the political case Kuhn remarks that there is a difference between the means standardly used in seeking change in non-revolutionary situations and the means used in revolutionary situations. By and large, the individuals in the non-revolutionary situation agree on the principles which are to govern decision making. In a revolutionary situation, agreement has broken down and an attempt is made to restructure by force the society in order to create a new framework for decision making. Kuhn is quite explicit in invoking this feature of the analogy. For in times of normal science there is agreement on the problems and agreement on what constitutes a solution. Kuhn thus corrects the simplistic Popperian model of science which tends to represent any experiment as a possible definitive test of a theory. Speaking of the scientist during a period of normality he says:[13]

> If it fails the test, only his own ability not the corpus of current science is impugned. In short, though tests occur frequently in normal science, these tests are of a peculiar sort, for in the final analysis it is the individual scientist rather than the current theory which is tested.

That there are periods in which experiments are seen in this light is clearly illustrated by noting our attitude to a student who in doing a routine experiment in a laboratory course gets a result at odds with the predicted result. The thought that the fault lies with the theory and not with him or his equipment is not even entertained. In the case of revolutionary science, on the other hand, the proponents of two competing paradigms face each other over the barricades without agreement on the principles governing the choice between paradigms.

The views that I have attributed to Kuhn can be construed as plausible, if somewhat obvious, sociological generalizations about the behaviour of the scientific community. As such their evaluation requires an examination of both the history of science and current scientific practice. At this juncture, however, Kuhn articulates a largely philosophical thesis to which historical and sociological factors are largely, if not entirely, irrelevant. At first glance the thesis looks as though it might be just another sociological claim:[14]

> As in political revolution, so in paradigm choice − there is no standard higher than the assent of the relevant community. To discover how scientific revolutions are effected, we shall therefore have to examine not only the impact of nature and of logic, but also the techniques of persuasive argumentation effective within the quite special groups that constitute the community of scientists.

This might be construed as the innocuous claim that propagandizing plays a role in the process of changing allegiances from one paradigm to another, which is something even rationalists can admit. However, Kuhn maintains not just that propagandizing plays a role but that nothing but propagandizing can play a role:[15]

> The normal-scientific tradition that emerges from a scientific revolution is not only incompatible but often actually incommensurable with that which has gone before.

That is, since the theories embedded in rival paradigms simply cannot be compared, there is no possibility of providing a rational explanation of scientific change. For in the case of incommensurable theories there are no objective theory-neutral principles relative to which the theories can be compared.

Kuhn offers Newtonian and Einsteinian mechanics as a specific example of incommensurability. Indeed, he rejects the standard derivation of Newtonian mechanics as a limiting case of Einsteinian mechanics for velocities low with respect to that of light as spurious on the grounds that the terms in the equations resulting from the derivation differ in meaning from the terms in the Newtonian theory. For in this derivation these terms are defined by reference not to the Newtonian concepts but to the Einsteinian concepts. We noted in Chapter I that the source of this doctrine of meaning variance lies in the positivistic and neo-positivistic holistic conceptions of the meaning of theoretical terms which give rise to the thesis of radical meaning variance, *RMV*. Kuhn does little to argue for this conception and simply assumes it to be correct. One cannot under-estimate the startling character of what we are consequently asked to accept. It means, for example, that there is no logical contradiction between Newton's assertion that simultaneity is not relative and Einstein's assertion that simultaneity is relative. It is ironic that someone who has urged us to take the actual practice of science seriously should be led to this conclusion. For this is certainly not how the scientific community views the Einstein-Newton controversy! In point of fact this is taken to be genuine head-on confrontation that does not represent a mere apparent incompatibility deriving from equivocation in the meanings of the crucial terms. In view, then, of these startling and unpalatable consequences we have every reason to refuse to accept the doctrine until we are presented with forceful arguments on its behalf. Since Kuhn has not offered the arguments for incommensurability due to *RMV*, we will defer further consideration of the case that can be made until Chapter VII. Kuhn's particular contribution has been to draw our attention to the surprising fact that a *prima facie* attractive theory of meaning leads to the consequences it does.

Given *RMV*, the problem of rationally comparing rival theories simply does not arise. Kuhn himself has remarked on this in the context[16] of withdrawing from his earlier more extreme position so as to allow for the possibility of partial communication between the proponents of competing paradigms. Since Kuhn no longer holds that extreme thesis of *RMV*, we have to look to his other reasons for likening the transitions between paradigms to a process of conversion or gestalt shift rather than to a rule-governed investigation which terminates in the grounded judgment that one paradigm is more justified than another. That is, even if we assumed invariance of meanings we would find, according to Kuhn, that in revolutionary periods there is a change in the standards of evaluation.

Kuhn's account of what it is that changes when such standards change is obscure. At times he talks of paradigm shifts as bringing about 'changes in the standards governing permissible problems, concepts and explanations'.[17] If it were the case that the very criterion of what constituted a good explanation changed radically as one paradigm replaced another, and if we lacked any paradigm neutral standard for evaluating criteria of explanation, we would have a problem. However, Kuhn does nothing to establish such an incommensurability between paradigms which we might call *incommensurability due to radical standard variance*. Indeed, he does not even show that the conception of what constitutes a good explanation has varied in the history of science. What is cited in justifying the claim that standards of explanation vary supports a quite different thesis. For instance, he says that the transition in the seventeenth century from the conception of gravity as having a mechanical explanation to the conception accepted by the mid-eighteenth century of gravity as being innate (and hence inexplicable) represents a shift in the standards of explanation.[18] But this undoubted transition is a transition in beliefs about what can be explained. There is no reason to think that it represents a change in the very criterion of what counts as a good explanation. It will be argued in Chapter IX that there are shifting conceptions of what constitutes an explanation, but that since there are rational considerations relevant to assessing these conceptions we do not have any reason to think that incommensurability due to radical standard variance is a real problem.

Kuhn offers another and more forceful reason for thinking that there may be problems involved in comparing theories across paradigms. Rightly remarking that we cannot choose between theories simply by reference to the number of problems they solve, because no paradigm ever solves all its problems and no two paradigms leave the same problems unsolved, he remarks that paradigm debates[19]

> involve the question: which problems is it more significant to have solved? Like the issue of competing standards, that question of values can be answered only in terms of criteria that lie outside of normal science altogether, and it is that recourse to external criteria that most obviously makes paradigm debates revolutionary.

If we formulate this problem of the significance of solved problems at a level of great generality it can look a very real problem. Suppose that theory T_1 solves a problem P_1 but not P_2 and that theory T_2 solves P_2 but not P_1. Let us imagine that the proponents of T_1 think that P_1 is significant and that P_2 is not, and vice versa for the proponents of T_2. What are we to do? We do not have any readily available criteria for assessing the significance of problems. This is not to say that we may not agree on some general considerations relevant to making such judgments in certain cases. For instance, if one party can point to the fact that the solution of one problem paves the way for further fruitful work, those who hold that the other problem is more significant should be expected to justify their position by showing either that this work is unlikely to be fruitful or that their own solution gives rise to further work which is at least equally fruitful. It may be that in the end we have to say that as things stand there is no reason to think that one problem is more significant than the other. It is none the less highly unlikely that this will generate a total stalemate. For it would be rare indeed if the only relevant factor at stake in the choice between competing theories turned on the question of the significance of their solved problems. Perhaps one theory generates a host of false predictions which the other does not. As an actual problem the problem of the significance of problems is not imposing. For it is unlikely that there will be many cases where the choice will rest entirely on unsettable judgments of significance. If it does in some cases this need not disturb the rationalist. For he ought to hold that sometimes the most rational thing is to suspend both belief and disbelief. If it is simply a difference as to significance, he ought to encourage the development of both theories with the reasonable expectation that some other more tractable difference will emerge.

3 THE FIVE WAYS

I have suggested that differences of opinion concerning the relative significance of problems is not likely to be as problematic in practice as Kuhn assumes. To this it might be objected that I have imagined resolving disputes in which there are differences of opinion as to relative significance of problems by appeal to other factors with respect to which there may not be any paradigm neutral agreement. Might not different paradigms come complete, not only with different conceptions of what is a significant problem, but also with different conceptions of what are the other good-making features of a theory? However, there does seem to be considerable consistency in what the scientific community in different cultures and different ages holds to be the good-making qualities of a theory. And, in any event, Kuhn certainly takes it that there is. For he offers us a partial list of the characteristics of a good scientific theory which he assumes will be agreed upon by the proponents of all paradigms. These characteristics, which I will call the *five ways*, are as follows:[20]

1 A theory should be *accurate* within its domain, that is, consequences deducible from a theory should be in demonstrated agreement with the results of existing experiments and observations.

2 A theory should be *consistent*, not only internally or with itself, but also with other currently accepted theories applicable to related aspects of nature.

3 It should have *broad scope*: in particular, a theory's consequences should extend far beyond the particular observations, laws, or sub-theories it was initially designed to explain.

4 It should be *simple*, bringing order to phenomena that in its absence would be individually isolated and, as a set, confused.

5 A theory should be *fruitful* of new research findings: it should, that is, disclose new phenomena or previously unnoted relationships among those already known.

Kuhn holds that these factors (together with others which are not specified) provide '*the* shared basis for theory choice'.[21] Thus we have at least five paradigm neutral courts of appeal in deciding between competing theories. But once this is conceded what is left of the claim that there may be variation in the standards employed from paradigm to paradigm? The remaining problem, as Kuhn sees it, is that while the parties in the dispute may agree, for instance, that simplicity is a good-making feature of a theory, they may differ in their judgments as to whether a given theory is simpler than another. It is argued,[22] for instance, that one might reasonably hold that Copernicus's system is simpler than Ptolemy's in respect of one aspect and not in respect of other aspects. That is, there may be disagreement as to how these factors apply in a given case. In addition, there may be disagreement as to the relative weight to be given to these factors when they point us in different directions. Therefore it will be convenient to leave the evaluation of this point until after we have considered the status of these five ways.

To this juncture I have been concerned only to make the point with which Kuhn himself has more recently expressed agreement: namely, that there is a consensus across paradigms concerning the features which make a theory a good theory. In *The Structure of Scientific Revolutions*[23] Kuhn notes that these factors can be appealed to in persuading scientists to change their minds. This suggests that these factors are not intended to play an evidential role. That is, while one scientist might get another to change his mind by pointing out it is inconsistent with his acceptance of these factors to hold the theory he does rather than the proffered rival theory, this does not show that there is evidence that the theory is better. For Kuhn the appeal to these factors has force only because of their general acceptance. That is, the generally agreed factors are ungrounded since there is no way of justifying them. This impression of his view of the status of these factors is reiterated in a later paper as follows (Kuhn refers to what I have called the five ways as the five scientific values):[24]

> Though the experience of scientists provides no philosophical justification for the values they deploy (such justification would solve the problem of induction), those values are in part learned from that experience, and they evolve with it.

If there were indeed no justification for these or any other factors which would play the role of what I called in Chapter I 'principles of comparison', the project of the rationalist is doomed. Thus, Kuhn, even having withdrawn from his earlier strong thesis of incommensurability due to radical meaning variance, and even accepting that there is agreement on the principles of comparison to be used in all paradigms, is still very much at odds with the rationalist whose position requires that principles of comparison be given a justification. Kuhn's scepticism derives from his view that if this were done, the problem of induction would be solved.[25] This problem, he says, cannot be solved, therefore this cannot be done. Which principle of induction is at stake? If Kuhn is basing his claim on a general scepticism about induction according to which nothing can ever constitute evidence for thinking that an empirical claim about the world is more likely to be true than false, his study of the history of science is simply irrelevant. His non-rationalist perspective follows immediately from this sceptical position without any need to look seriously at the practice of science. No mere historical study could support the philosophical doctrine of scepticism. If this is the basis of his non-rationalism, to expose its frailty we do not need to indulge in methodological investigations. This is not the place to enter into a full-scale attack on inductive scepticism. Suffice it to say that if Kuhn ultimately rests his case on inductive scepticism, his position is entirely devoid of interest. For his historical investigations are irrelevant to his non-rationalist model of science derived from philosophical scepticism concerning induction, and will be fraught with the same difficulties that face such inductive scepticism.

Even if we reject the sceptical position with regard to induction we are faced with the difficult task of identifying those principles which ought to guide us in deciding on inductive grounds which beliefs to hold. A more interesting postion will emerge if we assume that Kuhn is not a total sceptic and that by the problem of induction he means the problem of justifying particular inductive strategies. For instance, one of the five factors is simplicity. A non-sceptic ought seriously to ask whether there is any justification in treating this factor as an evidential one. To do so is to make the problematic assumption that simplicity is a guide to the truth (or whatever goal is posited for science).[26] Contrary to Kuhn, I think that particular inductive principles can be given a justification. It will take some time to lay the groundwork before an argument to this effect can be advanced in Chapter IX. What follows is merely a preview.

First, suppose that we are able to give a justification of the thesis of verisimilitude or *TV*. Suppose, further, that we succeed in isolating the particular principles that the scientific community has employed by and large in choosing between theories. The fact that science is progressing in the sense of generating theories of greater verisimilitude provides a reason for thinking that the methods employed (the principles of comparison) are in fact legitimate evidential principles. Obviously this argument needs much more elucidation and support (to be given in Chapters VIII and IX). For the moment my claim is only that if Kuhn has correctly identified the principles governing theory choice within the scientific community there is a promising line of argumentation which will, contrary to what he thinks, provide a justification for those principles. It should be stressed that Kuhn offers no reason for thinking that the five ways cannot be justified as evidential principles except for the vague reference to the problem of induction which we have considered.

It is possible that Kuhn has arrived at his non-rationalist position through an over-reaction to his sound, repeatedly made, but commonplace point that there is no algorithm for theory choice. That is, there is no rule to be discovered which would admit of mechanical application giving a definite answer in finite time to any question concerning which of a number of rival theories to prefer. Some of Kuhn's reasons for holding this we have elucidated above. Having pointed this out, Kuhn remarked, 'What better criterion than the decision of the scientific group could there be?'[27] As his critics were quick to note, this seems to make theory choice 'a matter of mob psychology'.[28] For if individual scientists have no grounds for their particular decisions, the collective decision of the group has no rational grounding. We cannot pull ourselves up by our own bootstraps in this way. Kuhn's response to his critics is to refer to the five ways which individual scientists are said to employ in arriving at their particular decisions. However, if these rules are not justified, the mere fact that they are employed only means that there is a pattern to the decisions made and not that the decisions are grounded. I described Kuhn as over-reacting to the discovery that there is no algorithm, for he seems to fail to appreciate that even if there is no rationally grounded algorithm to guide our decisions there may none the less be rational considerations which it is relevant to appeal to in justifying our decisions. Indeed he himself makes the point[29] that in ethical decision making there are considerations which influence conduct without constituting binding rules. In the same way (as we shall see in Chapter IX) there are considerations which guide our decision making in science even if they cannot be enshrined in binding rules.

Kuhn's over-reaction has served to counter the once popular position on the opposite extreme of the spectrum. For many philosophers of science thought that while the process of theory discovery was not rule-governed, the process of theory choice in the face of a given body of evidence was capable of being represented in a system of binding rules. Kuhn is correct in reminding us that even given the reports of experiments there is room for manoeuvre by the proponents of rival theories both of whom respect the need for consistency. In part Kuhn is echoing the thesis of Duhem and Quine that in the face of an anomaly there is a multitude of different moves that can be made. In addition he is pointing out that the various factors that can be appealed to in such a situation (simplicity, accuracy, etc.) may cut in different directions. Ultimately the scientist has to exercise his judgment. There is no more reason to think that this exercise of judgment can be replaced by a mechanical algorithm than there is to think that the judgment of a master chef might be made otiose by a computer-programmed super-cookery machine. This role for non-rule-governed judgment in the scientific enterprise will be explored in Chapter IX.

We can now see how to reply to Kuhn's point about differences in judgment concerning the application of the five ways and concerning their relative importance in cases where they point in different directions. For on the supposition that *TV* is true we can argue that the actual dialectical process which we do use in science to resolve these differences has served us well and hence we are justified in having general faith in it. Indeed, this procedure has resolved differences, for we are not faced with the spectacle of centuries of unresolved conflict concerning pairs of rival theories. It is not just that conflict has ceased, it has ceased in a not unfruitful way. For, given *TV*, it has brought us progress. This does not mean that we have justified some particular technique for resolving a dispute of this character. While we do not know which decision to make in a particular case we do have some reason for attempting to arrive at a decision in the ways standardly employed. This is what is right in Kuhn's rhetorical reference to the judgment of the scientific community as providing the best criteria. We have in that community the tradition of argument and counter-argument on these matters, and the success of science gives us reason to rely on the element of judgment that is inevitably involved in resolving these disputes.

4 DUCK-RABBITS

In 'Revolutions as Changes of World View'[30] Kuhn argues that a transition from one paradigm to another involves a change in world view. If by 'change in world view' we mean a change in our basic beliefs and/or attitudes this is merely a trivial consequence of the fact that in changing paradigms we are changing our theoretical assumptions. In some cases changing our theoretical beliefs may lead us to change other deep-seated beliefs. For instance, in opting for Quantum Mechanics we shall be led (if we accept the non-hidden variable interpretation) to think that determinism in its classical form is no longer tenable. Some (misguidedly, in my view) have tried to develop the consequences of this shift still further by arguing that it allows us to establish definitely the freedom of the will.[31] While some theoretical shifts may bring about quite extreme and unexpected revisions in our system of beliefs it is doubtful if many do have the far-reaching consequences that the adoption of Quantum Mechanics has been held to entail. Thus Kuhn is over-dramatizing in describing the sort of change in world view as being like that which would be experienced if 'the professional community had been suddenly transported to another planet where familiar objects are seen in a different light and are joined by unfamiliar ones as well'.[32] If the thesis that changes in world views follow changes in paradigms is construed as above it amounts to a rather contentless and hence uncontentious observation. However, Kuhn endeavours to give more content to the thought through the suggestion that 'the scientist with a new paradigm sees differently from the way he had seen before'[33] where 'see' is clearly taken not as a general term referring to how we think about the world but as referring to how we visually perceive it. There are two obvious ways in which a theoretical shift may bring about a shift in 'how we see things'. First, it will affect the way we describe the objects which are the causes of our visual experience. This can be illustrated by reference to Kuhn's own example of what he refers to as the minor paradigm shift involved in the acceptance of the possibility of undiscovered planets in the late eighteenth century.[34] What Herschel initially described as a comet came to be described as a planet (Uranus). Second, a shift in paradigm may influence not only how we describe what we see, it will also affect where and how we look for things. Once it was accepted that Uranus was a previously unknown planet the search began for other planets, leading eventually to the discovery of numerous asteroids. This much is uncontentious. However, Kuhn often writes as if a paradigm shift may actually bring about change in the objects which are the causes of our visual experience. Before pursuing this it will be fruitful to consider the mode of description Kuhn applies to the experience of one who undergoes a paradigm shift.

The shift in world view associated with paradigm changes are likened to the sort of gestalt shift one may have when, having first seen the notorious duck-rabbit as a duck, one suddenly sees it as a rabbit. By and large this analogy is absurdly far-fetched. For few of us had anything like this dramatic shift of attitude when, having learned Newtonian mechanics in school, we came slowly and perhaps painfully to appreciate the greater virtues of Einsteinian mechanics. None the less on occasion the innovative scientist may see the way ahead in a sudden flash. Even then it is unlikely that he will have the sort of alternating flashes – one moment seeing the old way as the way to truth and another seeing the new way as the way – just as one sees it now as a rabbit, now as a duck, now as a rabbit, and so on. For the innovative scientist it is much more likely that the new 'set' once grasped is fixed. Work then begins on elucidating and justifying the new approach without any backsliding.

Not only is the gestalt 'prototype' far-fetched as a model of paradigm shifts, it has several very misleading connotations. First, it suggests that the paradigms are incommensurable. One cannot simultaneously see the duck-rabbit as a duck and as a rabbit, and the analogy, taken seriously, would similarly suggest that one cannot simultaneously get at both theories for comparative purposes. It is for this reason that many have taken Kuhn to be committed to the extreme incommensurability thesis that he disavows. In addition, there is no way the duck-rabbit should be seen. The question of justifying a particular way of seeing it simply does not arise. There is no matter of fact at stake in this regard. Thus the analogy leads to the suggestion that Kuhn seems to intend, and that I have rejected, that similarly no question arises as to the justification of one paradigm over another in the case of a paradigm shift. A scientist

118

suddenly 'converted' to a new vision of the way forward cannot let matters rest there. The task of elaborating and justifying the new paradigm arises contrary to what the analogy with gestalt shifts would suggest.

5 WHERE IS TRUTH?

I return to the suggestion to be found in Kuhn that such a shift in paradigms not only brings about changes in how we describe the world and how and where we look at the world, but also brings about changes in the world itself. Kuhn writes as if he subscribed to this non-objectivist, idealist doctrine:[35]

> Something even more fundamental than standards and values is, however, also at stake. I have so far argued only that paradigms are constitutive of science. Now I wish to display a sense in which they are constitutive of nature as well.

> In a sense that I am unable to explicate further, the proponents of competing paradigms practise their trades in different worlds. One contains constrained bodies that fall slowly, the other pendulums that repeat their motion again and again. In one, solutions are compounds, in the other mixtures. One is embedded in a flat, the other in a curved matrix of space. Practising in different worlds, the two groups of scientists see different things when they look from the same point in the same direction.[36]

No passage in Kuhn's original essay has attracted as much attention or generated such heated controversy as this one. However, Kuhn has emphatically disavowed any idealist gloss which represents the contents of the world as changing at the behest of our theories.[37] Indeed, following the passage quoted above, he says of scientists in competing paradigms:[38]

> Again, that is not to say that they can see anything they please. Both are looking at the world, and what they look at has not changed. But in some areas they see different things, and they see them in different relations one to the other.

Thus, Kuhn's talk of a change in the world following a change in paradigms ought to be construed merely as a manner of speaking designed to draw our attention to the uncontestable and unexciting fact that the descriptions we make of the world may change as our theories change, and that theory change may prompt us to look at different aspects of the world. The world itself changes not in response to our changes of mind in matters theoretical. This is just as well, for we saw in Chapter II that the relativistic thesis involved in an idealist gloss of Kuhn is simply untenable.

It remains true that even if Kuhn does not have the idealistic tendencies ascribed to him by some critics, he is certainly not a realist. In *The Structure of Scientific Revolution* he makes the modest proposal (taken up by Laudan)[39] that we can explain 'both science's existence and its success' without the need to assume that there is some 'full, objective, true account of nature and that the proper measure of scientific achievement is the extent to which it brings us closer to that ultimate goal'.[40] Perhaps it is the case that scientific evolution is taking us nearer the truth. Be this as it may, the assumption that it is so is not needed for an adequate explanatory account for the scientific enterprise. In Kuhn's 'Postscript' this agnosticism is replaced by atheism:[41]

> One often hears that successive theories grow ever closer to, or approximate more and more closely to, the truth. Apparently generalizations like that refer not to the puzzle-solutions and the concrete predictions derived from a theory but rather to its ontology, to the match, that is, between the entities with which the theory populates nature and what is 'really there'.

> Perhaps there is some other way of salvaging the notion of 'truth' for application to whole theories, but this one will not do. There is, I think, no theory-independent way to reconstruct phrases like 'really there'; the notion of match between the ontology of a theory and its 'real' counterpart in nature now seems to me illusive in principle.

If, on the one hand, the absence of a viable theory-neutral notion of truth means that truth is relative to theory, we are back with the rejected idealist gloss. On the other hand it may mean that there is no technique which could be used by proponents of competing paradigms in arriving at reasoned judgments as to the relative degree of approximation to the truth of rival theories. However, through the argument of Chapters VIII and IX we will establish both *TV* and that there are evidential principles to guide us in assessing the relative degree of verisimilitude of rival theories.

There is a tension between his denial of any theory-neutral notion of truth and his more recent disavowals of the thesis of incommensurability due to radical meaning variance. There can be, he now maintains, partial communication across paradigms. Let us suppose that we are faced with a scientific community which holds a range of sentences $S_1 \ldots S_n, \ldots$ to be true. Suppose our partial translation scheme takes a sub-set of sentences $S_1 \ldots S_n$, onto sentences in our language $S'_1 \ldots S'_n$. If those whose theory we are endeavouring to translate associate with S_1 a different and entirely unrelated means for determining its truth-value than that which we associate with S'_1, what licenses us to assume that S'_1 is the translation of S_1? Or, to put the point more abstractly, if the meaning of a sentence is related to its truth-conditions, and if truth-conditions must be non-transcendent in the sense that it must be possible in principle at least for us to realize that they are, or are likely to be, in fact realized, the translation of sentences across language requires a theory-neutral notion of truth. Unless we share the same conception of what it is for a sentence in their language to have the same truth grounds as a sentence in our language, we cannot regard the sentences as equivalent in meaning. Thus to admit even the possibility of partial translation is to admit to that extent a theory-neutral notion of truth.

6 KUHN AND THE RATIONALISTS

On the interpretation that has been given, Kuhn is a temperate non-rationalist. For the rationalist presupposes that an objective justification can be given for his principles of comparison; and while Kuhn takes it that his five plus ways are generally accepted by the scientific community, they are, he holds, not capable of receiving the required sort of justification. This means that Kuhn rejects the view (described in Chapter I) that sociology accounts are required only for the explanation of non-rational transitions. All explanation of the evolution of science is to be done externally and not internally. That is, it must[42]

in the final analysis, be psychological or sociological. It must, that is, be a description of a value system, an ideology, together with an analysis of the institutions through which that system is transmitted

121

and enforced. Knowing what scientists value, we may hope to understand what problems they will undertake and what choices they will make in particular circumstances of conflict. I doubt that there is another sort of answer to be found.

I have described Kuhn as a temperate non-rationalist, for unlike Feyerabend he sees the scientific community as agreed on certain good-making features of theories. At times Kuhn gives a rationalistic-sounding perspective unlike that described in the above passage by stressing the role of internal factors in accounting for scientific change. For he argues that the build-up of anomalies in the case of a mature science is more important than the external factors in bringing about a paradigm shift.[43] However, in spite of the fact that he talks at times of the possibility of there being good reasons to prefer one paradigm to another,[44] he remains a non-rationalist. For, as we have seen, what are taken by the scientific community (according to Kuhn) to be good reasons for preferring one paradigm to another cannot be objectively justified. What makes the reasons 'good' is that they are generally accepted by the community, and if one wants to be a member of that community one will operate within the framework of this system of 'reasons'. Kuhn, in holding that there is a system of rules, differs dramatically from Feyerabend, the self-styled anarchistic non-rationalist, who denies that there is any agreement of this sort running through the historically evolving scientific community.

The description of Kuhn as a non-rationalist is premised on a particular construal of his view of the status of the five ways; and we must consider another serious tension that lurks slightly below the surface of Kuhn's text. Kuhn was trained originally as a scientist and has imbibed too much of the scientific ethos to want to do without a conception of progress: 'Later scientific theories are better than earlier ones for solving puzzles in the often quite different environments to which they are applied.'[45] And again: 'We must explain why science – our surest example of sound knowledge – progresses as it does, and we must first find out how, in fact, it does progress.'[46] These passages could be taken as pointing to a rationalist representation of science. For as I have defined the rationalist position, the rationalist is not committed *qua* rationalist to understanding the goal of the scientific enterprise in terms of truth or verisimilitude. Kuhn goes on, following the passages quoted above, to describe scientific progress as a matter of increasing puzzle-solving capacity in regard both to the improved precision of the solutions and to the wider range of puzzles solved. And, furthermore, he clearly thinks that the historically generated sequence of theories of a mature science is a sequence of theories having an ever-increasing puzzle-solving capacity. Given this construal of the goal of science and this belief that there has been progress towards it, if Kuhn were to argue that the five ways provide good grounds for making assessments of the likely puzzle-solving capacity of theories he would, in my ter-minology, be a rationalist. While his official position is that the five ways cannot be given such an objective justification, one senses at times that on the contrary he does regard them as providing good justifiable indications of puzzle-solving capacity. If we were to regard Kuhn as an embryonic rationalist, the following passage can be con-strued as giving a clear statement of a rationalist perspective on the sociology of scientific knowledge:[47]

> When scientists must choose between competing theories, two
> men fully committed to the same list of criteria for choice may
> nevertheless reach different conclusions. Perhaps they interpret
> simplicity differently or have different convictions about the range
> of fields within which the consistency criterion must be met. Or
> perhaps they agree about these matters but differ about the
> relative weights to be accorded to these or to other criteria when
> several are deployed together. With respect to divergencies of this
> sort, no set of choice criteria yet proposed is of any use. One can
> explain, as the historian characteristically does, why particular men
> made particular choices at particular times. But for that purpose one
> must go beyond the list of shared criteria to characteristics of the
> individuals who make the choice. One must, that is, deal with
> characteristics which vary from one scientist to another without
> thereby in the least jeopardizing their adherence to the canons
> that make science scientific. Though such canons do exist and
> should be discoverable (doubtless the criteria of choice with which
> I began are among them), they are not by themselves sufficient to
> determine the decisions of individual scientists. For that purpose
> the shared canons must be fleshed out in ways that differ from one
> individual to another.

If one assumes that the criteria referred to above can be given an objec-tive justification, there is nothing in Kuhn's perspective with which a rationalist need disagree at any fundamental level. For Kuhn would simply be insisting that in giving a full explanation of a scientific transition we must make reference not only to the objective criteria guiding theory choice but also to various pyschological and sociological factors. Only a rationalist who held the absurd view that scientific method consists of some binding algorithm which entirely determines the theory choices of scientists could disagree with the view that such factors have a role to play in the explanation of the evolution of science.

The position we have reached is that two Kuhns can be discerned. One, the temperate non-rationalist, takes it that while there is agreement on the factors which guide theory choice, these factors cannot be justified. The other, the embryonic rationalist, takes it that the five ways can be justified as the criteria to be used in achieving progress in science; that is, in increasing puzzle-solving capacity. This Kuhn is no realist, however, for progress is not related to truth or verisimilitude. Laudan, whose model of science we discuss in Chapter VIII, has sought to elaborate the sort of non-realist, rationalist perspective on the scientific enterprise of this latter Kuhn. However, as will be established, this will not do, since there is no viable notion of puzzle-solving or problem-solving (Laudan's phrase) capacity which does not make realist presumptions.

VI

FEYERABEND, THE
PASSIONATE LIBERAL

1 AGAINST METHOD

No more lively or entertaining critique of the scientific method has
been provided than that offered by Feyerabend in his *Against Method*,[1]
which might well have been called *Against Received Opinion*. Feyerabend
hopes that a perusal of this work will show us that there is no such
thing as scientific method. Science, it is argued, is just one tradition
among many. It is privileged neither in terms of methods nor in terms
of results; and in view of this we ought to remove science from its
pedestal and strive to create a society in which all traditions have
equal access to power and education. Among the traditions which
Feyerabend wishes to see benefit from this equal access are astrology,
witchcraft and traditional medicine.

Feyerabend's attempt to debunk the rationalist account of the
scientific enterprise rests largely on his attack on method, and consequently it will be fruitful to begin by reminding ourselves what it is
that is supposed not to exist. The study of scientific method has been
taken to cover two apparently different activities. One of these studies
would involve an attempt to discover rules or techniques to be employed in the discovery of theories. The other study would seek to
uncover objectively justifiable principles for the evaluation of rival
theories in the light of available evidence. Of these two activities it is
the former that is generally considered to be suspect. Most philosophers
of science hold that while the study of justification is a legitimate and
important enterprise, there is no systematic, useful study of theory
construction or discovery. For, it is argued, this is the lawless province

125

of intuition, inspiration, luck or unlucky hunches and guesswork. The claim that there is a distinction between discovery and justification, together with the claim that only the latter is the legitimate province of the philosophy of science, was one of the cardinal principles of the Vienna Circle. Thus, Feigl writes:[2]

> It is one thing to retrace the historical origins, the psychological genesis and development, the socio-politico-economic conditions for the acceptance or rejection of scientific theories; and it is quite another thing to provide a logical reconstruction of the conceptual structure and of the testing of scientific theories.

Feyerabend denies that there is any legitimate distinction between these two apparently different studies and, furthermore, he denies that there is method in science.

In due course (Chapter IX) it will be necessary to clarify what is supposed to be meant by 'method' in the sense of a logic of justification. However, the idea is clear enough for us to locate Feyerabend. He stands against the venerable tradition of searching for a system of rules which it is held ought to guide scientists in the business of theory choice. According to him no such system of rules can be found and to adopt any particular rules or methodology can only have the effect of impeding scientific progress: '*The only principle that does not inhibit progress: anything goes*'.[3] By this he means that if one wants to have exceptionless rules that can be applied come what may, they will be so empty and indefinite that nothing is ruled out by them.[4] Feyerabend is thus much more radical in his critique of rationalism than Kuhn. For Kuhn holds that there are rules held in common by all members of the scientific community. The application of the rules may be problematic and the rules cannot be given an objective justification. All the same there are rules (the five ways). For Feyerabend on the other hand no rules having any real content or force can be abstracted from scientific practice. Feyerabend is thus a paradigm case of what I called in Chapter I a non-rationalist. Attempts to appraise theories objectively in terms of content or verisimilitude are rejected on the grounds that theories are incommensurable.[5] Of principles of comparison that might be appealed to, Feyerabend claims, 'it is very difficult to find wish-independent arguments for their acceptability'.[6] Consequently the explanation of scientific change is to be done in external terms by reference to subjective preferences, propaganda, etc.[7]

Before proceeding to a detailed examination of Feyerabend's 'case' against method some remarks about my own philosophical methodology are in order. For Feyerabend, individuals are autonomous with regard to ideologies in the sense that the acceptance or rejection of an ideology is a matter for individual choice.[8] There are no considerations that could provide a reason for someone to adopt an ideology that would be a reason for anyone to do so regardless of his inclinations. Consequently, when we are faced with a conflict between scientific theories that involve a clash of ideology (among other such examples Feyerabend includes the clash between Lorentz and Einstein) there is nothing that could constitute a reason for adopting one theory rather than another which would be a reason for any individual regardless of his own ideological perspective. Feyerabend does seem to admit one exception to this general claim. For it is held that a theory or ideology can be shown to be objectively deficient if it can be shown that there is an inconsistency in the theory or ideology. The considerations that incline Feyerabend to the view that science is ideology would equally incline him to the view that philosophy is as ideological. Consequently one is inclined to ask what can possibly be the force of his philosophical arguments about the nature of science. Surely if philosophy is ideological in Feyerabend's sense of the term he cannot, *ex hypothesi*, provide a reason for believing his philosophical case which is a reason for anyone no matter what his ideological perspective. That being so, one must either leave Feyerabend alone (if we judge it not to be significant whether or not he is believed) or we must resort to the most effective means of bringing about a change in his views. The task in this case is not to reason with the philosopher but to change him. Happily the situation is not altogether desperate. For given that inconsistency provides an objective (i.e. non-ideologically based) reason for rejecting an ideology, even if a philosophical position is an ideological position we still have the minimal tool of *reductio ad absurdum*. On his own terms Feyerabend will have to accept a proof of an inconsistency in his position as a reason for abandoning that position. Consequently in what follows I will, as far as possible, restrict my criticism of Feyerabend to those criticisms that involve displaying internal tensions and contradictions in his position.

It might appear from some of Feyerabend's remarks that even finding an inconsistency in a system does not, according to him, show that there is anything wrong with the system. He asks rhetorically 'what is wrong with inconsistencies?'[9] and goes on to reject the standard defence of consistency, which consists in pointing out that from an inconsistency everything follows. For, he says, as inconsistent theories have brought progress in science, something is wrong with a logic which has the above consequence. But the fact that inconsistent theories have brought progress is no reason to revise logic by dropping the law of non-contradiction. Inconsistent theories have brought progress through their development into consistent theories. Indeed, the desire to modify theories because of inconsistency has been an important factor in bringing progress, as the example of a situation in set theory at the turn of the century illustrates. It was Russell's discovery that naive set theory was inconsistent that gave rise to the development of modern axiomatic set theory.

2 COUNTER-PRODUCTIVE METHOD

Feyerabend's attack on method begins on a plausible note:[10]

> The idea of a method that contains firm, unchanging and absolutely binding principles for conducting the business of science meets considerable difficulty when confronted with the results of historical research. We find then, that there is not a single rule, however plausible, and however firmly grounded in epistemology, that is not violated at some time or other. It becomes evident that such violations are not accidental events, they are not results of insufficient knowledge or of inattention which might have been avoided.

One can readily agree with Feyerabend's strictures against the notion of unchanging rules. If there is a method in science, we had to acquire knowledge of it. There is no reason to assume that such enlightenment was God-given in all its fullness at some moment of time. We can make discoveries in the area of methodology just as we make discoveries in science itself. There is, as Feyerabend reminds us, an inter-action between reason and research. If a line of research in which some methodology is being implicitly or explicitly followed is not delivering the goods, the way forward may well be to change the methodology. The all-important use of the statistical methods in the evaluation of hypotheses arose in just this way. But agreeing that method changes is no threat to the rationalist perspective. Nor need any rationalist maintain that the rules are absolutely binding and exceptionless. For these are inductive rules advising us as to which of a pair of rival empirical theories it is better to adopt in the face of available evidence. There is a logical gap between the evidence of a theory and its truth or approximate truth which is bridged by an inductive inference. As Russell colourfully reminded us, the best-laid inductions of men and chickens can go awry.[11] No matter how successful a rule is in general it may in some particular contexts lead us to choose what turns out to be the inferior theory. This is no mere logical possibility. For we should expect our rules to have a high risk factor. If our rules are too safe (i.e., requiring a vast amount of evidence before being applicable), they may cushion us from error at the cost of minimizing the number of contexts in which we actually end up adopting a theory. Thus, to have evidence of a number of occasions in which some rule has led us astray is not necessarily to have an adequate reason for doubting the acceptability of the rule. It may be, these exceptions notwithstanding, that our chance of progress in the long run is greater if we employ the rule. One might seek to show the unsatisfactory character of a particular rule by establishing that it has led us wrong more often than right. However, as we shall see in Section 4, to use this strategy in attacking method creates the destructive dilemma of invoking method against method.

Setting aside for the moment these initial doubts as to whether the conception of method which Feyerabend attacks would be shared by any contemporary rationalist, I turn to consider his particular strategy. This involves articulating two rules which he takes to have been standardly held by philosophers of science and arguing that in each case there is an equally acceptable but incompatible counter-rule. The given rules are not to be replaced by the counter-rules. Rather, Feyerabend hopes to undermine our faith in all rules of evidence by showing that any such rule has an equally plausible counter-rule the use of which would give opposite results.[12] Obviously this strategy will only bear fruit if the rules he identifies are rules that philosophers and/or scientists have tended to assume are used in theory choice. As we will see, he does not meet this condition. The first rule considered is what he calls the consistency condition '*which demands that new hypotheses agree with accepted theories.*'[13] But if we are to have a plausible case to discuss this rule needs at least three caveats. First, not even the most conservative of rationalists will deny that an unacceptable theory may have gained ascendancy. Hence it cannot be a constraint on one who wishes to evaluate a new theory critically that it must agree with any *de facto* accepted theories. At the very least the consistency condition needs to be modified to read: 'New hypotheses must agree with currently accepted *acceptable* theories'.

If the existence of a principle of comparison is taken as the existence of an algorithm providing a mechanical decision procedure for choosing which of a pair of rival theories is more worthy of adoption, even a committed rationalist will agree that there are no such principles. The believer in method will hold that there is a family of principles the members of which may on occasion point in different directions. It is for this reason that a rationalist will include within the statement of his principles of comparison a *ceteris paribus* clause. Applying this second caveat gives a consistency condition which reads: 'All things being equal, new theories should agree with currently accepted acceptable theories'.

A third and more important caveat is required if we are to have a plausible version of the consistency condition. Not even Popper (Feyerabend's particular *bête noire*) would accept it as it stands. For quite obviously it would impede theoretical growth in science. What one wants to preserve when faced with a choice between new rival theories is not the old theory itself but the observational successes of that theory. For instance, relativistic mechanics does not agree *simpliciter* with Newtonian mechanics. However, within the limits of experimental accuracy it does give the same predictions as Newtonian mechanics in those areas in which the latter is observationally successful. This means that the consistency condition should read as follows: 'All things being equal, new theories should agree with the observationally successful aspects of currently accepted acceptable theories'.

My consistency condition is at odds with Feyerabend's. He writes:[14]

Consider a theory T' that successfully describes the situation inside domain D'. T' agrees with a *finite* number of observations (let their class be F) and it agrees with these observations inside a margin M of error. Any alternative that contradicts T' outside F and inside M is supported by exactly the same observations and is therefore acceptable if T' was acceptable (I shall assume that F are the only observations made). The consistency condition is much less tolerant. It eliminates a theory or a hypothesis not because it disagrees with the facts; it eliminates it because it disagrees with another theory, with a theory, moreover, whose confirming instances it shares. It thereby makes the as yet untested part of that theory a measure of validity. The only difference between such a measure and a more recent theory is age and familiarity. Had the younger theory been there first, then the consistency condition would have worked in its favour.

It is very plausible to claim that my consistency condition (unlike Feyerabend's) is operative in science. In fact his condition has not been advocated by any influential scientist or philosopher in this century. For an illustration of the operation of my consistency condition, consider Everett's recent paper in which a rival to the Special Theory of Relativity is developed.[15] Everett, noting the dramatic observational successes of the Special Theory when used terrestrially, takes it as an explicit constraint of the construction of his rival theory that it should reproduce these observational successes. Neither scientists nor philosophers are likely to object to Everett's theory simply on the grounds that it is incompatible with the Special Theory. They certainly could be relied on to object reasonably if it gave results incompatible with the verified observational predictions of the Special Theory.

3 PROLIFERATION

As noted, Feyerabend's strategy is to weaken our allegiance to the consistency condition by developing a case for an incompatible counter-rule which in this case enjoins us to proliferate theories, especially theories incompatible with currently accepted ones. He offers the following as representing the 'reasonable core' of what he takes to be the standard case for his version of the consistency condition:[16]

> Theories should not be changed unless there are pressing reasons for doing so. The only pressing reason for changing a theory is disagreement with facts. Discussion of incompatible facts will therefore lead to progress. Discussion of incompatible hypotheses will not. Hence, it is sound procedure to increase the number of relevant facts. It is not sound procedure to increase the number of factually adequate, but incompatible, alternatives.

Feyerabend argues that this case rests on what he calls the 'autonomy principle' according to which the facts 'which belong to the empirical content of some theory are available whether or not one considers alternatives to *this* theory'.[17] The following plausible counter-example

131

is offered to the autonomy principle. Brownian motion is incompatible with phenomenological thermodynamics but it is unlikely that its relevance to phenomenological thermodynamics would have been appreciated without the development of the rival kinetic theory of heat. So, Feyerabend concludes, we should proliferate theories at odds with accepted theories in order to improve our chances of discovering facts relevant to assessing the acceptability of the original theories: 'Variety of opinion is necessary for objective knowledge'.[18]

This is a point of some insight. It may well be that facts relevant to the assessment of a given theory will be discovered only through the development of a rival. Everett, in the paper referred to above, points to possible experiments which would, depending on their outcome, tend to favour his theory or to favour the Special Theory. Without being aware of his theory one might not have thought of doing the particular experiments whose outcome would be relevant to assessing the Special Theory. However, as we shall see following a discussion of the proliferation maxim, a viable version of that maxim is not inconsistent with a viable formulation of the consistency condition.

Feyerabend's support for his proliferation counter-rule is reminiscent of Mill's arguments for freedom of opinion,[19] which can be adapted as follows to support proliferation. Since we are not infallible we should recognize that theories incompatible with our currently accepted theory may be true and consequently we should permit other theories to flourish. An unfashionable theory may in time be developed in such a way as to be more acceptable than any theory developed out of our current favourite. Even if our current theory is true, proliferation of rivals should be permitted and, indeed, encouraged. For we shall not fully appreciate the grounds in favour of our own theory unless we are forced to deal with objections to it:[20]

> But on every subject on which difference of opinion is possible,
> the truth depends on a balance to be struck between two sets
> of conflicting reasons. Even in natural philosophy, there is always
> some other explanation possible of the same facts: some geocentric
> theory instead of heliocentric, some phlogiston instead of oxygen;
> and it has to be shown why that other theory cannot be the true
> one: and until this is shown, and until we know how it is shown,
> we do not understand the grounds of our own opinion.

Mill also noted that a theory incompatible with our current theory while in error may contain 'a portion of truth' and[21]

132

since the general or prevailing opinion on any subject is rarely or never the whole truth, it is only by the collision of adverse opinions that the remainder of the truth has any chance of being supplied.

While Mill, like Feyerabend, would encourage proliferation he is very much the rationalist in thinking that we are 'capable of rectifying ... mistakes, by discussion and experience', which is why, according to Mill, there is 'a preponderance among mankind of rational opinions'.[22] Mill would no doubt advise putting most of our collective resources at work on those theories which come out best under dispassionate, rational assessment, while advising that some encouragement should be given to heretics. Feyerabend, who adds non-rationalism to his liberal roots,[23] would like to see each rival theoretician (including astrologers and witches) have an equal share in society's resources!

More recently Feyerabend has remarked[24] that he has not shown that proliferation should be encouraged but only that the rationalist cannot exclude it. But, as my adaptation of Mill's argument shows, the rationalist has good reasons to encourage a degree of proliferation. Such proliferation would be incompatible with Feyerabend's implausible consistency condition. But it is not incompatible with my weakened consistency condition if we construe that condition as one which is to operate in general; that is, as a condition that the majority of scientists should follow most of the time. No doubt in the long run scientific progress requires that the scientific community contain some heretics who receive some support. But science would not flourish if everyone was all the time trying to develop his own totally unique theory. Thus Feyerabend's particular strategy has failed. In so far as there is a case for a proliferation counter-rule that counter-rule is compatible with a (properly construed) consistency condition.

4 THE FAILURE OF THE GENERAL STRATEGY

The rationalist regards his principles of comparison as inductive rules to be used to guide us in the choice between rival theories in the face of the available evidence. It is the characteristic mark of inductive reasoning that something can be a good supporting reason for a hypothesis even though that hypothesis turns out to be false. Thus it cannot count against a particular inductive rule that it has on some occasion led us to hold false beliefs. To have reason to abandon such a rule we would have to have reason to think that it has led us wrong more often than right. The way in which Feyerabend regards putative counter-productive instances to a principle of comparison indicates that he erroneously assumes that the rationalist is committed to believing in exceptionless algorithmic principles of comparison:[25]

> Now, what our historical examples seem to show is this: there are situations when our most liberal judgments and our most liberal rules would have eliminated an idea or a point of view which we regard today as essential for science, and would not have permitted it to prevail —and such situations occur quite frequently. . . The ideas survived and they can *now* be said to be in agreement with reason. They survived because prejudice, passion, conceit, errors, sheer pigheadedness, in short because all the elements that characterize the context of discovery, *opposed* the dictates of reason *and because these irrational elements were permitted to have their way.* To express it differently: *Copernicanism and other 'rational' views exist today only because reason was overruled at some time in their past.*

Of course, our principles of comparison may on occasion point us in the wrong direction. No rationalist need dispute this truism. If historical evidence is to count against a particular principle of comparison we need more than anecdotes about failures, we need a proof that it has led us wrong more often than not. That would require a massive historical investigation which Feyerabend does not even begin to provide. In any event there are more than mere practical problems involved in carrying out such an investigation. For how do we know that a particular rule has led us to make unfortunate choices? We have no omniscient God to whisper the answers in our ears. Trapped as we are within the scientific enterprise without such a divine road to knowledge, we have no recourse but to make such judgments on the basis of other principles of comparison. Thus any historically based attack on a particular methodological rule of the sort being envisaged will presuppose the viability of other such rules. The best one can do through an historical investigation is to take up a single plank of the ship of methodology while the rest remain, for the moment at least, firmly in place. An attack on a particular aspect of method presupposes method. And it is just incoherent to suppose that method in general should be rendered suspect by this sort of argument. Thus Feyerabend's easy defeat of a straw man (the rationalist who believes in infallible exceptionless rules) is construed by him as a victory over a real man (the rationalist who believes in general guiding fallible principles of comparison) who is in fact enlisted in the battle with the straw man!

No historical study can justify dispensing with a methodological rule unless it is shown by reference to justifiable methodological rules that that particular rule has led us wrong more often than not. Feyerabend does not even begin to amass the sort of details that would be required. Neither does he provide us with any criterion whereby the particular rule may be assessed. What he says is that all methodological rules inhibit progress. Of progress, he remarks with disarming frankness:[26]

> Incidentally, it should be pointed out that my frequent use of such words as 'progress', 'advance', 'improvement', etc., does not mean that I claim to possess special knowledge about what is good and what is bad in the sciences and that I want to impose this knowledge upon my readers. *Everyone can read the terms in his own way* and in accordance with the tradition to which he belongs. Thus, for an empiricist, 'progress' will mean transition to a theory that provides direct empirical tests for most of its basic assumptions. Some people believe the quantum theory to be a theory of this kind. For others, 'progress' may mean unification and harmony, perhaps even at the expense of empirical adequacy. This is how Einstein viewed the general theory of relativity. *And my thesis is that anarchism helps to achieve progress in any one of the senses one cares to choose.* Even a law-and-order science will succeed only if anarchistic moves are occasionally allowed to take place.

Suppose one took it that the notion of progress was to be construed in terms of increased verisimilitude (however analysed). Nothing in Feyerabend's historical studies has established that a viable form of the consistency condition (by that I mean my modified form) has tended to move us away from the goal of increasing verisimilitude. A few isolated examples do not add up to a general refutation. In any event, given his specification of progress, this style of argument would not sustain a wholesale attack on method. At best it could point to a tension between a particular methodological principle and some other principle or principles.

I would not deny that an historical study could undermine our faith in methodology. Suppose we listed a historically generated series of theories for some subject matter which we take as a sequence of ever better theories. Suppose that no family of rules could be abstracted from a consideration of this series of theories adequate to more or less generate the series. Suppose further that any reassessment of the relative merits of the theories left us with a sequence of theories for which there was no generating principle. In such a case our faith in the existence of articulatable rules of methodology ought to be shaken. We would either have to abandon the notion that there was any objective content to the relation of being better than as applied to theories, or to regard that objective relation as something about which we could make intuitive judgments without being able to articulate the grounds for making the judgments.

This is not what Feyerabend has in mind. For in his discussions of Lakatos he concedes that Lakatos can generate a set of rules fitting his (Lakatos's) selection of progressive sequences of theories. His objection to Lakatos is not that he cannot generate a system of methodological rules but rather that Lakatos can give no rational justification for the rules selected. That is, Lakatos's rules cannot be given more than a descriptive force. For, according to Feyerabend, one could equally abstract a system of rules from a consideration of magic, myth or early science. No rational case can be developed for giving a privileged normative status to those which characterize the evolution of contemporary science. However, if we accept that scientific method evolves through time it is not fair to face Lakatos with alleged counter-examples drawn from magic, myth or early science. For Lakatos is concerned with the methods of contemporary science.

5 COUNTER-INDUCTION *VIS-À-VIS* FACTS

Our naive view that theories ought to fit with the outcome of observation is a barnacle on the ship of progress according to Feyerabend. To sweep away this obstacle we need only embrace the second counter-rule:[27]

> The second 'counter-rule' which favours hypotheses inconsistent with *observations, facts and experimental results*, needs no special defence, for there is not a single interesting theory that agrees with all the known facts in its domain. The question is, therefore, not whether counter-inductive theories should be *admitted* into science; the question is, rather, whether the *existing* discrepancies between theory and fact should be increased, or diminished, or what else should be done with them.

136

As usual there is behind Feyerabend's extravagance a point of interest. For, as we noted in our discussion of Popper, no theory is free of anomalies and it would not be very shrewd to abandon a theory just because it faces an anomaly. The man who has no friends except those without fault has few, if any, friends. The man who rejects any theory which has an anomaly has no theory whatsoever. But as usual Feyerabend is not merely making a humble point with a colourful flourish. That humble point would not sustain an injunction to favour a hypothesis because it disagreed with the facts. What is intended is a castigation of the notion that there are objective facts to which we have access through observation and experiment:[28]

> It is this *historico-physiological character of the evidence*, the fact
> that it does not merely describe some objective state of affairs *but
> also expresses some subjective, mythical, and long-forgotten views*
> concerning this state of affairs, that forces us to take a fresh look at
> methodology. It shows that it would be extremely imprudent to
> let the evidence judge our theories directly and without any further
> ado. A straightforward and unqualified judgment of theories by
> 'facts' is bound to eliminate ideas *simply because they do not fit
> into the framework of some older cosmology.* Taking experimental
> results and observations for granted and putting the burden of
> proof on the theory means taking the observational ideology for
> granted without having ever examined it.

Feyerabend, in rejecting the idea that experience provides unproblematic evidence for the assessment of theories, again echoes Mill, who held that while we are capable of rectifying our mistakes this cannot be done by experience alone. There must be discussion to show how experience is to be interpreted.[29] For Feyerabend the development of theories incompatible with our considered judgments about the observational facts will assist us in helping to improve those judgments through exposing untenable assumptions which may be implicit in these judgments:[30]

> Therefore, the first step in our criticism of customary concepts
> and customary reactions is to step outside the circle and either to
> invent a new conceptual system, for example a new theory, that
> clashes with the most carefully established observational results
> and confounds the most plausible theoretical principles, or to
> import such a system from outside science, from religion, from

mythology, from the ideas of incompetents, or the ramblings of madmen. This step is, again, counter-inductive. Counter induction is thus both a *fact* — science could not exist without it — and a legitimate and much needed *move* in the game of science.

One may agree with Feyerabend that our observational judgments may embody assumptions which are unnoticed and untenable. It may be a useful heuristic device in uncovering such assumptions to approach the familiar subject matter in the face of which these judgments are made through the perspective of a radically different theory. This may be useful even if the rival theory is not itself tenable. We may, for instance, become aware of unexamined assumptions in a certain philosophical tradition through working seriously in a rival tradition. As was argued in Chapter II, judgments made at the observational level in science do have theoretical presuppositions. However, it is not obvious that the sorts of implicit theoretical assumptions can be detected only through the extreme device that Feyerabend suggests. He has done nothing to show by way of example that a careful scrutiny within a particular theoretical framework will not unearth the assumptions of that framework. We are not, unfortunately, treated to examples of such unearthings through the study of the views of incompetents, madmen, or even persons of religion. As we will see his own example (relating to Galileo) is not of this interesting character.

I have written as if the point of looking at our judgments from the perspective of a radically different framework was heuristic, in that it might assist us in coming to maximize the rationality of our beliefs. In so doing I have assumed both that there are facts and that we can have rationally grounded beliefs as to what the facts are, and that radically different frameworks are commensurable. But if, as Feyerabend assumes, they are incommensurable, the perspective of such a framework could tell us nothing whatsoever about our own perspective. Hence his position at this point is just inconsistent. Even if this inconsistency is set aside, other tensions and contradictions surface. This can be seen if we note that I have placed a certain gloss on Feyerabend's remarks in order to render them plausible. I have taken it that it is possible to have rationally grounded beliefs concerning the facts and that the point of the exercise of disengagement is to assist in maximizing the rationality of our beliefs. At times Feyerabend writes as if this is his position. We are told that observational judgments not merely describe objective states of affairs but they also embody 'subjective, mythical and long-forgotten views'.[31] This suggests the gloss I have given. We are to indulge in disengagement in order to pare away the non-objective components in our judgments. Feyerabend's considered and more contentious view is incompatible with this. For it is not that our observational judgments may have an ideological component, our observational judgments have no components that are not ideological. However, as was argued in Chapter II (cf. pp. 27–8), even if some of our observational judgments need correcting because they embody false presuppositions, we have good reasons for relying in general on such judgments. I turn now to consider Feyerabend's example of disengagement, an example which does not give support to this more extreme claim that all observational judgments are essentially ideological.

The process of disengagement is to assist us in uncovering what Feyerabend calls natural interpretations, 'ideas so closely connected with observation that it needs a special effort to realize their existence and to determine their content'.[32] Feyerabend attempts to illustrate the importance of disengagement through a discussion of Galileo's attempts to promote the Copernican system. The natural interpretation implicit in the observational judgments prior to Galileo is said to be that all motion is motion in absolute space and that all motion is 'operative'. By 'operative' Feyerabend means that any motion will have detectable effects. His suggestion is that within this framework the tower experiment provides experiences which contradict the hypothesis of the motion of the earth. For if the earth moves it must move absolutely and this must have some effect on the falling stone: namely, the stone will move obliquely. As the stone does not, the experience described within this framework disconfirms the hypothesis of earthly motion.

Feyerabend claims that not all motion was seen as operative. He suggests that there was a rival paradigm of motion illustrated by the motion of objects in boats, coaches and other moving systems. I give below one of the rather nice passages from Galileo quoted by Feyerabend:[33]

> *Salviati*: . . . imagine yourself in a boat with your eyes fixed on a point of the sail yard. Do you think that because the boat is moving along briskly, you will have to move your eyes in order to keep your vision always on that point of the sail yard and follow its motion?
> *Simplicio*: I am sure that I should not need to make any change at all; not just as to my vision, but if I had aimed a musket I should never have to move it a hairsbreadth to keep it aimed, no matter how the boat moved.

Salviati: And this comes about because the motion which the ship confers upon the sail yard, it confers also upon you and upon your eyes, so that you need not move them a bit in order to gaze at the top of the sail yard, which consequently appears motionless to you.

Feyerabend construes Galileo as attempting to convert the refuting experience into a confirming experience by replacing the observation language used in the initial characterization of the experience by a different observational language. In this new language the natural interpretation involves relative motion that is not operative. The motion of the earth means that there is no relative motion between the starting point and the stone in the horizontal direction. Galileo is supposed to have propagandized his contemporaries into adopting this new observational language and hence to have moved them along the way to Copernicanism:[34]

An argument is proposed that refutes Copernicus by observation. The argument is inverted in order to discover the natural interpretations which are responsible for the contradiction. The offensive interpretations are replaced by others, propaganda and appeal to distant, and highly theoretical, parts of common sense are used to defuse old habits and to enthrone new ones. The new natural interpretations, which are also formulated explicitly, as auxiliary hypotheses, are established partly by the support they give to Copernicus and partly by plausibility considerations and *ad hoc* hypotheses. An entirely new 'experience' arises in this way.

This is a fascinating little story but it in no way vindicates the non-rationalist themes Feyerabend draws from it. First, by no stretch of the imagination can this be regarded as a case of a new observational language. For, as Feyerabend himself notes, there was already an ordinary language mode of description which treated as operative only relative motion. That is why Galileo is able to offer an alternative way of describing the tower experiment by thinking of it as analogous to the motion of objects in boats and carriages. Second, in unearthing the alleged implicit assumption (all motion is operative) we have not had to move to some extreme alternative perspective (no madmen, magicians or incompetents enter into the story). Two paradigms of motion were available. One is represented by the situation of a hunter watching a deer run through the forest, the other by the relation between a pen, a piece of paper and a ship sailing the seas. Galileo is suggesting that the relation of the ball to the tower should be conceived on the latter model. Finally, the rationalist will not be particularly interested in the claim, even if warranted, that Galileo succeeded only because of rhetoric, persuasion and propaganda. His claim is not that these never play a role but that a rational case can be constructed. He will argue that the rational case is to be constructed through showing that this re-construal of the motion of the ball and the tower is justified in virtue of the fact that it is part and parcel of a general theory of motion superior to the pre-Copernican one.

It may be that a case could be constructed in favour of one of the themes Feyerabend advances: namely, that Galileo's triumph does not fit the rational model. On the evidence available at the time of Galileo's triumph the Copernican theory may not have been superior. It may be that it triumphed not because of a perceived or apparent superiority but simply through Galileo's successful advertising trickery. But that is no threat to the rationalist programme in so far as that programme articulates a model which can be used to assess whether or not a given transformation is rational. The sort of thing that would threaten the rationalist case, such as, for example, establishing the essentially ideological character of observational judgments or the incommensurability of Copernican and non-Copernican theories, is not supported and could not be supported by the kinds of historical argument that are adduced.

It must be remembered that there are two different aspects to what I called the rationalist model of science. On the one hand, the rationalist argues that there are objectively justifiable principles of theory comparison which he hopes to articulate. Nothing in Feyerabend's attack on method has established the untenability of this presumption. Indeed, in developing the case for the proliferation rule he can be seen to have contributed to the rationalist programme. On the other hand, the rationalist hopes to explain scientific change in terms of the model. The central tenet of this book is that the first aspect of rationalism is correct. However, we shall see in Chapter X that the explanation of scientific change is not to be handled in the simple-minded rationalistic manner of Lakatos and his followers. Consequently, we shall come to agree with one of Feyerabend's central theses. For he has argued with conviction that a whole host of factors, many having nothing to do with science, played a role in the triumph of the Copernican revolution:[35]

Not one reason, not one method, but a variety of reasons made active by a variety of attitudes created the 'Copernican Revolution'. The reasons and attitudes converged but the convergence was accidental and it is vain trying to explain the whole process by the effects of simplistic methodological rules.

However, that such a variety of factors needs to be appealed to in giving a full explanation of the transition does not show that the transition was not objectively justifiable.

6 INCOMMENSURABILITY

Feyerabend, like Kuhn, rests his case against the rationalist in part on the alleged existence of incommensurable theories. In such cases none of the methods which the rationalists wants 'to use for rationalizing scientific changes can be applied'.[36] Not all theory change generates incommensurability. The context in which it is said to arise is described as follows:[37]

> We have a point of view (theory, framework, cosmos, mode of representation) whose elements (concepts, 'facts', pictures) are built up in accordance with certain principles of construction. . . . Let us call such principles *universal principles* of the theory in question. Suspending universal principles means suspending all facts and all concepts. Finally, let us call a discovery, or a statement, or an attitude *incommensurable* with the cosmos (the theory, the framework) if it suspends some of its universal principles.

If it is only the abandonment of 'universal principles' that generates incommensurability, it is crucial to be able to identify such principles. But Feyerabend provides no help. Indeed, we are told that the vagueness of the characterization 'reflects the incompleteness and complexity of the material and invited [*sic*] articulation by further research'.[38] At best we are given alleged examples. Newtonian mechanics is said to be incommensurable with relativisitic mechanics (if both are construed realistically) on the grounds that the latter suspends a universal principle of the former 'that shapes, masses, periods are changed only by physical interactions'.[39]

Given Feyerabend's insistence on the untranslatability between incommensurable frameworks, the picture is that the meaning of all

142

terms is dependent on their connection with the 'universal principles'. Alter a universal principle, and all meanings change. Preserve the principles, and meanings can be constant across theory change. It is well-nigh impossible to evaluate this picture. For we are not told how the principles are to be identified, nor are we provided with a theory of meaning which would display how it is that changes in these principles bring about radical meaning variance. Consequently, I shall treat his discussion as simply presenting a challenge to be met in the next chapter by showing that such scientific theories which he offers as putative cases of incommensurability can in fact be compared.

7 THE IDEOLOGY OF SCIENCE

Ultimately, for Feyerabend, science is but one ideology among many. The only constraint on an ideology (or theory or tradition, to use other terms that Feyerabend employs more or less interchangeably) is coherence:[40]

> There is only *one* task we can legitimately demand of a theory, and it is that it should give us a correct account of the world, i.e. of the totality of facts *as constituted by its own basic concepts.*

> Incommensurable theories, then, can be *refuted* by reference to their own respective kinds of experience; i.e. by discovering the *internal* contradictions from which they are suffering . . . Their *contents* cannot be compared. Nor is it possible to make a judgment of *verisimilitude* except within the confines of a particular theory (remember that the problem of incommensurability arises only when we analyse the change of *comprehensive cosmological points of view* — restricted theories rarely lead to the needed conceptual revisions). None of the methods which Carnap, Hempel, Nagel, Popper or even Lakatos want to use for rationalizing scientific changes can be applied, and the one that *can* be applied, refutation, is greatly reduced in strength. What remains are aesthetic judgments, judgments of taste, metaphysical prejudices, religious desires, in short, *what remains are our subjective wishes*: science at its most advanced and general returns to the individual a freedom he seems to lose when entering its more pedestrian parts, and even its 'third world' image, the development of its concepts, ceases to be 'rational'.[41]

143

Feyerabend has not established that there is nothing to guide us in science except 'subjective wishes'. While there are no binding, changeless algorithms there are general guiding principles (an account of which will be given in Chapter IX). Feyerabend passes from this false belief about the complete autonomy within science to the conclusion that in an ideally free society all traditions, including witchcraft, magic and science, would be autonomous in the sense of having 'equal rights and equal access to the centres of power'.[42] Science is but one human activity among others, having its costs and its benefits. No doubt we should take a dispassionate look at our priorities in this regard. The world would be a better place if the time and money spent on pursuing the truth about quarks could be used to end starvation. Some might even argue that we should wind up all pure research, resting content with the knowledge already acquired, devoting ourselves to raising and equalizing standards of living with a view to furthering the pursuit of the pleasures of, say music, social interaction, and so on. This is a matter of what human goals ought to be pursued.

Even the believer in method can argue against continuing to attach the high priority we do to science. Feyerabend takes it that the priority attached arises from our belief in method:[43]

> The reason for this special treatment of science is, of course, our
> little fairy-tale [the myth of method] : if science has found a
> method that turns ideological contaminated ideas into true and
> useful theories, then it is indeed not mere ideology, but an objective
> measure of all ideologies. It is then not subjected to the demand
> for a separation between state and ideology.
> But the fairy-tale is false, as we have seen. There is no special
> method that guarantees success or makes it probable.

This puts things the wrong way round. It is because of a belief in the worth of its products that science has achieved its privileged position. In so far as we believe that there is something special about its results we believe that there is something special about its methods. Even Feyerabend concedes that science has made 'marvellous contributions to our understanding of the world and that this understanding has led to even more marvellous practical achievements'.[44] He is mindful of the fact that some may wish both to explain why it has achieved this position and to defend the maintenance of this position by reference to its results. That is, someone might argue that science is privileged in virtue of its fruits even if its practice is more aptly described by Feyerabend than by rationalists. However, replies Feyerabend, to show that it is so privileged one would have to show: (a) that no other view has ever produced anything comparable; and (b) that the results of science are autonomous, they do not owe anything to non-scientific agencies.[45]

But just what other tradition has produced anything comparable in regard to our ability to predict and manipulate the physical world? Feyerabend talks of the ability of Stone Age man in a pre-scientific world to build seaworthy vessels which they navigated quite impressively. But impressive as it may have been it is hardly on a par with twentieth-century physics. In any event there is no reason not to regard Stone Age man as operating with primitive scientific techniques. One imagines that these vessels were produced through a process of conjecture and experimental testing. The same point applies to acupuncture, which so impresses Feyerabend. One imagines it too developed through a process of trial and error (I make for the sake of argument the assumption that Feyerabend is right in holding that acupuncture is in fact causally efficacious in medical treatment). Contemporary medical researchers stick medicine in people and investigate the effects just as no doubt the developers of acupuncture stuck needles and observed the effects with the hope of finding methods of diagnosis and cure. There is every reason to see these traditions as pre-scientific rather than as non-scientific. Whether we see these traditions as non-scientific or as pre-scientific is not important for our present purposes, for there is no doubt these traditions have not delivered the goods. But, Feyerabend retorts, the reason is simply that the game has been fixed: 'Today science prevails not because of its comparative merits but because the show has been rigged in its favour'.[46] We are told that *'the apostles of science were the more determined conquerors'* and that they *'materially suppressed* the bearers of alternative cultures'.[47] How did the apostles of science come to have this alleged power to suppress other traditions? Feyerabend supplies no explanation. One wants to know what is wrong with the obvious answer that the other traditions failed to thrive for the simple reason that men came to perceive correctly that they were not delivering the goods. We have every reason to suppose that even if each tradition had an equal access to power and even if each individual had a free choice as to which tradition to adopt, the scientific tradition would triumph in virtue of its fruits.

Turning to (b), there is just no incompatibility between the claim that science has been more fruitful than any other tradition in generating an understanding of the physical world and the claim that many of the ideas around which theories in science are built had their origins in other traditions. Perhaps, as Feyerabend claims, medicine profited from 'herbalism, from the psychology, the metaphysics, the physiology of witches, midwives, cunning men, wandering druggists'.[48] Why should the fact that some scientific theories arose from such sources detract from the success claims of science? The salient point is that the scientific tradition has evolved methods for evaluating and successfully developing such primitive beliefs and speculations. Feyerabend has done nothing to show that any other tradition has produced or even could provide that kind of understanding of the physical world which brings with it the predictive and manipulative powers of modern physics. One may not value the goal of achieving this and may therefore wish to give one's allegiance to another tradition. But if one's goal is that kind of understanding, science wins hands down and its success is explicable only on the assumption that there is method.

How has the rationalist fared in the face of Feyerabend's onslaught? First, we have seen that his attack on method at best scores a hit on a straw man. No rationalist need be committed to (and few have taken it that they are) a conception of method as a system of binding, unchanging, exceptionless algorithmic rules. Furthermore, Feyerabend's critique of method presupposes the viability of method (on a more reasonable construal of what that involves). The rationalist certainly can concede that the motivational factor governing scientists is not simply and exclusively the disinterested pursuit of approximate truth. Other interests do lead him at times to indulge in 'propaganda and trickery'. Conceding this does not destroy the rationalist perspective so long as this is not generally the case. Feyerabend has not shown that it is in general the case, even if he has drawn attention to the fact that the record is not unblemished. Rationalists do face difficult problems concerning in particular the problem of meaning variance across theories and the analysis of the notion of approximation to the truth, to which we turn in the next two chapters. Feyerabend's disinterest in any questions relating to the concept of meaning (problems concerning which lie at the heart of these difficulties) has the consequences that the rationalist gets off most lightly at his hands just where he is most vulnerable. Feyerabend's response to the results of his reflections is to become a Dadaist:[49]

A Dadaist is convinced that a worthwhile life will arise only when we start taking things *lightly* and when we remove from our

speech the profound but already putrid meanings it has
accumulated over the centuries. . . . I hope that having read the
pamphlet the reader will remember me as a flippant Dadaist and
not as a serious anarchist.

There is every reason to believe that his wishes will be realized.

VII

THEORIES ARE
INCOMMENSURABLE?

---

1 TYPES OF INCOMMENSURABILITY

The thought that theories are incommensurable is the thought that theories simply cannot be compared and consequently there cannot be any rationally justifiable reason for thinking that one theory is better than another. Expressed in this bold universal form, the thesis that theories are incommensurable is extremely implausible. This requires the caveat that it is implausible in so far as it is intelligible. Taken literally, it is implausible because it suggests that I could never have rationally justifiable grounds for holding any belief whatsoever, say, that I now see a typewriter, rather than a belief incompatible with it, say, that I do not see a typewriter. For if I could have grounds for rationally preferring one of those beliefs to the other why could I not have grounds for preferring one theory to another? That is, why should theories, as complex webs of beliefs, be any different from simple, humble everyday beliefs? The implausibility of this consequence or apparent consequence ought to prompt us to consider what motivates those who articulate the thesis of the incommensurability of theories. This is done below, for one presumes that they are not merely offering a thinly disguised version of traditional scepticism.

First, I note that the intelligibility of the thesis is questionable. The problem is supposed to be that since theories are incommensurable we cannot justify a preference for one rather than another. However, if the theories are genuinely incommensurable why should I be faced with the problem of choosing between them? Why not believe them all? The early Kuhn would have said that this cannot be done since some of

148

them are incompatible with others. For he wrote: 'The normal-scientific tradition that emerges from a scientific revolution is not only incompatible but often actually incommensurable with that which has gone before'.[1] But one wants to know how theories can be incompatible if incommensurable. There must be some sense in which they can be compared if the judgment of the incompatibility can be justified.

Enough has been said to reveal that the most pressing problem at this juncture is to formulate the thesis more perspicuously. If to start with we take the incommensurability of theories to refer to the alleged lack of rational grounds for choosing between theories, we can identify three alleged sources of incommensurability. Two of these will be explicated only briefly, as I have considered them in Chapter V. The first alleged source of incommensurability will be referred to as *incommensurability due to value variance.* Kuhn takes it that in some cases the disagreement between scientists as to which of a pair of theories to prefer arises from disagreements about values. In his 'Postscript' he writes:[2]

> What it should suggest, however, is that such reasons [accuracy, simplicity, fruitfulness and the like] function as values and they can thus be differently applied, individually and collectively, by men who concur in honouring them. If two men disagree, for example, about the relative fruitfulness of their theories, or if they agree about that but disagree about the relative importance of fruitfulness and, say, scope in reaching a choice, neither can be convicted for a mistake. Nor is either being unscientific.

Kuhn is advancing two claims which if accepted would generate some incommensurability where incommensurability is understood as indicating a limitation on the possibility of making rationally justifiable choices between theories. The first thesis is that in justifying my preference for one theory over another I shall have to appeal to value judgments. The second is that value judgments are autonomous in the sense that ultimately no rational considerations can be adduced for favouring one value judgment over another (given that the condition of internal consistency of one's value system would be met by either choice of values). This would mean that there could be cases where no rational consideration could be adduced to favour one theory over another. For instance, let us suppose that we have two theories which are under-determined by all actual observational data available to date one of which is more 'fruitful' than the other, the other of which is simpler. If no rational considerations can be adduced for favouring simplicity over 'fruitfulness', we might well (on Kuhn's assumpton) be faced with a choice which could not be rationally grounded. As I argued in Chapter V, this is a largely if not entirely spurious source of incommensurability.

A second related source of incommensurability would arise if in some cases of scientific conflict the rival scientists disagreed as to the principles of comparison and there was no possibility of rationally justifying one of these sets of principles over the other even though the difference did not arise from a disagreement over values. In this event there would be cases of incommensurability in the sense that there would be no possibility of adducing rational considerations favouring one theory over the other. This source of incommensurability, which I call *incommensurability due to radical standard variance*, will be set aside, as it was considered in detail in my discussions of Kuhn and Feyerabend.

Having set aside two putative sources of limitations on the possibility of rationally justifying the choice of one theory rather than another, I turn to the most extreme and therefore the most interesting claim concerning such limitations. This is incommensurability due to what I called *radical meaning variance*, a description I borrow from Kordig.[3] It will be fruitful to start with a relatively modest version of the thesis which will be called the *thesis of the radical meaning variance of theoretical terms*, hereafter cited as *RMVT*. For the sake of argument let us suppose that there is an observation-theory dichotomy and consider the *RMVT* to be the thesis that the meaning of a theoretical term within a theory may change if certain alterations are made in that theory. Suppose, for instance, that the change from Newtonian mechanics to relativistic mechanics was of such a character that the meaning of 'mass' changed radically. In this case there is only the appearance of logical incompatibility between the Newtonian assertion that, say, 'mass is invariant' and the relativistic assertion that 'mass is not invariant'. Given that there has been a shift in meaning, these assertions represent equivocation and not contradiction. This is a surprising result. For our naive view of the matter is that Newton and Einstein are in fact contradicting each other. Before developing further the consequences of admitting this meaning variance, it will be instructive to consider the chain of reasoning that gave rise to the thesis of the *RMVT*. To see this we need to begin with some reflections on the problems of the meaning of theoretical terms.

150

In the positivist tradition, which, as we shall see, is the generator of the thesis in question, theoretical terms were taken to be particularly problematic from the semantical point of view in a way that the meaning of observational terms were not. For it was held that the meaning of observational terms, or O-terms, could be specified directly through their connection with experience. To understand the meaning of an observational predicate was to grasp the kinds of experience that constituted evidence for the application of the predicate and to grasp the kinds of experience that constituted evidence against the application of the predicate. Theoretical terms, or T-terms, were problematic for, since they were not applied to items directly given in experience, their meaning could not be explicated in this fashion. Nor could their meaning be specified in terms of antecedently understood observational terms. For if a term is definable in terms of a complex of O-terms, that term could not play the role that T-terms were required to play in a theory. For T-terms were to play a role in the explanation of observations. If such terms were definable in terms of observational terms, talk of theoretical items would not be talk which could serve as an explanation of the observations. Such talk would merely constitute a trivial, non-explanatory re-description of the observations. It would not involve the postulation of underlying, non-observable items causally responsible for the observations in question. Neither could the meaning of all T-terms be given in terms of other T-terms 'on pain of a circle or an infinite regress'.[4]

2 THE RECEIVED VIEW

The response to this situation was to suppose that the meaning of the T-terms was implicitly defined through some of the postulates, the meaning postulates, of the theory. Some postulates in this set would connect a T-term with other T-terms within the theory; other postulates would connect the T-term with observational or O-terms. Thus, the T-term '... is an electron' might be connected with another T-term in the postulate 'Electrons have negative charge' and with an O-term in the postulate 'Electrons leave tracks in cloud chambers (in certain conditions)'.

Strictly speaking, the set of meaning postulates could not serve to define implicitly the theoretical term in question. If the meaning postulates for a T-term t did implicitly define t, the extension of t, would be fixed in any interpretation of the language which fixed the extension of the other terms occurring in the set of meaning postulates. In the case of the examples standardly offered this condition is not met.[5] That, however, may not itself be an objection to the meaning postulate account. What it shows is that meaning postulates do not strictly speaking implicitly define the T-terms in question. Instead, the meaning postulates might be described as partially defining T-terms in the sense that the fixing of the extension of O-terms only constrains or partially fixes the extension of T-terms. That these terms are only partially defined will seem a merit of this account to those who take it that T-terms are in any event partially indeterminate with regard to meaning.

On the meaning postulate approach, the postulates specify all there is to be specified concerning the meaning of T-terms. Consequently not all changes in theory involve changes in the meaning of T-terms across the theories. For on this account we might have two incompatible theories having the same meaning postulate set for the T-terms. Thus the meaning-postulate approach provides us with a framework within which it makes sense to ask if a given T-term means the same within theory T_1 as it does within theory T_2. But the proponents of this approach owe us an account of how one picks out which postulates of a theory are meaning postulates. One source of disenchantment with the approach is the difficulty in providing any satisfactory answer to this question. In general meaning postulates (hereafter cited as MP) were regarded as analytic truths.[6] On this construal of the MPs, the approach would have to be abandoned given that the Quinean claim that the very notion of analyticity is devoid of content could be sustained.[7] Even those who reject the strong Quinean claim may come to be sceptical of the particular MP approach which construes the MP as analytical on the grounds that we have no viable technique for determining which postulates of a theory are analytic. That is, even if one thought that the notion of analyticity had content and that there were some analytic truths, one might think either that the sorts of postulate offered as MPs were not analytic or that the notion of analyticity did not have a determinate extension in the field of postulates of scientific theories. In that case there would be little or no justification for holding that there was a set of analytic postulates for any given theory which could serve as MPs. Rather than argue directly against the MP approach, I will show it to be untenable through first displaying the unsatisfactory consequences of the approach and, second, through providing an alternative account of the meaning of T-terms that is free of these unhappy consequences.

The *MP* approach applied to *T*-terms but not to *O*-terms provides what we will call the *first degree of meaning variance*. In this case theory change, such as the shift from Newtonian to Einsteinian theories of mechanics, does not necessarily produce changes in the meaning of *T*-terms. Whether there is a change in meaning depends on the particular changes made in the theory (i.e., it depends on whether the changes involve changes in the meaning postulates). Interestingly, Carnap himself noted as early as 1956 that the *MP* approach can give rise to meaning variance of *T*-terms, as the quotation below reveals. A *T*-term is significant for Carnap if it has some connection with observation. *T*, below, refers to the set of purely theoretical postulates of a theory plus the set of correspondence rules which contains all postulates having both *T*-terms and *O*-terms:[8]

> Perhaps the objection might be raised that, if significance is
> dependent upon *T*, then any observation of a new fact may
> compel us to take as non-significant a term so far regarded as
> significant or vice versa. . . This class will generally be changed
> only when a radical revolution in the system of science is made,
> especially by the introduction of a new primitive theoretical term
> and the addition of postulates for that term.

Thus Carnap acknowledged the first degree of meaning variance and in so doing came to hold a view not dissimilar to Kuhn's.[9] For Kuhn maintained that meanings vary only across dramatic theory changes and that they are more or less invariant under minor theory changes.

If one rejected the assumption that there is a distinction in kind between meaning postulates and non-meaning postulates while retaining the general idea of the *MP* approach that meaning of *T*-terms is to be specified through a specification of the role of the term in the theory, one would be led to embrace *the second degree of meaning variance*. The thesis of the second degree of meaning variance is that the meanings of all *T*-terms change under theory change while the meaning of *O*-terms remains constant. For if to specify the meaning of a *T*-term is to specify all the postulates of the theory in which the term occurs, any change in a theory which involves a change in a postulate containing *T* will involve a change in the meaning of *T*. As that term is likely to be connected through the postulates with all other *T*-terms, all other *T*-terms would have their meaning altered. At a later stage Carnap included in the meaning postulates of a theory not only all the purely theoretical postulates and all postulates which contain both *T*-terms and O-terms but also all purely observational postulates.[10] This committed Carnap to the second degree of meaning variance. For now any change in a theory will bring about a change in the meaning of its T-terms. However, O-terms, for Carnap, have a meaning that is constant through theory change.

In discussion of incommensurability there has been a tendency to focus on questions of meaning and not on questions of reference and truth − a tendency which we shall see is regrettable. In reconstructing the so-called problem of incommensurability I will for the moment indulge in this tendency. Having reached the second degree of meaning variance we can articulate what the problem of incommensurability has been supposed to be. Taking Einsteinian and Newtonian theories as our examples, the problem can be posed as follows. Some of the theoretical assertions of Newton seem incompatible with some of the theoretical assertions of Einstein. For example, Newton says 'mass is invariant' and Einstein says 'mass is not invariant'. Given that the second degree of meaning variance obtains, these assertions represent mere equivocations. In fact the situation would be more perspicuously represented as follows: 'mass$_N$ is invariant, mass$_E$ is not invariant'. Since 'mass$_N$' and 'mass$_E$' differ in meaning these latter assertions are not logically incompatible. If this applies to all T-terms Einstein and Newton are not contradicting one another at the theoretical level.

At the second degree of meaning variance it is taken that O-terms have invariant meaning across theory change. This would give a way which theories could be contradictories of one another notwithstanding the variation in the meaning of the T-terms. This would arise if, given a common statement of initial conditions and a common auxiliary theory, one theory entailed an observation statement O and the other theory entailed the observation statement not-O. In this case the theories would be in genuine conflict and there would be the possibility of rationally justifying a choice between the theories by reference to the outcome of experiments designed to determine the truth-value of O and other such observational statements. However, as noted in Chapter II, the assumption that there is a difference in kind of either an epistemological character or a semantical character between so-called O-statements and so-called T-statements is untenable. Given the second degree of meaning variance, rejecting the observation-theoretical, O/T, distinction leads to the *third degree of meaning variance*. On the third degree the assumption of a theory-neutral meaning invariant observational language is dropped and it is taken that the meaning of all terms is determined through their role in a theory with the consequence that any change in the theory brings a change in the meaning of all terms. Thus, on this third degree meaning variance (hereafter referred to as *radical meaning variance*, or *RMV*) different theories cannot be logically incompatible and it is no longer possible to justify rationally choices between the theories by reference to the observational level.

One route from *RMVT* to *RMV* involves arguing against the putative observation-theory dichotomy. Another route is to note the tension between *RMVT* and the claim that there is a theory-neutral observation language which arises for those who hold that there are analytically true meaning postulates linking *T*-terms and *O*-terms. To see this, suppose we have a *T*-term, t, which occurs in theories T_1 and T_2. Given *RMVT*, the meaning of t is not invariant across T_1 and T_2. Suppose T_1 contains the analytic meaning postulate $(x)\,(t(x) \to O)$ where '*O*' is an *O*-term. If that sentence is also analytically true in T_2, O has changed meaning as '$t(x)$' has changed meaning. Equally, if that sentence is not analytically true, '*O*' has changed meaning as it is no longer analytically tied to '$t(x)$'.

There is an ironic twist in the route to the third degree of meaning variance, *RMV*. Popper, Lakatos, Kuhn and Feyerabend see themselves as anti-positivists and cite their rejection of the *O/T* distinction as an important ground for rejecting positivist and neo-positivist approaches. Popper and Lakatos reject *RMV* without unfortunately providing any adequate positive account of the meaning of scientific terms which would justify this rejection. Kuhn and Feyerabend embrace *RMV*. The irony is that Kuhn and Feyerabend have inherited from positivism the general holistic conception of the meaning of a term as given by the role of the term within a theory. Having accepted this legacy and having rejected the *O/T* distinction, they are led to embrace *RMV*. Thus there is a sense in which their rejection of positivism is superficial. As we shall see, what is required is a much more radical critique of positivism than they provide.

Kuhn does not unequivocally subscribe to *RMV*. For Kuhn, we have the third degree of meaning variance only in the case of a paradigm shift. Slight theory change during periods of normal science does not give rise to meaning variance. However, as was argued in Chapter V, Kuhn does not provide an adequate criterion for determining how much change is required before there is a change in paradigm. This means that he has not provided a means of determining which theory changes generate variation in meaning. Feyerabend, as we saw in Chapter VI,

155

holds that *RMV* arises only when theory change involves 'suspending universal principles.' We are not given any useful guidance as to how to determine whether there has been any 'suspension'.

Before turning to consider strategies to be deployed in the face of *RMV*, it is of interest to note a reflexive problem that arises for the advocates of *RMV*. If scientific terms change meaning with change in theory, presumably the terms used in the philosophy of science such as, 'theory', 'explanation', 'truth', etc., change in meaning with change in philosophical theory. This means that, say, Kuhn and Popper differ in what they mean by the crucial terms in their philosophical theories; and the attempts of Kuhn to deny what Popper asserts represent an equivocation in the same way that, *à la* Kuhn, an encounter between a Newtonian and an Einsteinian represents an equivocation.

3 STRATEGIES FOR DEALING WITH *RMV*

In reaching the third degree of radical meaning variance, the conception of what a theory is has been considerably broadened (at least implicitly). For the so-called *O*-terms the meaning of which is said to be sensitive to theory change are terms which occur in ordinary non-scientific discourse. Consequently the role they play in that discourse is partly constitutive of their meaning. Thus, if we are to say that the meaning of a term is a function of its role in a theory we shall have to take a theory to include not just the theory proper but all other sentences involving the terms (or terms connected with those terms) to which someone assents. In this case the conception of meaning involved is approaching that of Quine. However, there is an important difference between the position we have arrived at and that of Quine. According to Quine, we are not licensed to talk of the meaning of a term within a theory. For, given a theory, there will be more than one translation manual which could be employed in translating that theory into our own language. This claim that there is a multiplicity of empirically adequate translations of a theory into our own language, together with the assumption that there is no matter of fact at stake as to which is the correct translation, is the infamous thesis of the indeterminacy of translation.[11] Given this thesis, there is no content to talk about *the* meaning of a term within a theory.

Neither Kuhn nor Feyerabend accepts the indeterminacy of translation. Kuhn is quite happy to talk of the meaning of a term within a theory and he takes it that, say, Einstein can come to see what Newton meant by his terms. Einstein can discover in principle at least what role the terms play for Newton and hence come to understand what he meant. It does not follow that Einstein can express what Newton meant within his, Einstein's, theoretical language. For he has no term within his language which plays the role, that, say, 'mass' plays within Newton's theory. This is an intelligible situation. Consider learning a foreign language *ab initio* and coming thereby to understand a term which one might recognize as having no equivalent in English as it stands. That this is Kuhn's view is suggested by his claim that there may be partial translation between the proponents of competing paradigms.[12] For while there may be no term within Einstein's language that plays the role 'mass' plays in Newton's theoretical language, there may be a term which approximates that role to some extent. I leave for the moment the question of the tenability of the thesis of the indeterminacy of translation and its relevance to the issue of incommensurability. For the sake of argument I assume that it is legitimate to talk of the meaning of a term within a theory and I construe the thesis of *RMV* as the claim that in any theory change the meaning of all terms within the theory changes.

A number of different strategies have been deployed by those sceptical of the thesis of *RMV*. Some have sought to confute the thesis by arguing that its consequences are sufficiently absurd to justify its rejection. For instance, one finds it said that regardless of what justification there may be for holding that 'mass' has changed its meaning under theory change, it would just be absurd to claim that scientists operating in different paradigms meant something different by, say, 'The pointer is at the 4'. This is not a very convincing strategy. Perhaps after all the truth is ultimately absurd! In any event it is not a satisfying style of argument. For it rests on agreement that a certain result is absurd, without providing any framework within which to justify the claim that the result is indeed absurd. It has also been argued by Kordig that the thesis of *RMV* is 'methodologically undesirable'.[13] Among the undesirable consequences according to Kordig are that 'no theory could be tested or falsified by any observations or observation reports'; that 'scientific change could not constitute progress'; that 'true communication in a sense between holders of different theories would be impossible'; that 'no theory could contradict or agree with another'; that 'one could not learn a new theory'. Even granted that these are indeed consequences of *RMV* (this might well be questioned in some cases), this is an unhappy strategy to deploy in dealing with a proponent of *RMV*. At best it raises our interest in the thesis by showing some of its intriguing consequences. Some, such as Feyerabend, who advocate *RMV* positively relish these consequences. Even if one did not welcome these conclusions, the conclusions are not self-evidently absurd. Indeed, any attempt to justify the claim that they are false will involve complex and controversial argumentation. One would also like to know what Kordig means by 'methodologically undesirable consequences', a notion he fails to explicate. If it means that adopting *RMV* would hinder scientific activity (i.e., it would be to embrace a bad methodology), this does not show that *RMV* is false. It only shows that practising scientists should be persuaded not to believe in it. It may, after all, be methodologically desirable to hide the truth from the scientist.

I am not objecting to the claim that *RMV* has untenable consequences. I shall argue in Chapter VIII in favour of *TV* (the thesis of verisimilitude), and given *TV* there is something wrong with a position which rules out the very possibility of its holding. We shall see that *RMV* does rule out *TV*, and this ought to prompt us to consider an alternative approach to the meaning of terms within scientific theories which does not give rise to *RMV*. To this task I turn in the later part of this chapter. For the only satisfying strategy for dealing with *RMV* is one that proceeds to vindicate a theory of meaning which does not generate *RMV*.

4 REFERENCE, TRUTH AND RADICAL MEANING VARIANCE

In the discussions of incommensurability too little attention has been given to the notions of truth and reference. Unless we focus on these notions we shall not be able to appreciate the full anti-rationalist consequences of *RMV*, nor shall we be able to see the way forward to a theory of meaning that avoids *RMV*. To develop the full consequences of *RMV*, consider again the example of Newton and Einstein. Our naive pre-*RMV* intuition is that their theories are logically incompatible. But given *RMV* Newton and Einstein are equivocating and their theories are logically compatible. This has been taken to mean that the theories are not in competition.[14] However, as Kuhn and Feyerabend are well aware, this conclusion is so unacceptable that if it was indeed a consequence of *RMV*, *RMV* would have to be rejected. Can we find a sense in which these theories are in competition notwithstanding

RMV? Kuhn himself offers no help on this point, for he inconsistently explicates the notion of competition in terms of the notion of logical incompatibility.[15] And Feyerabend talks of the theories as being rivals without explicating in what the rivalry consists. We can come to their aid, for the theories are in what I will call *pragmatic tension*.

Suppose we are faced with two theories, T_1 and T_2, which pre-reflexively we would regard as logically incompatible accounts of some phenomenon. Given *RMV* there would be no logical inconsistency in adopting both T_1 and T_2. Let us assume with Kuhn and Feyerabend that while we cannot express one theory in terms of the language of the other, we can come to have some understanding of both theories. On a realist construal of theories, adopting T_1 will lead us to posit the existence of various theoretical entities and states. If we adopt T_2 we shall be led to posit the existence of other entities and states. While there would be no logical inconsistency in adopting both T_1 and T_2, pragmatic considerations militate against this. For having adopted, say, T_1, we shall have an account of the phenomenon in question and there is no point in adopting T_2 as well. Indeed, an application of Occam's razor gives a reason for not also adopting T_2. For nothing is gained by positing the existence of more than is needed to explain the phenomenon the observation of which gave rise to the desire to produce an explanatory theory. There is no point in populating the world with more things than are needed in giving an explanatory theory. To adopt both T_1 and T_2 would be to violate this maxim. The theories T_1 and T_2 are in pragmatic tension in the sense that there is no need for explanatory purposes to adopt both, and adopting both would have the consequence of pointlessly bloating our ontology.

If the proponent of *RMV* can give sense to the notion of a comparison between theories, what after all is worrying about the consequences of his thesis? The problem is that *RMV* does not fit with the realist construal of theories which we have adopted. For, as realists, we ask of any pair of theories in pragmatic tension, which is more approximately true? And, in view of the fact that there is growth in scientific knowledge, we cannot accept any answer to this question which amounts to saying that our current theory is to some degree approximately true and that any past theory in pragmatic tension with that theory is to no degree approximately true. To see that *RMV* leads to this unacceptable answer, let us compare our current theories of the electron with the theories which Thomson (who is usually credited with having discovered the electron) and Bohr held about what they called 'electrons'.

Naively (that is, pre-*RMV*) one would say that we, Thomson and Bohr, held beliefs about electrons which are pair-wise incompatible, i.e., any two of these belief sets are inconsistent. Thomson thought that electrons were well-defined in regard to spatial volume. Bohr would agree with us that they are not. Bohr thought that electrons could have any energy level, whereas we would deny this. Given *RMV*, the meaning of the term 'electron' shifts from Thomson to Bohr and again from Bohr to ourselves. Let us suppose with Kuhn that we can come to understand what Bohr and Thomson meant by 'electron'. Remembering that all terms shift their meaning given *RMV* we can schematically represent the situation as follows:

Thomson : Electrons$_T$ are $F_1, F_2, \ldots F_n$.
Bohr : Electrons$_B$ are $G_1, G_2, \ldots G_n$.
Ourselves:: Electrons$_O$ are $H_1, H_2, \ldots H_n$.

These schemes give a partial specification of the meaning of the terms in their respective theories by relating the term to other predicates in the theory that are said to hold of what the term applies to. The specification is only partial, for given *RMV* we can only fully specify the meaning of the term 'electron' by giving the entire theory in which it occurs. However, nothing in my argument will be affected if for ease of exposition we suppose that the meaning is more or less given by a list of predicates with which the term is connected in the theory.

What are we to say about the truth-value of Thomson's assertion that electrons are F_1 or Bohr's assertions that electrons are G_1? In pursuing this question two assumptions will be made. First, that adequate reasons have already been provided in Chapter II for rejecting any relativisitic construal of truth, and that theories are to be construed realistically so that in holding something to be true we are holding that the world is as it says it to be. Second, that we can recognize what Thomson and Bohr meant by the terms of their theories. To establish the truth-value of, say, Thomson's assertion 'Electrons are F_1' we have first to discover what, if anything, he was referring to by the term 'electron'. If he did succeed in referring to something we have to discover if those things had the property in question. If it turns out that Thomson did not succeed in referring to anything, all his assertions involving the term 'electron' will be false, for he has not expressed a truth about any existing thing. If what Thomson meant by 'electron' is 'anything having the properties of $F_1 \ldots F_n$' we shall be forced to the conclusion that he failed to refer to anything. For from the perspective of our current beliefs we shall not find any constituents of matter answering to the description Thomson associated with the term 'electron'. Similarly we find that Bohr's important work on electrons amounts to nothing more than a tissue of falsehoods, since he too failed to refer to anything. But it is at the very least offensive to be driven to the conclusion that neither Thomson whom we think of as having discovered the electron nor Bohr whom we think of as having made important discoveries about the electron said anything true about electrons.

We have been assuming with the proponents of *RMV* that the meaning of a term is given by its role in a theory and that the referent, if any, of a term is determined by the meaning of that term. The consequence of these assumptions is that if we look at the theories of Thomson and Bohr from the perspective of our current theories, we shall have to say that there are neither such things as Bohr electrons nor such things as Thomson electrons. For we shall not find anything having the properties which their theories associate with being an electron. Since they attempted to discourse about what does not exist, all their assertions involving the term 'electron' are false. Thus, their theories are totally false. This is incompatible with our assumption that there has been growth in scientific knowledge to which their theories contributed. This result generalizes so that given *RMV* all past theories turn out to contain no truth whereas our current theories, we believe, have some truth in them. Consequently, *RMV* is not compatible with the thesis of verisimilitude, *TV*, according to which there has been an accumulating increase in truth-content.

The importance of the holism involved in *RMV* in the above argument can be brought out if we consider the following simple example assuming a non-holistic approach to meaning. Suppose that the speakers of one linguistic community have stipulated that 't_1' means 'the first star to appear in the evening' and that the speakers in another community have stipulated that 't_2' means 'the last star to disappear in the morning'. Suppose further that each community has a range of further beliefs which they take to be beliefs about t_1 and t_2 respectively where these two ranges of beliefs are inconsistent with each other. If the other predicates which each community associates with 't_1' and 't_2' respectively do not enter into the meaning of 't_1' and 't_2', and if it is the case that the first star to appear in the evening is the last star to disappear in the morning, each community can give a charitable construal of the referential activities of the other notwithstanding the fact that they mean something different by 't_1' and 't_2'. However, on a holistic account of meaning which would require that the meaning of 't_1' involve all the predicates the one community takes to hold of 't_1' (and similarly for 't_2'), each community will hold that the other has failed to refer to anything. For given the tension between their beliefs, each will hold that there is nothing picked out by the term in question by the other community.

5 WHAT SHOULD A NICE THEORY OF MEANING LOOK LIKE?

What should a theory of meaning for scientific terms look like if it is not to undercut *TV*? It is crucial that the theory be charitable in the following sense. It should allow us to determine the reference of singular terms of previous theories in such a way that on some occasions at least a singular term has a referent which is the same as the referent assigned to the corresponding term in our current theories; and, second, the extension of predicates must on some occasions at least overlap with the extensions we would assign the corresponding predicate in our current theories. For instance, if we construe what Newton meant by 'mass' along the lines of *RMV* we shall be required to say that Newtonian mass did not exist and consequently that all of Newton's assertions about mass are false. Even if Newton pointing to a stone says that it has mass he does not say something true, for nothing has mass if 'mass' is defined in terms of the Newtonian theory. If on the other hand we can construe what Newton meant charitably so that he is taken as referring to what we refer to by 'mass' we can regard Newton as having talked about what we talk about when using the term 'mass', in which case at least some of the things he said about mass will be held by us to be true. Thus, if he said 'mass is invariant' he would have spoken falsely. However, if he said 'The amount of mass affects the gravitational force acting on a body' we would regard him as having spoken truly. We could not do so if we had assigned no referent at all to the term 'mass' as he used it.

One way in which a theory of meaning might achieve charitable status would be to minimize the meaning it assigned to terms within a theory. Suppose that an earlier scientist holds that a predicate 'E' is satisfied if and only if predicates 'P_i', . . ., 'P_n' are simultaneously satisfied and suppose that we hold that 'E' is satisfied if and only if a range of predicates 'P'$_i$, . . ., 'P'$_n$ are simultaneously satisfied. The smaller the number of predicates that are taken to be constitutive of the meaning of 'E' in each theory, the greater the chance that we shall be able to say with justification that what was referred to by 'E' in the previous theory is what we refer to by 'E'. This point can be expressed more generally. A non-holistic theory of the meaning of scientific terms is likely to have a greater chance of being charitable than a holistic account. The less the meaning is determined by the role in theory; or, to put the point another way, the less the meaning of a term is a function of the beliefs of the proponents of the theory about the putative referent of that term, the greater the chance that we can regard proponents of different theories as referring to the same thing by the same expression.

It is fashionable to argue in some quarters that one can transcendentally justify a principle of charity which ordains us to endeavour to maximize the ascription of true beliefs in the interpretation of the discourse of others.[16] My reference to charity is not to be taken as endorsing this view. My point is rather that the particular theory of meaning which I shall offer tends to provide ascriptions of more true beliefs to previous scientists than any holistic theory of meaning. This is important because, as we shall see in the next chapter, there are contexts in which we can argue for *TV*. Given this, it will count against a theory of meaning that it has uncharitable consequences which are incompatible with *TV*. However, we do not always want to be charitable. Whatever plausibility the claim has that the principle of charity is a sort of *a priori* constraint on the interpretation of the ordinary discourse of others, it has no plausibility as a constraint on the interpretation of the theoretical discourse of others. The simple reason is that we well understand how easy it is to have a theory that turns out to be totally incorrect. While it may be hard to see how a group of people could cope with the everyday world in the face of massively mistaken beliefs (this is what gives the principle of charity its plausibility), it is easy to see how a group can be utterly mistaken at the theoretical level. Mary Hesse is guilty of making this slide from the principle of charity as applied to ordinary discourse to a much more contentious application of charity to theoretical discourse.[17]

In addition, a theory of meaning that will help with the current problem will have to be fine-grained. Theories of meaning according to which the meaning of a sentence is given by the truth-conditions or assertability-conditions of the sentence within which they occur would be a coarse-grained and not a fine-grained theory. Against the background of such a coarse-grained theory of meaning we want to be able to say something more specific about the meaning of different classes of expression. A sufficiently fine-grained theory to provide a framework within which to answer questions about the referent, if any, of 'Newtonian mass' and 'Thomson electron' is required; and that is likely to require that we consider in turn different types of expression and offer accounts of meaning specific to expressions of that type.

6 THE APPROACH OF CAUSAL REALISM

I propose to develop a suggestion of Putnam's concerning the meaning of terms for physical magnitudes. Put in a nutshell, Putnam's thesis is that terms for physical magnitudes which are discovered through their effects are introduced into the language as terms for the physical magnitude responsible for certain effects.[18] Following Putnam I will call the description of the effects in question the *introducing event*. What we find if we consider the history of the use of the term 'electricity', to use his example, is that there is no description of electricity common to all users of the term. What unites the users is the intention to use the term to refer to whatever magnitude it is that is responsible for certain effects: namely, those specified by the introducing event. Notwithstanding the fact that Gilbert, Franklin, Maxwell and contemporary scientists held or hold radically different beliefs about electricity, they are referring to the same thing. If we put too much into what they meant by the term we shall have meaning variances and shall consequently be led to uncharitable construals of their attempts to refer. However, if all that they mean by 'electricity' is just 'that magnitude responsible for certain (specified) effects' and if either they agree on the effects in question or agree that the effects in question are whatever effects the original introducer of the term had in mind, we believing, as we do, in the existence of a physical magnitude responsible for the effects in question, will be able to give a charitable construal of their attempts to refer.

It is interesting to note that scientists in explicating what they mean by 'electric charge' do so by reference to phenomena produced by electric charge. Gilbert in his *De Megnete* wrote:[19]

> For it is not only amber and jet that attract small bodies when
> rubbed. The same is true of diamond, sapphire, carbuncle, iris

gem. . . . Feeble power of attraction is also possessed under a
suitable dry sky by rock salt, mica, rock alum. This one may observe
when in midwinter the atmosphere is sharp and clear and rare —
when the emanations from the earth hinder *electrics* less, and the
electric bodies are harder.

Maxwell, in his *Treatise on Electricity and Magnetism*, wrote:[20]

Let a piece of glass and a piece of resin, neither of which exhibits
any electrical properties, be rubbed together and left with the
rubbed surfaces in contact. They will still exhibit no electrical
properties. Let them be separated. They will now attract each
other.

If a second piece of glass be rubbed with a second piece of resin,
and if the pieces be then separated and suspended in the
neighbourhood of the former pieces of glass and resin, it may be
observed —
(1) That the two pieces of glass repel each other.
(2) That each piece of glass attracts each piece of resin.
(3) That the two pieces of resin repel each other.
These phenomena of attraction and repulsion are called Electrical
phenomena, and the bodies which exhibit them are said to be
electrified, or to be *charged with electricity*.

The explanation of the term 'electrical charge' in elementary textbooks is not dissimilar. Consider, for instance, the following passage
where the term is first introduced in a standard text:[21]

If a second glass rod is rubbed with silk and held near the rubbed
end of the first rod, the rods will repel each other. On the other
hand, a hard-rubber rod rubbed with fur will *attract* the glass rod.
Two hard-rubber rods rubbed with fur will repel each other. We
explain these facts by saying that rubbing a rod gives it an *electrical
charge* and that the charges on the two rods exert forces on each
other.

It is certainly a virtue of Putnam's account that it explicates the meaning
of physical magnitude terms in the manner employed by practising
scientists.

If 'e', a physical magnitude term, has its meaning specified through
the scheme: e is that magnitude which is causally responsible for . . .

(where the blank is to be filled out by a specification of the effects in question) then, in keeping with actual scientific practice, the meaning is not explicated by giving the role of the term of a theory. We do not explain what we mean by 'electric charge' by giving a list of properties of electrical charge. The account is simple and so nicely supports our belief in *TV* that what is required, as well as an articulation and defence of the theory, is an explanation which will be given in Section 8 below of why it is that this account has had no prior currency.

There are two areas of unclarity in the account. First, what description is it appropriate to use in specifying what, say, electrical charge is? Second, what is the nature of the link between the description and the term? If, considering the first question, we were to survey competent users of the term 'electric charge', asking them which effect they would cite in explaining what, say, electric charge is, it is unlikely we should find a single preferred description. Indeed, some relatively competent users of the term might not be able to supply any such description. The approach that Putnam favours in singling out a privileged description to be used in the schema is called the *historical-causal approach*. On this account what a speaker of the language intends to refer to by the term 'electric charge' is that which was responsible for the effect cited in the original act of introducing the term into the language, given that current usage is connected by the appropriate sort of causal chain to that original 'baptism' of the magnitude in question. Let D be that effect. For Putnam the assertion that electric charge is that which causes D is not analytic. The description serves to determine the reference of the term without becoming analytically tied to the term in question.

The historical aspect of this account has struck some as implausible. In view of this we should note that one can develop a non-historical variant of this account which shares with the historical version its chief merit. On the non-historical variant we would say that what a scientist intends to refer to by 'electric charge' is that magnitude which is causally responsible for an effect or effects which he describes. The non-scientist in the linguistic community who uses the term with some competence may not be able to supply any such description. Thus we need to modify the schema given as follows. What I intend to refer to by 'electric charge' is that magnitude responsible for the effect or effects which the experts take it to be responsible for. Thus the ability of a layman who lacks any appropriate description to refer to a magnitude is parasitic on the experts possessing a description of the effect in question.

The mode of description involved is implicitly indexical in that the description is intended to pick out the cause of that phenomenon in this world. That is, for a magnitude to be an electric charge it has to be the same magnitude as that magnitude which causes the phenomenon in the world. To decide whether a magnitude is the same as a given magnitude one has to have recourse to our physical theories about magnitudes. In terms of the apparatus of possible worlds, we can say that a magnitude in a given possible world is electric charge if and only if that magnitude shares its nature with the magnitude which in the actual world causes the phenomenon in question. Just what its nature is is something which we hope to discover through our physical theories.

It is held by Putnam that this makes certain statements which traditionally would have been held to be contingently true to be in fact necessarily true. Assuming it is the case that, for example, electric charge obeys an inverse square law, Putnam would argue that in any possible world in which that magnitude is present, it will obey the inverse square law. Since all possible worlds in which there is electrical charge are worlds in which charge obeys an inverse square law, that electrical charge does obey such a law will be a necessary truth. While necessarily true, this truth is discovered *a posteriori* because our discovery that it is part of the nature of electric charge in this world to obey the inverse square law is done and could not but be done *a posteriori*. This claim, that there are necessary truths — logically necessary truths — whose truth can be ascertained only *a posteriori* has been greeted with considerable hostility. This misplaced hostility derives from a number of sources. One is the belief that the approach commits us to admitting the legitimacy of possible world semantics. The other is the belief that it commits us to *de re* necessity. I shall argue that both beliefs are mistaken in the context of considering the area of language (natural kind words) in regard to which this approach has been most highly developed.

For Putnam to give the meaning of a natural kind term such as 'water' is to provide an account of how one definitively determines its extension. That is, an explanation of the meaning of 'water' tells us what conditions must be satisifed by a liquid for it to count as being water. One might seek to do this by providing a list of some of the characteristics, $C_1, C_2, \ldots, C_n$, which we believe water to possess and claiming that 'water' just means anything that has these characteristics. For instance, one might say that a liquid is water if and only if it is clear, drinkable, tasteless, etc. There are difficulties, arguably insurmountable ones, in specifying a precise set of characteristics which provide logically necessary and sufficient conditions for something to count as water. The problem is to determine which of our beliefs about water are constitutive of the meaning of the term 'water'. The problem is exacerbated by the fact that the scientific community would not count anything as water unless it were H_2O whether or not it were to have the characteristics we might list. Does this mean that we have meaning variance between ordinary discourse and scientific discourse involving the term 'water'?

Putnam has made a proposal concerning the meaning of 'water' which avoids both the problem of specifying its meaning in ordinary discourse in terms of a set of characteristics constitutive of water and the problem of relating the meaning of 'water' in ordinary discourse to its meaning in scientific discourse. The proposal provides a way of determining the referent of the term in all possible worlds. This is important. For we might enable someone who could determine the extension of 'is a creature with a kidney' to determine the extension of 'is a creature with a heart' successfully in this world by saying that any creature with a heart is a creature with a kidney. This works in this world because it is true as a matter of fact that all creatures with hearts are creatures with kidneys. However, someone who thought that the extension is fixed in this way would not understand the meaning of 'is a creature with a heart'. For we can imagine situations (possible worlds) in which creatures with kidneys lack hearts, and so the person determining the extension of 'is a creature with a heart' by reference to the possession of a kidney would make erroneous applications of the predicate. For Putnam the crucial schema in explicating the meaning of 'water' is the following:[22]

(For every world W) (For every x in W) (x is water iff x bears same$_1$ to the entity referred to as 'this' *in the actual world W_1*).

We can understand the reference to every possible world as meaning simply 'in any conceivable circumstances'. The schema presupposes that we ostensively identify some liquid in this world. Perhaps we stand on the shores of Loch Lomond and say: 'This is water'. We determine what else is water by determining what bears the relation *same$_1$* to this ostended liquid. For something to bear this relation to the stuff in Loch Lomond is for it to share its nature in the following sense. Whatever it is about the stuff in Loch Lomond (whatever attributes it has) which explains why it has the phenomenal or observable qualities it does have (i.e., drinkable, clear, etc.) is its nature. In point of fact we believe that the nature of water is to be H_2O. Given that belief we will not count anything as water unless it is H_2O. It is to be noted that it is not part of the meaning of 'water' that water is H_2O. The explication of the meaning of 'water' refers only to the sharing of a common nature with the stuff in Loch Lomond and not to the fact that its nature is to be H_2O.

This approach has attractive features. First, we have avoided having to decide which phenomenal characteristics are constitutive of the meaning of 'water'. Second, we have an account of the meaning of 'water' which gives constancy of meaning across ordinary discourse and scientific discourse. Furthermore, if it is the case that the nature of water is to be H_2O, then under this assumption anything that is water must be H_2O. If water is H_2O there will be no conceivable circumstances in which something which is not H_2O can count as water. This explains the conviction of many scientists that nothing which is not H_2O is water without making it a matter of definition (and thereby making 'water' mean something different for the scientist and the man beside the Loch). Thus it is a necessary truth that water is H_2O − given that water is in fact H_2O. This is a necessary truth that has been discovered through an empirical investigation of the world and not through an analysis of the meaning of 'water' alone.

On this approach, having associated the term 'water' with an os- tended liquid, we determine the further extension of the term through discovering the nature of the sample. To specify the nature is to specify those properties possessed by the liquid in question which explain its properties and behaviour. In talking of the method by which we deter- mine the extension we are not referring to actual procedures followed. In actual practice we shall most often simply apply the term to other liquids which look, feel and taste the same. Determination refers instead to the definitive test for ascertaining the extension. To discover the nature of something we have to develop an explanatory theory about it. Such a theory, like any scientific theory, is defeasible and may need to be modified in the light of further investigation. However, if our current theory that water's nature is to be specified by saying that water consists of a collection of H_2O molecules is true, any sample of water must be H_2O. That water is H_2O is necessarily true but it is not analytically true. For we cannot arrive at that truth through an analysis of the meaning of the term 'water'. A meaning analysis will only yield the analytical truth that water is a liquid having some nature or other and not that it has any particular nature.

In outlining the doctrine Putnam makes use of the apparatus of possible worlds. Many would reject the approach of causal realism if it presupposed this controversial device. Happily this is not the case and those who are dubious about possible worlds can re-cast the doctrine as follows: nothing *counts* as water unless it shares its nature with this ostended sample of liquid. To specify the nature of water is to specify those features which play a fundamental role in the explanation of the properties and behaviour of water. Assuming that water's nature is specified by saying that it is H_2O, nothing counts as water unless it is H_2O. Thus we can re-cast the doctrine in a manner that does not presuppose an ontology of possible worlds. We simply say that we do not count something as water unless it shares it nature with the stuff in Loch Lomond.

There is a philosophical tradition of being willing to countenance only *de dicto* necessities and not *de re* necessities. Some of those who follow this tradition charge that the Putnamesque account introduces, objectionably, *de re* necessities. We shall see, following a clarification of this distinction, that this objection lacks force. A necessary truth is *de dicto* if its necessity arises from our linguistic practices. For instance, it is necessarily true that all bachelors are unmarried. Nothing would count as a bachelor if it were married. That this is so arises simply from the linguistic conventions covering the use of the terms 'bachelor' and 'unmarried'. A necessary truth is *de re* if its necessity arises from the way the world is. Using my modification of Putnam's schema, given that water is H_2O, then necessarily water is H_2O, for nothing will count as water unless it is H_2O. This makes it look as though there is a necessary connection between being water and being H_2O, a necessary connection that arises from the way the world is. If this is indeed so anyone of Humean persuasion who thinks that there are no necessary connections in nature will object to the causal-realist account of meaning. However, there is in fact nothing involved in this account that need disturb one hostile to *de re* necessities. Certainly it is the way the world is that makes it true that water is H_2O. But what makes this truth necessarily true is not the way the world is, apart from our linguistic practices. For the necessity is a reflection of a general institutionalized linguistic practice of determining the extension of natural kind words by reference to the nature of ostended paradigm instances of the kind in question. The necessary connection between being water and being H_2O is imposed by us on the world. For given that water is H_2O our practice is not to count as water anything that does not have this nature. Water can fail to be such that most humans like to swim in it for it is not part of our practice to require instances of natural kinds to share more than their nature. There is no harm or mystery involved in saying that water is necessarily H_2O so long as we remember in virtue of what it is that this is so. It is so in virtue of the fact that water is H_2O and our general linguistic practice of requiring all instances of a kind to share the same nature. The necessity is *de dicto* in that it reflects nothing more than the way we talk, given our belief that water is H_2O.

We have seen that causal realism does not commit us to using possible world semantics, nor does it commit us to *de re* necessity. At this juncture it is imperative that we consider an objection to my non-historical version of causal realism. I suggested that the meaning of physical magnitude terms was to be given by reference to a schema of the form:

x is that magnitude which is causally responsible for certain (specified) effects

where the effects are the effects we would cite. These are not necessarily those cited when the term was first introduced into the language. The objection is that this modification lands us with meaning variance again. Suppose we have two scientists each of whom uses the term 'electric charge' but takes it to denote the cause of a different phenomenon. A perspicuous representation of this situation would be:

Scientist$_1$: Electric charge$_1$ is that which is responsible for P_1.
Scientist$_2$: Electric charge$_2$ is that which is responsible for P_2.

This meaning variance is innocuous enough. For if from the perspective of scientist$_2$ it is said to be the case that that which is causally responsible for P_1 is that which is causally responsible for P_2, S_2's assignment of a referent to S_1 in his use of 'E_1' will be charitable. This is to be contrasted with the unhappy sort of meaning variance where descriptions are associated with 'E_1' which S_2 holds do not apply to anything. For instance, if for S_1 part of what he meant by 'E_1' has to be that E_1 is a substance (as scientists in the eighteenth century tended to assume) S_2 would have had to assign no referent to S_1's use of 'E_1' with a consequential uncharitable assessment of the truth-content of S_1's theory.

We have been considering a modification of Putnam's view according to which for each user of the term in question there is a privileged description of the effects of the magnitude in question and there may be variation through time or through the community of users at a time as to which that description is. Making this modification does not generate uncharitable construals of the referential endeavours of previous scientists. For in the standard case, later scientists will agree that that which is the cause of the phenomenon previously associated with the term is the cause of the phenomenon now associated with the term. Consequently they will have to be able to act charitably with regard to their predecessors. The grounds of my claim are as follows. The sort of case in which we wish to be charitable to our predecessors is one in which their theory had some area of success. Setting aside fancy philosophical argumentation for the moment, it simply is a brute fact that in such cases later scientific theories in a mature science generally succeed in that area and in other areas as well. Hence one would expect to find that from the perspective of a later theory, the phenomenon associated with the term in earlier times has the same cause as the phenomenon associated with the term in later times.

Unlike Putnam's account, mine is non-historical in that current users of a term for a physical magnitude intend to refer to what causes a certain phenomenon specified by the current experts. They do not intend to refer to that which causes the phenomenon cited when the term was originally introduced into the language. However, we shall achieve constancy of reference across possible variation in observable effects in any case in which we hold that there is a lawlike connection between the disposition of a system to produce the effect specified in the introducing event and its disposition to produce the effect currently used in specifying the magnitude.

This non-historical account allows us to meet the objection of Fine[23] that the Putnam account enforces constancy of reference across theories. Fine rightly objects to any account such as Putnam's that it precludes the possibility of variation of reference of a term across theory change. My account allows for such variation. To see this let I be the original introducing event for a magnitude term 'M' and let E be the type of event we would currently cite in identifying the magnitude we call 'M'. If we hold that there is no lawlike connection between a system's disposition to produce an effect of type I and its disposition to produce an effect of type E, we shall hold that 'M' has changed its referent. Depending on the details of the case it may be that 'M' as used by previous scientists failed to refer or referred to a different magnitude.

However, in most cases the requisite lawlike connection will obtain and hence there will be constancy of reference.

Things may not always be as simple as I have suggested, and in Section 9 below I turn to examine one possible complexity which will require a considerable elaboration of the general schema. Before doing this attention should be given to another class of terms, to forestall the suspicion that the account reflects some peculiarity of terms for physical magnitudes. Perhaps the most important class of terms in contemporary physics are those terms for what we might call the constituents of matter, i.e., 'molecule', 'atom', 'electron', 'quark' and so on.

7 THE CONSTITUENTS OF MATTER

Surprisingly little attention has been paid in discussions of the meaning of theoretical terms to the manner in which those terms were originally introduced into scientific discourse. If we attend to the procedure whereby the term 'electron' was added to the vocabulary of science, we shall see how to develop the programme of causal realism. During the nineteenth century it was noted that in certain circumstances an illuminated patch was seen in a cathode ray tube at the end opposite to the cathode. The variation in the patch under variation of the parameters involved could be explained under the supposition that particles travelling in straight lines were emitted from the cathode. It was subsequently supposed that there were such particles and the term 'cathode ray particles' was introduced to refer to them. At this stage there was no presumption that cathode ray particles formed a natural kind. However, J. J. Thomson was able to determine that the charge to mass ratio of all particles so produced was constant. This led to the supposition that only one type of particle was being produced, the electron, discovery of which is therefore usually credited to Thomson.

The predicate '. . . is an electron' was introduced with the intention of picking out a kind of constituent of matter; namely, that constituent causally responsible for the cathode ray phenomenon. There is no suggestion that it is necessary or sufficient for something's being an electron that it actually has produced this effect in this way. To be an electron is rather to be a particle of the same type as the particles responsible for the cathode ray phenomenon. In spite of the great variation since Thomson's time in beliefs about electrons, we are united with him in that the things we call electrons we recognize as

173

being the things responsible for the cathode ray phenomenon, and thus we can treat Thomson charitably when awarding prizes in the verisimilitude stakes.

Someone might object that what is meant by 'cathode ray phenomenon' has, or could, shift in meaning to such an extent that what we now denote by that description is not what Thompson would have intended to pick out. That is, it will be asked, are you not assuming an invariant observational language in which the cathode ray phenomenon can be described? This objection is out of place in the context of the current debate. For, after all, the reason for thinking that there was meaning variance at the observational level was that there is variance at the theoretical level which would filter down through to the humbler levels of language. However, the model of meaning being advanced for theoretical terms is one in which either there is no meaning variance or meaning variance of a harmless sort. The existence of this model calls into question the holistic model implicit in the thesis of *RMV* and hence undercuts the only grounds that had been advanced for supposing that there is serious meaning variance at the humble non-theoretical level of discourse.

8 THE TRUTH OVERLOOKED

I have referred to the above account of the meaning of theoretical terms as a theory of causal realism: causal because the scheme which allows us to determine reference or extension does so by specifying the referent or extensions as that which causes a certain phenomenon in certain ways. This means that my reasons for using the label 'causal' are not the reasons of Putnam. For I have not adopted the view that to determine what one is referring to in one's use of a theoretical term one needs to determine the terminus of a causal chain taking us back to the original act of introducing the term into the language. The account is realist in that it commits the user of theoretical terms to giving a realist construal of theoretical entities. That is, one cannot accept this account and regard theoretical terms as non-denotational terms introduced into theories to facilitate observational prediction.

The reason for the lack of appreciation of this model of meaning lies in this very fact — the fact that it is a realist account. For the dominant trend in the philosophy of science this century has been positivistic, with its attendant hostility to the postulation of entities

174

which could not be observed in a fairly direct way. If one wishes either to take a non-realist line concerning theoretical entities or even if one wishes to be neutral on this issue, one cannot accept what I have called the causal realist approach. Consider in this light Mach, who in spite of the attempts of the early Einstein remained firmly convinced that atoms did not exist and that the term 'atom' was introduced merely to simplify calculations:[24]

> The atomic theory plays a part in physics similar to that of certain auxiliary concepts in mathematics; it is a mathematical *model* for facilitating the mental reproduction of facts.

Given that view, it is hard to see what could be said about the meaning of 'atom' except that its meaning is given by specifying its role in the theory. We have seen where that approach leads, and we see now why the approach I have been developing would not have commended itself to a hard-line positivist.

Causal realism, if adopted as our theory of meaning for scientific terms, will have the effect of inclining us to see invariance in meaning and reference through theory change. For scientists in different paradigms are more likely to agree on what we might call the privileged effects of some magnitude; and if what they mean by a particular magnitude term is 'that magnitude which is responsible for those effects' they will agree on meaning. They may not agree on the effects, but this is not so important. For so long as the later scientists agree that that which causes the phenomenon they take to be privileged is that which caused the phenomenon which earlier scientists took to be privileged, their interpretation of the preceding theories will be charitable and *TV* will be preserved.

I have provided a general framework within which to represent the meaning of terms in scientific discourse. While the approach advocated does not generate the holism which gives rise to *RMV*, it remains very much a framework within which to operate. Attempts to apply it in the analysis of actual case studies of scientific change will no doubt show the need for refinement and modification. For instance, we noted that on our non-historical causal approach, the way in which the referent of a term is fixed may change with time. In some cases we have constancy of reference across this change and in other cases we have not. Kitcher,[25] operating within, broadly speaking, the same framework, has argued that a particular case study (that of dephlogisticated air) shows the need to make the theory context-dependent. For, according to

Kitcher, during a time in which the mode of fixing the reference is changing and bringing about a change in what is referred to, we have to look at the actual context to determine what the scientist is referring to. At some time he may be referring to what is picked out by one specified effect and at other times he may be referring to what is picked out by the other specified effect. What he is referring to on a particular occasion is, for Kitcher, that which best explains his use of the term on that occasion. This elaboration is needed and further historical studies will no doubt reveal others.

9 A POSSIBLE COMPLICATION

I have assumed that when theory T_1 containing the term 't' is replaced by theory T_2 containing the term 't', we can determine from the perspective of T_2 whether 't' has the same referent in both cases. It has been suggested that in the normal sort of theory change in mature sciences (which will be called *containment change*) one will find in general that the referent of the term is the same in both theories. A complication would ensue if we were faced with what Hartley Field has called *denotational refinement.*[26] In the case of denotational refinement we find that the later theory T_2 contains two terms, 't_1' and 't_2', each of which has some claim to have the same referent or extension as 't' in T_1. The example offered by Field is the term 'mass' in Newtonian mechanics and in relativistic mechanics. As Field rightly notes, in relativistic mechanics one can distinguish between proper mass and relativistic mass. Proper mass is in some ways like Newtonian mass and is in some ways different from Newtonian mass. This is also true of relativistic mass. Field's suggestion is that there is no matter of fact as to whether Newton denoted proper mass or relativistic mass by 'mass'. I do not think that Field has made out his case with regard to this particular example. There are good reasons (some of which have been cited by Earman and Fine[27]) for holding that proper mass is the proper concept of mass and that Newton denoted proper mass by 'mass'. That being so it remains possible, however, that other examples of denotational refinement will be forthcoming, and it is worth pursuing Field's suggestion as to how one might cope with the situation. Before doing that it is worth noting that 'mass' does not easily fit the scheme I advanced. For unlike other physical magnitude terms, 'mass' is not introduced as the magnitude responsible for certain effects. It tends, in fact, to be explicated by reference to other physical magnitude terms. For instance, Mach attempted to define 'mass' in terms of ratios of acceleration and in relativity 'mass' can be defined in terms of energy. I mention this to draw attention to the dangers of assuming that one uniform micro-account can be given of the meaning of all T-terms even within a specific class of terms.

Denotational refinement might well arise. For instance, suppose it had turned out that what was taken to be the extension of 'water' at one time turned out to be generally a mixture of two chemically different liquids the phenomenal properties of which were indistinguishable, whether mixed or pure. Within the scientific context we might well introduce the terms 'water$_1$' and 'water$_2$' to distinguish these two liquids. Let us imagine that chemists prior to this realization had made what they regarded as discoveries about water; some of the properties they ascribed to water hold of water$_1$ and not water$_2$ and vice versa. If we suppose that the earlier chemists did not denote anything we shall be uncharitable in our construal of their theories. If we have no reason to suppose that it was water$_1$ and no reason to suppose that it was water$_2$ that they denoted, we may wish to regard this as a situation in which there is no matter of fact at stake as to what they denoted. We cannot suppose that they denoted both water$_1$ and water$_2$, because they treat 'water' as a singular term for a liquid and these are two different liquids. Field's interesting suggestion for coping with such a situation is that we introduce a notion of a partial denotation and an associated referential semantics which would allow us to be charitable. The details which I give below can be skipped by readers not interested in the technicalities of formal semantics. The intuitive idea is that assertions made by the earlier scientist come out true only if they would be said to be true both of water$_1$ and of water$_2$. Assertions are false only if they are false under both the construal of water as water$_1$ and as water$_2$; otherwise their assertions lack a determinate truth-value.

On Field's notion of partial denotation, singular terms may partially denote more than one thing. 'Mass' for Newton is said to denote partially proper mass and partially relativistic mass. In this case the term is said to be referentially indeterminate. If it partially denotes only one thing it is fully determinate. This notion is extended to predicates which partially signify different extensions. Within this framework we define truth as follows:[28]

A structure for a sentence is a function that maps each name or quantity term of the sentence into some object or quantity, and maps each predicate into some set. The structure *m corresponds* to the sentence if each name or quantity term of the sentence partially denotes the thing that *m* assigns to it, and each predicate signifies the set that *m* assigns to it. Now, for each structure *m*, we can apply the standard referential (Tarski-type) semantics to determine whether the sentence is *m-true* or *m-false*, i.e., true or false *relative to m* (to say that the sentence is *m*-true is to say that it would be true if the denotations and extensions of its terms were as specified by *m*). We can then say that a sentence is true (false) if it is *m*-true (*m*-false) for every structure *m* that corresponds to it. Putting all these definitions together, we get definitions of truth and falsity in terms of partial denotation and partial signification.

Field provided an attractive framework within which to deal with any case of denotational refinement. For it allows us to be charitable and it fits with our intuitions. If we are faced with a scientist who in a sense does not know what he is talking about because his term suffers from referential indeterminacy we would be inclined to award him marks for insight and truth only if what he claimed to have discovered held of both types of item partially denoted by his term. For instance, suppose there are mathematicians who take it that the numbers are what they would be on the Zermelo construction of the numbers (i.e. the sequences of sets $\emptyset, \{\emptyset\}, \{\emptyset, \{\emptyset\}\}, \ldots$), and suppose that there are mathematicians who take it that the numbers are what they would be on the Von Neumann construction (i.e. the sequence of sets $\emptyset, \{\emptyset\}, \{\{\emptyset\}\}, \ldots$). Suppose we come to the conclusion (the false conclusion) that no other objects could be the numbers. Under these assumptions we should regard it as indeterminate which of these two systems of objects are the numbers. In such a case our inclination would be to regard as true only those assertions of mathematicians which were true of both systems. If one says that 2 is an element of 4, this would be indeterminate as to truth value since it is true on the Zermelo construction and false on the von Neumann construction; 4 is greater than 2 on either construal, and hence this would be true. Thus, the approach of partial denotation seems to accord with our intuitions about the assessment of truth in the context of indeterminacy of reference. It is not merely a device introduced *ad hoc* to allow us to

178

be charitable. That being said, it is not clear that we are faced with any situations within which the reference of theoretical terms is indeterminate.

10 INDETERMINACY OF TRANSLATION AND INCOMMENSURABILITY

Following Kuhn and Feyerabend, I assumed that it makes sense to suppose we can come to understand what previous scientists meant by the terms within their theories. On occasion we may see that they meant the same as we do, and on occasion we may see that they meant something different. Even in the latter case we may be able to determine that they were talking about the same thing, and thus we may be able to satisfy the thesis of verisimilitude. Thus, from the important point of view — that of truth — meaning variance in science is of more interest but of no more harm than that which arises if Icabod means by 'Phosphorus', 'first star to appear in the evening' and Isabel means by 'Phosphorus', 'last star to disappear in the morning'. They, and we, can discover that in spite of the difference in sense there is sameness of reference. Icabod and Isabel will not be precluded from making a charitable assessment of each other's pronouncements containing the term 'Phosphorus'.

This assumption about the possibility of coming to glimpse what is meant on the other side of the paradigm divide has been challenged. For given Quine's thesis of the indeterminacy of translation, there will be empirically equivalent but logically incompatible translation manuals which I can bring to bear on the theories of my predecessors (and my compatriots, for that matter). Further, according to Quine, there is no fact of the matter at stake with regard to the questions as to which of these competing manuals is the correct one. That being so, there is no such thing as what the previous scientist meant. There are simply different and equally viable ways of construing his assertions. According to Quine, indeterminacy of translation gives rise to the inscrutability of reference.[29] This is the thesis that we can give alternative equally viable construals of the referents of the terms of someone's theory, and that there is no fact of the matter at stake as to which one is correct. If reference is inscrutable there is no way I can penetrate through the veils of indeterminacy to discover what it is that my predecessor was talking about. This means that I may be faced with different construals of his theory which from the persepective of my own theory will seem to fare differently with regard to how approximately true they are. This would provide a dramatic source of incommensurability. One cannot compare theories without a translation and a specification of reference, and if Quine is right and there is no unique translation and no unique specification of reference there will be no determinate answer to the question: does his theory have more or less truth than my own?

Quine's argument for indeterminacy rested on an unargued assumption, that of the strong under-determination thesis, an assumption about which he himself has come to have serious doubts.[30] Consequently, I would claim that there is no good reason to take this source of incommensurability seriously. Happily we can do better than simply returning the ball to the opposition court. For we have already argued that we cannot make the scientific enterprise intelligible except on the assumption of realism. This style of arguing — that we ought to opt for realism on the grounds that it provides the best explanation of certain crucial features of the scientific enterprise — is a style that should commend itself to Quine, given his general position that there is no essential difference between the methods of philosophy and the methods of science. For it is, after all, the style of argumentation standardly employed in scientific contexts. Given, as I argue below, that indeterminacy of translation is incompatible with the thesis of realism, and given that we have respectable reasons for adopting realism and no respectable reasons for adopting the thesis of the indeterminacy of translation (what after all would be explained by the supposition of its truth?), we need not take indeterminacy seriously.

The reason for holding that indeterminacy and realism are incompatible is quite simple. Realism is the thesis that the world makes how theories say it to be either true or false. If indeterminacy obtains, there is no such thing as how a theory says the world to be. Indeed, it is not even clear that there is anything to be a candidate for being true. For not even Quine would hold that it is uninterpreted sentences which are true or false. It is interpreted sentences that are so. However, there is no way of determining the correct or the uniquely preferable interpretation of a sentence of a theory under which it could be said to be true or false. At least this is so for Quine, once we have gone beyond humble observation sentences the meaning of which is more or less exhausted by a specification of their stimulus meaning. The realist can allow that some sentences are not determinate as to their meaning; he can even allow that most sentences may have limits to their determinacy; but he cannot allow that there is the sort of unlimited indeterminacy that Quine supposes to obtain. To do so is to lose that which can be true or false. The realist pictures the world as being more or less determinate and takes it to be possible to frame assertions which express the state of the world. This is only possible if sentences have more or less determinate sense.

Lest anyone think that this line of argument is unfair to Quine, consider his remarks about truth given towards the end of one of his discussions of under-determination:[31]

It [under-determination] sets one to wondering about truth. Perhaps there are two best theories that imply all the true observation conditionals and no false ones. The two are equally simple, let us suppose, and logically incompatible. Suppose further, contrary to our last conjecture, that they are not reconcilable by reconstrual of predicates [i.e., they are not merely notational variants of some one theory], however devious. Can we say that one, perhaps, is true, and the other, therefore, false, but that it is impossible in principle to know which? Or, taking a more positivistic line, should we say that truth reaches only to the observation conditionals at most, and, in Kronecker's words, that *alles übrige ist Menschenwerk?*

I incline to neither line. Whatever we affirm, after all, we affirm as a statement within our aggregate theory of nature as we now see it; and to call a statement true is just to reaffirm it. Perhaps it is not true, and perhaps we shall find that out; but in any event there is no extra-theoretic truth, no higher truth than the truth we are claiming or aspiring to as we continue to tinker with our system of the world from within. If ours were one of those two rival best theories that we imagined a moment ago, it would be our place to insist on the truth of our laws and the falsity of the other theory where it conflicts.

This has the ring of cultural relativism. That way, however, lies paradox. Truth, says the cultural relativist, is culture-bound. But if it were, then he, within his own culture, ought to see his own culture-bound truth as absolute. He cannot proclaim cultural relativism without rising above it, and he cannot rise above it without giving it up.

Quine is right. This has the ring of cultural relativism. It is no comfort to learn that to proclaim that doctrine lands us in paradox. At best that would leave us in a *Tractatus* silence. If Quine is right we have been shown that there is truth in cultural relativism even though (because of that paradox) we cannot say that there is truth there. The point is that Quine seems to recognize that the positing of under-determination (from which he argues to indeterminacy) of theory-truth takes us (given the response to this that Quine prefers) to the indeter-minacy of theory-truth. On this line of argument there is no fact of the matter at stake with regard to truth. Realism must be rejected. Indeed, Quine explicitly rejects it in rejecting the very idea of extra-theoretical truth. But, as has been argued and will be further argued in the next chapter, there is no tenable construal of science that is not basically realistic. Therefore, we have good reason to reject the indeterminacy of translation since it precludes a realistic account of the scientific enterprise.

VIII

THE THESIS OF VERISIMILITUDE

1 THE WHOLE DEPRESSING STORY

Science, viewed *sub specie eternitatis*, can seem a depressing business. For, as we noted in Chapter I, there are good reasons for adopting what was called the pessimistic induction. Past theories have turned out to be false, and since there is no good reason to make an exception in favour of our currently most cherished theories, we ought to conclude that all theories which have been or will be propounded are strictly speaking false. *Prima facie*, this induction, if granted, does more than a little to tarnish the image of science as the very paradigm of institutionalized rationality. For if we have inductive evidence that the goal is not ever to be reached, how can it be rational to continue to pursue it? As Laudan has put the problem:[1]

> If rationality consists in believing only what we can reasonably presume to be true, and if we define 'truth' in its classical non-pragmatic sense, then science is (and will forever remain) irrational.

It is, if not downright irrational, certainly pretty unpalatable to play a game which you have reason to believe cannot be won.[2] In such circumstances the reasonable man may well opt to change the rules of the game. And much recent work in philosophy of science amounts to attempts to reconstruct the aim of the scientific enterprise in the hope of delivering a more accessible target. The least radical of these attempts to take the sting out of the pessimistic induction do so by making what I called the *Animal Farm move*. True, it is said, all past and present theories are false and, indeed, the evidence is that any theory which is the product of finite minds like ours will turn out to be false. However, some theories are falser than others. In Lenin's words, 'we draw closer and closer to objective truth (without ever exhausting it)'.[3] While the historically generated sequence of theories of a branch of a mature science are all, strictly speaking, false, the theories are increasing in verisimilitude; that is, in the degree to which they are approximately true. In this case we would have progress after all, for our theories would be capturing more and more truth about the world. This thesis, to be argued for in this chapter, I have called the thesis of verisimilitude or *TV*. On this account of the matter rationality consists in believing in those theories which it is most reasonable to presume have the highest degree of verisimilitude among the available rival theories.

This attempt to maintain a conception of rationality linked to truth in the face of the pessimistic induction is most closely associated with Popper. Unfortunately, as we saw in Chapter III, his own particular attempt to do this is a dismal failure. For on Popper's analysis of verisimilitude no pair of false theories can be ranked in terms of comparative verisimilitude. Even setting aside the intractable difficulties involved in his analysis, Popper has not given (and in view of his horror of 'pernicious inductivism' cannot consistently give) any reason for thinking that the methods of science as he construes them are taking us in the direction of the goal of increased verisimilitude. His ban on all inductive argumentation precludes him from giving a reason for thinking that the systematic replacement of falsified theories by as yet unfalsified theories of greater content will increase truth-content without increasing falsity-content. In view of the inaccessibility of the goal of science according to Popper, I will characterize his as a *transcendent strategy*. For it involves positing a goal – increasing the verisimilitude of our theories – which is simply not accessible by the methods taken to be constitutive of science: bold conjecture and refutations. Perhaps the strategy is none the less a step forward in the face of the pessimistic induction. For science is not seen as positively irrational. However, it is hardly the paradigm of a rational activity, given that we can have no reason to think that its methods will take us towards its goal.

A more extreme response, which we will call the *atheistic response*, can be discerned in Feyerabend's writings. 'And as regards the word "truth" ', Feyerabend advises, 'we can say at this stage only say that it certainly has people in a tizzy, but has not achieved much else.'[4] We are advised to let Reason join the other abstract monsters – 'Obligation, Duty, Morality, Truth'[5] and to slay the lot with gay abandon. We thereby save ourselves the task of facing the problem through the simple expedient of jettisoning the concepts in terms of which it is formulated. Taken on its own Feyerabend's position is not nearly so unattractive as it comes to appear in contrast to Popper's. For if truth is utterly inaccessible, as Popper holds, what point is there in assuming that there is any truth at all? Seen in this light, Feyerabend's atheism amounts to the application of Occam's razor to Popper's transcendentalism. However, reasons have already been advanced in Chapter II for adopting a realist construal of scientific theories. Consequently we cannot avail ourselves of what would be Feyerabend's cavalier dismissal of the problem generated by the pessimistic induction. In this chapter I defend the Animal Farm move, arguing in favour of the thesis of verisimilitude and providing an analysis of the notion of verisimilitude. This will be offered following a critical evaluation of the attempt by Laudan to develop a model of science which is intended to show science to be progressive notwithstanding the pessimistic induction by assuming a goal other than truth or increasing verisimilitude. Laudan's strategy is to interpose between the extremes of Popper and Feyerabend what amounts to an *agnostic position.*

2 THE AGNOSTIC STRATEGY

Laudan remarks that setting up truth or verisimilitude as goals for scientific inquiry[6]

> may be noble and edifying to those who delight in the frustration
> of aspiring to that which they can never (know themselves to)
> attain; but they are not very helpful if our object is to explain
> how scientific theories are (or should be) evaluated.

Laudan is no atheist. He does not wish to deny the existence of truth. Rather, he simply has no need of that hypothesis, the thesis of verisimilitude. For he holds science to be essentially 'a problem-solving activity' and regards progress in science as a matter of increasing the problem-solving capacity of research programmes (cited hereafter as *RP*). His crucial assumption (to be examined later) is that judgments of the problem-solving capacity of a theory are logically independent of judgments of its truth or degree of verisimilitude. However, as shall be shown, his strategy fails. First, I shall argue that his notion of problem-solving capacity is not neutral with regard to truth and verisimilitude in the way he requires. Second, I shall point out that his own position is vulnerable to the objections he advances against those who have used a notion of verisimilitude.

First what is problem solving? We are told that 'any theory, T, can be regarded as having solved an empirical problem, if T functions (significantly) in any scheme or inference whose conclusion is a statement of the problem'.[7] Progress is not simply a matter of solving problems, it involves in addition avoiding anomalies and conceptual problems. So progress is a matter of increasing problem-solving effectiveness where this is determined 'by assessing the number and importance of the empirical problems which the theory solves and deducting therefrom the number and importance of the anomalies and conceptual problems which the theory generates'.[8] As Laudan notes, this account of problem solving is reminiscent of the deductive-nomological account of explanation. However, we are warned against the temptation to 'translate the claims I shall make about the nature and logic of problem solving into assertions about the logic of explanations'.[9] On the deductive-nomological model (hereafter cited as the *DN* model) it is a necessary condition of a deductively valid argument's providing an explanation that the premises be true or well-confirmed (depending on the particular version of the *DN* model). In this regard Laudan's account of problem solving diverges radically from the *DN* model. For Laudan takes it that questions as to whether a theory solves a problem can be settled without settling issues as to the truth or well-confirmedness of either the theory or the statement of initial conditions or the statement whose querying generates the problem.

If we were to focus exclusively on the problem-solving capacity of an *RP* (that is, the ability of the *RP* to solve empirical problems) without regard to its problem-solving effectiveness (that is, its ability both to solve empirical problems and to avoid anomalies and conceptual problems), this would make science so easy that we could all become Laplacian super-scientists. All you would need to do would be to take your favourite proposition and formulate a theory whose only postulates are that proposition and its negation. Let 'Q' be a statement of any problem you like. As 'P and not-P' entails 'Q', the problem is solved. Since any contradiction entails any proposition, this theory solves any empirical problem. Laudan is saved from this promise of instantaneous success. For he holds that the displaying of a non-localizable contradiction within a theory is conclusive grounds for refusing to accept the theory.[10] I make this blatant misconstrual of his position to stress a point with which he agrees which emerges if we ask why we are inclined to lay down a constraint excluding inconsistent theories. The answer is quite simply that we think that theories are to be evaluated through the categories of truth and falsehood, and a theory which is inconsistent is to be rejected because it cannot be true. And unless we are intuitionists, to reject '*p* and not-*p*' is to embrace '*p* or not-*p*'. Hence our rejection of a theory for being inconsistent is tantamount to embracing the claim that any sentence of a theory is either true or false. The reason why Laudan will not disagree is that he is not a semantical instrumentalist.[11] The sentences of scientific theories are either true or false. However, holding that all theories are false, he is what I called an epistemological instrumentalist. And since he rejects the notion of verisimilitude, the fact that sentences are true or false cannot play a role in any account of scientific progress. Laudan, then, agrees that the sentences of theories are either true or false. However, judgments as to which truth value sentences have is to play no place in the evaluation of rival *RP*s.

Having reached agreement that theories are true or false even though we may not be entitled to say of any given theory which it is, I turn to the problem of problems. It must be remembered that for Laudan a theory solves a problem if and only if the theory entails a statement of the problem. Questions concerning the truth or warranted assertability of the theory or the statement of the problem are simply beside the point. Suppose that I, having read Laudan, decide to set up in business as a scientist solving a range of problems. Suppose further that I am going to work on such problems as: why will sugar never dissolve in hot water? why are swans green? why does matter repel? why do freely moving bodies accelerate in the absence of force? and so on. Certainly I have got problems, but not the right sort of problems. One wants to respond that these are not genuine problems because the proposition queried is in each case false and known to be false. Even if I had some grand theory that enabled me to derive statements of a host of these and other problems, no Nobel Prize would be forthcoming. Our untutored inclination is to assume that our concern ought to be with what we might call non-spurious problems. That is, with problems whose corresponding statement is such that we have good reason to believe it to be true or to believe it is more likely to be true than false.

My concern is not to challenge Laudan's conception of what counts as a problem. Let us be generous to the point of allowing as he does

187

that the *esse* of problems is their *percipi*. The point of my caveat is that in the assessment of theories credit should be given only for solutions of non-spurious problems. Laudan would reject any caveat restricting the evaluation of a theory to an assessment of its capacity to solve non-spurious problems (and to avoid non-spurious anomalies). For instance, he writes:[12]

> Certain presumed states of affairs regarded as posing practical problems are actually *counter-factual*. A problem need not accurately describe a real state of affairs to be a problem: all that is required is that it be *thought to be* an actual state of affairs by some agent.

I take it that Laudan means by 'counter-factual problem' simply a problem whose statement is false and not one whose statement has the form of a counter-factual. If Laudan were rejecting the caveat because he holds that there are counter-factual problems in this latter sense of the term and that as counter-factuals lack truth-conditions they cannot be assessed in the categories of truth and falsehood, it would be a simple matter to modify the caveat as follows. Counter-factual problems count as non-spurious only if we have reasonable grounds for asserting the counter-factual (where 'grounds for asserting it' does not mean 'grounds for asserting it to be true').[13]

Given that we would not prize and, indeed, would not even be interested in a theory which solved only spurious problems and avoided spurious anomalies, why does Laudan want to take into account all problems where for the problems *esse est percipi*? We are told:[14]

> If factuality were a necessary condition for something to count as an empirical problem then such situations [the speculations concerning the behaviour of hypothetical sea serpents by early members of the Royal Society] could not count as problems. So long as we insist that theories are designed only to explain 'facts' (i.e., true statements about the world), we shall find ourselves unable to explain most of the theoretical activity which has taken place in science.

But there is certainly something unhappy about the endeavours of the early members of the Royal Society in the face of the tales of sea serpents. Undoubtedly our ideal (formulated within the rhetoric of problem solving) is a theory that solves non-spurious problems. We want to count it against our sea serpentologists and in favour of, say,

Harvey that in the former case the problems were spurious and that in the latter case they were not. Any tenable model of science must allow for this sort of differential assessment. The problem-solving model can aspire to do this only if the only solved problems which count in favour of an *RP* are problems we have reason to believe to be non-spurious. Adding a caveat to this effect in no way precludes us from doing justice to the laudable endeavours of our sea serpentologists. To see this we need only remind ourselves of the fact that the rational assessment of belief has two dimensions. Given that someone has a belief, *p*, we want to ask both whether the belief is true (judged from our own perspective) and whether on the evidence available to the person it was more reasonable for him to believe *p* than to disbelieve *p* or to suspend belief. The prize in the rational assessment stakes goes to the one who scores on both points. Of course, there are consolation prizes for those who score on one or the other dimension without scoring on both.

Our sea serpentologists certainly had a problem – a spurious problem. However, let us suppose that it was reasonable for them to think it was a genuine problem, so they can score on the other dimension. Unhappily but reasonably they expended their energies on a spurious problem. Happily they coped admirably (or can be imagined to have) in producing a theory designed to deal with this problem. If the theory arrived at meets our criteria for being a good theory we can give them credit for this. We can explain in this way their activity and represent it as rational while noting the unhappy feature of their activities that precludes them from admission to the Scientific Hall of Fame. They were rational to the extent to which they had reasonable grounds on the basis of the available evidence for thinking their problem to be non-spurious, and to the extent to which they had reason to believe that their theory did entail a statement of the problem.

It might be thought that my spurious theory could be rejected within Laudan's framework by reference to its anomaly-generating capacity without appeal to the caveat that problem-solving capacity is to be restricted to the solution of non-spurious problems. Laudan rightly employs a generous notion of an anomaly. He is correct in holding that one wants to take into account not only the generation of false predictions but also the generation of conceptual problems under the heading of 'anomaly'. Laudan's view that a false prediction counts as an anomaly only if another theory solves that problem, means that with ingenuity I could generate a spurious theory which was anomaly-free by constructing a theory from which I could derive a large number of falsehoods the negations of which were not the consequence of any known theory. Let us leave aside this more outlandish speculation and consider a pair of theories, T_1 and T_2, which are such that by and large if a statement of a problem is entailed by T_1, its negation is entailed by T_2. Suppose further that by and large we are inclined to believe the consequences of T_1 and disbelieve the consequences of T_2. We can explain our inclination to prefer T_1 either by saying that T_2 solves only spurious problems (problems the statements of which we have reason to believe false) or, equivalently, by saying that T_2 generates anomalies (generates false predictions). Either way we have to admit accessible truth and falsity into the picture. The expression 'accessible truth and falsity' is meant to refer to statements which are such that we can have reasonable grounds in certain contexts for thinking that they are true (or are likely to be true) and reasonable grounds in other contexts for thinking that they are false (or are likely to be false).

If we refuse to do this Laudan's model of science simply does not latch on to the world. Unless truth plays a regulative role, we can each select on the basis of our whims our own set of sentences which are statements of problems for us just because we so choose to regard them. We each then erect our own theories for solving these problems. Never mind how the world is, just solve your own problems! We should be faced with the unedifying spectacle of a plurality of free-floating sets of problems and their associated theories, where some of the theories would rate equally well on the theory assessment scale. It simply is just utterly implausible to suppose that progress could arise through a developing sequence of theories solving ever more spurious problems.

This model makes nonsense of the entire scientific enterprise. For truth does play a regulative role in the sense that theories designed to solve a problem whose corresponding statement has been shown to be false (or likely to be false) are condemned for that very reason. Of course, while we would condemn the theory for this reason we might none the less laud the theoretician if he had reasonable grounds for his false beliefs, and erected a theory that would have been reasonable had those beliefs been well-grounded.

If we are to latch our theories on to the world using a problem-solving model of science, we have to admit what I will call *an empirical basis*. This is a range of sentences which are such that we can have reasonable beliefs (in principle at least) about their truth value. If we can at the level of the empirical basis distinguish between spurious and non-spurious problems we can avoid the problem outlined above. In this case the solution of non-spurious problems will count in favour of a programme, and the solution of spurious problems will count against it. At some points Laudan seems to admit the need for such an empirical basis:[15]

> If we ask, 'How fast do bodies fall near the earth?', we are assuming there are objects akin to our conceptions of body and earth which move towards one another according to some regular rule. That assumption, of course, is a theory-laden one, but we none the less assert it to be about the physical world. Empirical problems are thus *first order problems*: they are substantial questions about the objects which constitute the domain of any given science. Unlike other higher order problems . . ., we judge the adequacy of solutions to empirical problems by studying the objects in the domain.

This suggests that the 'solution' of the problem 'why p?' obtained by deriving 'p' from a theory is to count for the theory only if we have good reason to think on the basis of a study of the objects in the domain that 'p' is true or more likely to be approximately true than not.

It turns out that Laudan is not referring to the low-level empirical problems which arise when we ask 'why p?' where 'p' is an observation sentence. The qualification 'empirical' is intended to differentiate between empirical and such *conceptual* problems as, say, the question of the intelligibility of absolute space. Examples given by Laudan of empirical problems include Brownian motion, the null result of the Michelson-Morley effect, and the photoelectric effect.

Laudan is on the horns of the following dilemma. If, on the one hand, we do not consider when assessing a theory from which we can derive a sentence, 'p', whether or not we have reasons to believe that 'p' is true, is likely to be true, is probably approximately true, etc., he faces the 'problem of problems' outlined above, and his model is no model of science as it is practised or as it should be practised. If, on the other hand, we are to take such judgments into account in evaluating a theory and count only the solution of non-spurious problems in favour of a theory, he cannot contrast his position with that of one who takes it that the goal of science is the production of good *DN* explanations. For requiring that 'p' not only be derivable from a theory but that the theory be true or corroborated is just what a *DN* model of explanation requires. On this construal of Laudan's intentions, he cannot consistently maintain the thesis that it is more important to ask whether theories 'constitute adequate solutions to significant problems than it is to ask whether they are "true", "corroborated", "well-confirmed" or otherwise justifiable within the framework of contemporary epistemology'.[16] For in asking whether they provide an adequate solution we shall have to ask these sorts of question of the sentences of the theories which are used in the derivations which constitute the solution of problems.

Furthermore, if we can make assessments of the reasonableness of believing in the truth of any empirical sentence, why should we not make assessments of theories which are just conjunctions of such sentences? Laudan's answer no doubt will be that the pessimistic induction gives us good reason to assume that all theories are false. And, as there is no viable notion of verisimilitude, we cannot take the sting out of the induction by making the Animal Farm move. Thus Laudan is committed to giving a different sort of assessment of individual sentences and theories. However, as we shall now see, Laudan's method for assessing theories faces precisely the same problems that are involved in analysing the notion of verisimilitude.

3 LAUDAN'S METRICAL PROBLEMS

My second major objection, which is a *tu quoque*, I press in order to reinforce my argument for operating within the traditional framework of verisimilitude. One of the advantages Laudan claims for his model is that: '(1) *it is workable*: unlike both inductivist and falsificationist models, the basic evaluation measures seem (at least in principle) to pose fewer difficulties'.[17] His measure was defined as follows:[18]

> The overall problem-solving effectiveness of a theory is determined by assessing the number and importance of the empirical problems which the theory solves and deducting therefrom the number and importance of the anomalies and conceptual problems which the theory generates.

Laudan gives us some principles which it might reasonably be held ought to guide our judgments as to the importance of problems and anomalies. However, we are a millennium away from having anything like a technique for measuring the importance of a problem or of an anomaly. It is bold (to say the very least) to claim that his evaluation measure poses fewer problems in principle.

In any event there is a more serious prior problem. Just how do we assess the number of problems solved by a theory? We are not provided with any principle of individuation of problems, and lacking that we are in no position to count up the number of problems. Why should one assume (in the absence of such a principle of individuation) that the number of problems solved by a theory is even finite? Let us suppose for the sake of argument that there are an infinite number of problems. One might be inclined to say that a physical theory which predicted the motion of each body in an infinite sub-set of the set of all particles solved an infinite number of problems. Suppose further that we have a rival theory which also provides an account of the motion of an infinite sub-set of all bodies, a sub-set that overlaps with, but is distinct from, the sub-set which the other theory deals with. How in this case are we to compare the theories as to problem-solving capacity? One might think that the example is far-fetched on the grounds that there are not an infinite number of particles and, consequently, there are not actual situations in which we have to face the problem of comparing theories which have an infinite problem-solving capacity. However, one can simply take any two rival theories and regard them as solving an infinite set of problems, given that time is either dense or continuous.[19] If, for instance, the theories make predictions about the state of a physical system at each instant of time, they will solve an infinite number of problems. For, for each instant, there is a problem concerning the state of the system at that instant. This means that the rhetoric of problem solving fails to evade what Laudan regards as the crucial challenge to the Popperian approach. Measuring the problem-solving capacity of a theory is too intimately related to measuring the content of a theory for us to be optimistic that the former is a less intractable problem than the latter.

It might be objected that I am using too fine a specification of the notion of a problem. To this one might rhetorically respond that as Laudan regards the *esse* of problems to be their *percipi*, it is enough that I feel that these are all problems. That alone makes them problems. More seriously, the actual state of a system at each instant of time is a potential falsifier of the theory (to put the point in Popperian terms) and thus is a potential anomaly. Why should not each prediction of the state of the system at a moment of time count as a solved problem?

Perhaps Laudan would seek to solve this problem by introducing a coarser notion of a problem so that, for instance, we only count the theory as solving the single general problem: how does the system evolve through time? and not the infinite set of problems of the form: what is that state of the system at instant t? – for each t. In that case the onus is on him to provide some criterion for the individuation of problems, and the development of this is likely to prove as difficult as the development of a content measure. So one might retort that as no one has even told us what we mean by 'greater problem-solving capacity', let alone how to measure it, we ought to be wary of using the notion.

Laudan, when pressed on this point,[20] claimed that there is general agreement among members of the scientific community about the individuation of problems. However, it is far from clear that they do agree in the case of theory clash as to whether one theory solves more problems than another. In any event, what is required is an articulation and justification of the principles they do use or ought to use in individuating problems for the purposes of comparing theories as to problem-solving capacity. And one can object *ad hominem* that if this sort of appeal to the ordinary discourse of practising scientists is in order, the defenders of the Animal Farm move can, with equal justice, appeal to the fact that scientists do talk of some theories containing more truth than other theories.

These problems do not exhaust the difficulties in Laudan's approach. Perhaps the deepest problem concerns the constraint his position places on the theory of meaning. For if meaning is to be given in terms of truth-conditions, and if truth-conditions cannot be transcendent, if, that is, it must be possible in principle at least to have evidence for and evidence against any statement that can be true or false, there will be insurmountable problems for Laudan and any other epistemological instrumentalist. Interestingly, Popper seems dimly aware of this difficulty, a difficulty which had driven him to embrace a Platonic scientism about meaning, whereby understanding a sentence is not a matter of grasping the evidential conditions of the sentence but of being in a quasi-causal relation to the proposition in the Third World earmarked by the sentence in question.

Finally, Laudan seems to have forgotten that we accept theories as a basis for action. Plainly the reason we do so is that we assume that the theories on which we act capture to some degree important truths about the world. But if (1) the rational acceptance of a theory is to be determined on the basis of its problem-solving capacity; (2) the problem-solving capacity of a theory can be determined without reference to the truth or falsity of its constituent hypotheses; and (3) the success of a theory as a problem solver provides no evidential support for the truth or truthlikefulness of a theory, it would be irrational in the extreme to act on a theory which turned out to be acceptable on Laudan's model. To accept a theory rationally as a basis for action just is to accept it as telling us something or other about how the world is, and that is to accept the theory as being more or less true.

4 THE TRANSCENDENTAL STRATEGY

Laudan and others have been far too swift in rejecting the theses that the goal of the scientific enterprise is to be understood in terms of progress towards increasing verisimilitude, and that we can have reasons (on occasion at least) for believing that we have indeed made progress. Unfortunately, some of those (i.e. Popper) who hold this position have been ill-equipped, given their anti-inductivism, to argue for *TV*. My strategy, which will be called the *transcendental strategy*, involves arguing for *TV* using what Popper would regard as 'pernicious inductivism'. Until the argument has been advanced I am not going to consider the qualms that many have concerning the notion of verisimilitude.

The contemporary trend in the philosophy of science is to take science seriously. Kuhn, Feyerabend, and others urge us (in their differing ways) to set aside our rational reconstruction of scientific theories and our philosophers' conceptions of method and look closely at the scientific process with the intention of learning and not instructing. In view of this it is surprising how rarely philosophers of science (including those cited above) attempt to employ in their philosophical writings the patterns of inference standardly employed in science. This is particularly surprising in view of the additional fact that the methods of science and philosophy are not as distinct as philosophers once fancied. One thinks here not only of the general approach of Quine but also of the difficulties in separating empirical and philosophical considerations in the evaluation of particular theories as illustrated in, for example, Sklar's study of absolutist-relativist controversy concerning space and time.[21] The particular style of argumentation whose time has come in the philosophy of science is inference to the best explanation.[22] Within physics we frequently find a particular hypothesis about, say, the constituents of protons supported by the claim that that hypothesis provides the best explanation of the observed phenomenon. To take science seriously is to admit as legitimate such a style of argumentation. Admittedly, like all inductive argumentation, it has its risks. For it may be that lack of ingenuity has left unarticulated a better explanation of the phenomenon in question. However, this possibility does not undercut the grounds for tentatively adopting the proffered hypothesis.

In the present context the phenomenon that calls out for explanation is the undeniable fact that in a mature science like physics, contemporary theories provided us with better predictions about the world than their predecessors and have placed us in a better position to manipulate that world. The impressive technological spin-off of contemporary physics is just one measure of this increased predictive and manipulative power. Interestingly, this phenomenon is acknowledged both by hard-line rationalists such as Popper, soft-line non-rationalists such as Kuhn, and hard-line non-rationalists such as Feyerabend. Of course, Feyerabend is given to adding the quite compatible claim that there are areas in which magic, traditional medicine and forgotten science had particular achievements not encompassed within contemporary science. He also retorts that there are other fun things to do beside predicting and manipulating the world.

The problem whose solution we seek is: how is it that contemporary theories are more useful in doing what they manifestly are more useful in doing? If *TV* is true we have an answer. If theories are increasing in truth-content without increasing in falsity-content, one would expect an increase in predictive power. Indeed, it would be totally mystifying that this increase should occur if it were not for the fact that theories are capturing more and more truth about the world. Thus I suggest we have more reason to believe in *TV* than in its denial, and that we should consequently tentatively adopt that hypothesis.[23] If someone is able to offer a better explanation, we shall have to withdraw the hypothesis. As things stand, we do not find any available alternatives whatsoever.

In developing this argument I have sought to derive support for *TV* from a premise common to all parties in the rationalist/non-rationalist controversy. For Popper, Lakatos, Kuhn, Laudan and even Feyerabend agree that within a mature science like physics there has been an impressive improvement in the predictive power of theories. To argue from this phenomenon to *TV* we need the following crucial premise:

If a theory T_2 is a better approximation to the truth than a theory T_1, then it is likely that T_2 will have greater predictive power than T_1.

This premise has a strong intuitive appeal. For if a theory has latched on to more theoretical truth about the world one would expect it to give better predictions. However, in view of the crucial role played by the thesis of TV we shall have to do more than rely on this appeal to mere intuition by providing a justification of the premise based on an analysis of the notion of verisimilitude or approximation to the truth. This will be done in the next section, which is technical. While further use will be made of TV, an understanding of the technical details of the analysis of verisimilitude will not be required to follow the argument in the remaining chapters. Similarly, we need to give more precise content to the notion of increased predictive power, which will be provided in Section 6.

The most sensitive of the Achilles' heels in this argument is the cavalier manipulation of the unanalysed notion of verisimilitude. Laudan, for instance, objects that 'no one has been able even to say what it would mean to be "closer to the truth"', let alone to offer criteria for determining how we could assess such proximity'.[24] On the first point it must be conceded that no one has given a satisfactory analysis of the notion of verisimilitude and that Popper's spirited attempt to do so is a dismal failure. However, that in itself is not a telling objection. Here again we can learn something from the practice of science. It is standard practice to introduce a concept in a theoretical context even if one cannot at the time give a satisfactory philosophical analysis of it. Indeed, such a concept can have a fruitful scientific career while the seas of philosophical controversy rage endlessly around it. Think, for instance, of the concept of spacetime, and the semantical controversies concerning this concept (i.e., is a reductive or non-reductive analysis appropriate?). Or, to take an historical example, think of the controversies about the meaning of 'field' which continued alongside the development of successful field theories. If the concept of verisimilitude is required in order to give a satisfactory theoretical explanation of an aspect of the scientific enterprise, why not use it and leave to Locke's 'underlabourers' the matter of analysis? No doubt some will feel that this is letting the side down, as philosophers are supposed to be exemplary in subjecting concepts to rigorous scrutiny; and so in the next section I develop a preliminary analysis of verisimilitude.

5 VERISIMILITUDE

The argument for TV will not be fully convincing unless we can defend the crucial premise that if a theory T_2 has greater verisimilitude than a theory T_1, T_2 is likely to have greater observational success than T_1. Thus far I have taken this to be intuitively plausible, given our intuitive grasp of the notion of verisimilitude. However, the failure of Popper's theory of verisimilitude which did seem plausible must make us wary of relying on intuitions in this area. And Laudan has quite rightly objected to my argument on the grounds that in the absence of any analysis of the notion of verisimilitude we are not entitled to assume that what holds for truth, holds for verisimilitude. That is, if a theory is true, any consequent is true. But why should we assume that if a theory has high verisimilitude a consequent of it is more likely to be true than false? In this section I provide an analysis of verisimilitude which will justify the premise in question. My approach will be very abstract and will involve making a number of simplifying assumptions. If the analysis has something in it, one hopes that further work will lead to a less simplifying analysis. As things stand, there is no other way of proceeding, for we are in effect in the process of creating a concept of verisimilitude.

It is important to be clear about what it is hoped the analysis will achieve. The argument for TV requires the assumption that greater verisimilitude entails the likelihood of greater observational success. It is essential that this be an entailment. For if the crucial premise were taken as an empirical, inductive claim asserting a correlation between higher verisimilitude and greater observational success the argument for TV would fail. For we have no direct access to the relative verisimilitude of rival theories and hence we cannot seek to correlate inductively degree of verisimilitude and degree of observational success. The hope is that a satisfactory analysis will establish the entailment. Furthermore, the analysis must show that there is no entailment in the opposite direction. For if greater observation success entailed greater verisimilitude, we would in effect have defined verisimilitude in terms of observational success. In this case we could not explain observational success by reference to verisimilitude. To guard against raising expectations too high it should be said at the outset that the analysis of verisimilitude to be given cannot be used to ascertain directly in any practical way the relative degree of verisimilitude of rival theories. For the moment I am only interested in saying what is to be meant by 'verisimilitude', leaving until the next chapter the question of how one could in fact justify judgments concerning the relative verisimilitude of theories.

It will be helpful to begin by reviewing the central problem involved in any attempt to define verisimilitude. As we noted, there would be no problem if theories contained only a finite number of sentences. For in that case we could compare the theories by counting up the number of truths and the number of falsehoods contained in each theory. However, any interesting pair of theories, each of which has something going for it, will contain the same number of truths and the same number of falsehoods: namely, an infinite number. No one has succeeded in defining a measure of the size of infinite sets of sentences analogous to the measures defined in geometry giving the lengths of line intervals all of which contain the same infinite number of points. My aim is the ambitious one of providing a solution to this problem for the infinite case.

In aiming at increasing verisimilitude we are aiming at getting more truth. We are not simply trying to increase the chances that an arbitrary consequence of our theory is true. If that were our aim we should proceed by continually weakening our theories. For instance, an arbitrary consequence of the first two of Newton's laws of motion probably is more likely to be true than an arbitrary consequence of a theory consisting of the three laws of motion together with the universal law of gravitation. However, the latter theory has much greater content than the former theory, and in spite of having some falsity-content has impressive truth-content that the former lacks. This suggests that our definition should satisfy the following constraint which, at this stage, can only be understood intuitively. If T_2 has greater verisimilitude than T_1, T_2 should have at least as much content as T_1 (it should say at least as much about the world). It should contain more truth in its content and if it also contains more falsehood that increased falsehood should be offset by a much greater improvement in its truth-content.

In view of the importance of the notion of content our first task must be to analyse it. In doing so the following terminology will be used. By a *theory* I shall mean the deductive closure of a set of theoretical postulates together with an appropriate set of auxiliary hypotheses; that is, everything that can be deduced from this set. By an *observational consequence* of a theory I mean those observational conditionals which can be derived, the antecedents of which specify initial conditions and the consequents of which specify final conditions. Attention is restricted to theories that can be represented by a first-order recursively axiomatized theory. That is, the theoretical postulates and the auxiliary hypotheses can be written in a standard first-order language, and there is some mechanical procedure for recognizing whether a sentence of the language is either a theoretical postulate or an auxiliary hypothesis. This procedure might take the form of a finite list of these. A theory that satisfies this condition is recursively axiomatizable and it therefore follows that the set of consequences (the deductive closure) is recursively enumerable. This means that this set can be mechanically produced in a sequence and each consequence can be assigned a positive integer corresponding to its position in the sequence. For details see Hunter (1971), Enderton (1972), or Boolos and Jeffrey (1974).

One aspect of our intuitive idea of one theory's having more content than another is that one theory answers more questions than another. It is this aspect which I wish to clarify. A theory answers the question '?p' if it contains as a consequence either 'p' or 'not-p'. If a theory contains either 'p' or 'not-p' I will say that it *decides* 'p'. In developing this notion of content attention will be restricted to theories which either have the same vocabulary, or the vocabulary of one contains the vocabulary of the other. Let T_1 and T_2 be two such theories. As we are interested in empirical content let t_1 and t_2 be enumerations respectively of the consequences of T_1 and T_2 from which all logically true sentences have been deleted. Furthermore, let us suppose that if a formula A occurs in the enumeration, all logically equivalent formulae following A in the enumeration have been deleted.

Our aim is to explain what it means to say that one of these theories answers more questions, i.e., decides more sentences than the other. To this end consider the sequence t_1 associated with T_1. Any member of that sequence is either decided by T_2 or it is not. If it is decided by T_2, either t or not-t is in T_2. If it is not decided by T_2 neither t nor not-t is in T_2. For any n there is the ratio of the number of sentences among the first n of t_1 which are decided by T_2. Let R^1 be the infinite sequence of such ratios. The sequence might look like the following if T_2 tended to be a theory which decided most of the sentences of T_1: $^1/_1$, $^1/_2$, $^2/_3$, $^3/_4$, $^4/_5$, ... Such a result tells us only that T_2 has at least as much content as T_1. It may be that T_1 decides most of the sentences of the sequence associated with T_2. Therefore we repeat the above process using the random sequence of T_2 to define in the same way a sequence of ratios R^2. We compare the two sequences of ratios, R^1 and R^2, by taking the difference between corresponding terms. If for sufficiently large n the absolute value of the differences tends to be small and constant, the theories are of roughly equal content. If, on the other hand, for sufficiently large n the terms of the one sequence, say R^1, tend to be larger than the corresponding terms of the other sequences, R^2, the theory T_2 generating has greater content than theory T_1.

We can gain some confirmation that this explication of content captures our intuitive ideas by considering the special case of two decidable theories T_1 and T_2. In virtue of being decidable, any sentence, 's', expressible in the languages of T_1 and T_2 respectively is such that either 's' is a theorem of the theory or 'not-s' is a theorem of the theory. Intuitively we would expect that if T_1 entails T_2 and T_2 does not entail T_1, then T_1 has greater content than T_2. This is indeed the case. Suppose that T_1 entails T_2 but not vice versa, then any sentence decided by T_2 is decided by T_1 but not vice versa. Therefore, as n increases the difference between the ratio of sentences decided by T_1 to sentences decided by T_2 is bound to be non-zero.

As so far explicated this notion of relative content is vague and qualitative. The vagueness arises from the fact that we have said that T_2 has greater content than T_1 if for sufficiently large n the terms in the sequence of ratios R^1 tend to be larger than the terms in the sequences of ratios R^2. It would be nice to be able to attach a measure to the content of T_2 relative to the content of T_1. Suppose that the infinite sequence of differences between the ratios of R^1 and R^2 has a limit. Could this serve as a measure of the degree to which the content of T_2 exceeds the content of T_1? Unfortunately there is a complication due to the fact that the limit, if any, of an infinite sequence depends on the order of the terms in the sequence. In order to see how we might cope with this problem it will be instructive to consider the analagous problem which arises in the frequency theory of probability.

Suppose we toss a coin 1000 times with a view to determining the probability of heads. We cannot define the probability of heads as the ratio of heads to tosses in 1000 tosses. For suppose we had 600 heads in the first 1,000 tosses but 50,000 heads in the first 100,000. We should revise our estimate of the probability from 6 in 10 to 1 in 2. The solution proposed by the frequency theory of probability is to define the probability as the limit of the infinite sequence of ratios of heads to tosses in finite sequences of tosses. That is, we take the sequence of ratio of heads to tosses in one toss, in 2 tosses, in 3, in 4, . . . Of course we cannot actually toss the coin an infinite number of times. Consequently, following von Mises, frequentists define probability for a mathematical entity called a *collective* which can be supposed to represent an idealization of an empirical situation. A collective is an infinite set of outcomes (which we can think of as outcomes of tossing a coin). We take an infinite sub-sequence of this set and form the infinite sequence of ratios of heads to tosses. To say that the probability of getting heads is defined on this collective is to say that this sequence of ratios has a limit which is the probability of the outcome given the following additional constraint. The limit defined is insensitive to reasonable place-selection; that is, if for all reasonable selections of infinite sub-sequences of the given sequence the resulting sequence has the same limit. We cannot require that the limit be preserved under all place selections, for one could select *all* the heads assuming there is, say, 50 heads every 100 tosses and obtain the limit 1 even if it is a fair coin. The usual strategy is to specify reasonable place selection, as, say, any selection obtained by taking every nth outcome for every n. Such selections are called *Bernoulli sequences*. It is provable both that such sequences exist and that there are such sequences which are insensitive to place selection under more sophisticated rules for generating sub-sequences.

I propose simply to borrow from the frequency theory of probability, and in talking of the insensitivity of the limit of the sequence of ratios to reasonable place selection I mean the place selection rules allowed by the frequency theory of probability. As a matter of terminology and not as a sleight of hand I will define a notion of *respectability* on a pair of theories as follows:

> T_1 and T_2 are *respectable*$_1$ if and only if the sequence of absolute differences of the corresponding terms in the sequence of ratios R^1 and R^2 has a limit and that limit is insensitive to reasonable place selection on the sequences of sentences t_1 and t_2.

I do not know that any pair of actual theories are respectable. But in this regard my approach fares no less well than does the frequency theory of probability. Frequentists posit that if for large n the relative frequencies observed in the tossing of a coin appear to stabilize then the set-up does approximate to that of a collective, in the sense that the observed outcome is an initial segment of a sequence from a collective and that the observed relative frequency approximates the probability in the collective.

202

Similarly I would argue that if for sufficiently large n the difference in the corresponding ratios of R^1 and R^2 tends to stablize, we should posit that that value represents a reasonably approximate measure of the difference in content between the two theories. It must be conceded that this is a theoretical procedure. Practical application faces severe problems. First, we have to generate at least an initial sequence of, say, 1000 sentences of each theory. Second, we have to ask of each such sentence whether it is decided by the other theory. In most cases there will not be any mechanical way of doing this. That a sentence s is not decided by T_1 will be a conjecture based on our inability either to derive s in T_1 or to derive not-s in T_1. All that I claim is that this definition captures an important ingredient in our idea of the relative content of theories. The idea is intelligible even if we cannot except in special circumstances employ it to reach a reasonable conjecture about the relative content of a pair of theories.

The definition of content given treats all questions on a par. In comparing theories as to content some may wish to invoke a notion of significance. To put the objection intuitively: one theory might answer more questions of a trivial sort than another theory which answered more questions of great significance. The procedure given can be used none the less. For one simply deletes from the list of, say, the first 1000 sentences in the enumeration those which are deemed non-significant.

We have explicated a notion of relative content for respectable$_1$ theories. The next stage in moving towards an approximation to the truth about verisimilitude requires defining a notion, to be called *relative truth*. Our final definition of verisimilitude will be in terms of these two notions. Consider as before theories T_1 and T_2 with associated sequences of consequences $t_1 = t_1^1, t_1^2, t_1^3, \ldots$ and $t_2 = t_2^1, t_2^2, t_2^3, \ldots$ We define a new sequence of ratios, called *truth-ratios*, the nth term in the sequence gives the ratio of the number of truths in the first n terms of t_1 to the number of truths in the first n terms of t_2. For instance, if t_1^1, t_1^2, t_1^3, are true and t_1^4 and t_1^5 false and if $t_2^1, t_2^2, t_2^3, t_2^5$ are true and t_2^4 false, the 5th term is $3/4$. If the ratios tend to be greater than one we consider the sequence of inverses of the terms in this sequence. That is, we want to take the ratio of truths in finite sequences of sentences in the theory that fares best to truths in finite sequences of sentences in the theory that fares worst. We define a *respectable$_2$* pair of theories as a pair of theories in which either the ratio of T_1 to T_2 or the ratio of T_2 to T_1 has a limit and any infinite sub-sequence of the original sequences of sentences obtained by reasonable place selection gives the same limit. We define the truth-ratio of the poorer to the better theory as this limit.

The use of the notion of relative truth as defined is a matter for God, not man. Even if we take, say, the first 1,000 sentences in the respective enumerations of T_1 and T_2 we cannot fix their truth-value in a theory-neutral way. Admittedly one would expect to encounter low-level observational conditionals the truth or falsity of which we can expect to be able to determine in principle at least. However, we shall also expect that there will be highly theoretical sentences, and for these we have no theory-neutral way of discovering their truth. This means that if positing that these sentences are either true or false we are presupposing some transcendent notion of truth. That is, we are assuming we understand what it is for them to be true or false notwithstanding the fact that we have no procedure for determining whether they are true or false. Many will have qualms which I share about such a notion of truth (cf. pp. 53–4). One possibility is to determine the truth-ratio of T_1 and T_2 relative to some theory T_3. We might take T_3, for instance, to be our current theory. In that case we determine the ratio of truths in T_1 to T_2 in the first n sentences in the enumeration by reference to T_3. Alternatively we might take T_3 to be that theory which in the ideal long run will become the accepted total theory of nature in the Peircean sense. The former alternative has the attractive feature of being more usable than the latter, given our ignorance of the final state of science. Our definition of relative truth given below leaves the specification of T_3 open:

> T_2 has a greater truth relative to T_3 than T_1 if and only if the infinite sequence of ratios giving the ratio of truths in T_1 to the truths in T_2 judged by reference to T_3 has a limit less than 1 which is unaffected by reasonable place-selection.

Using the notion of relative content and relative truth, we define relative verisimilitude as follows:

> T_2 has greater verisimilitude than T_1 if and only if both:
>   (1) the relative content of T_2 is equal to or greater than that of T_1;
>   (2) T_2 has greater truth relative to T_3 than T_1.

This definition captures a central strand in our notion of approximation to the truth. For one theory to be nearer the truth than another it must have greater content and more of its content must be true. The definition of relative truth means that less of its content will be false. It follows from this definition that if one theory has greater verisimilitude than another it is likely to have greater observational success. For the greater relative truth of T_2 means that an arbitrary consequence of T_2 is more likely to be true than an arbitrary consequence of T_1. Furthermore, this cannot be true of T_2 simply because T_1 is the weaker theory. For by the first clause in the definition T_2 has more content than T_1. If one wants both to say more about the world and to say more true things in so doing, T_2 is the theory to adopt. The fact that an arbitrary consequence of T_2 is more likely to be true than an arbitrary consequence of T_1 means that an arbitrary observational condition in T_2 is more likely to be true than an arbitrary observational condition in T_1. It might be objected that this is a *non sequitur*. From the fact that an arbitrary child of ten is likely to live to 50 it does not follow that an arbitrary child who will become a heavy smoker will live to 50. This is because smoking is relevant to the outcome. Being red-haired is irrelevant to the outcome, so the probability that a red-haired child of ten will live to 50 is unaffected by this additional information. Similarly, just being observational is not relevant to the outcome. Being observational just means being a sentence of the sort we feel we can test for truth and be confident in our results. Being observational is like being red-haired, and hence we are entitled to maintain that if an arbitrary consequence of T_2 is more likely to be true than an arbitrary consequence of T_1, this holds for arbitrary observational consequences.

The entailment must not run the other way, for if it does we shall have defined verisimilitude as the likelihood of observational success and thereby be deprived of using TV as an explanatory hypothesis to explain increasing observational success. Quite obviously the entailment does not run the other way. For from the fact that one theory is observationally more successful than another we cannot infer anything about the relative content of the two theories. Having given content to the notion of verisimilitude we have vindicated the crucial premise in argument for TV. Before turning in the next chapter to showing how we can have fallible indications of the relative verisimilitude of rival theories, we need to complete the process of clarifying the notions employed in the argument for TV by looking at the notion of observational success.

6 OBSERVATIONAL NESTING

There is general agreement that contemporary theories provide greater observational success than their predecessors. In specifying in what that success consists it will be helpful to focus on a case which virtually everyone regards as a paradigm: the transition from Newtonian mechanics to relativistic mechanics. There are three aspects to the observational improvement of relativistic mechanics over Newtonian mechanics. First, if Newtonian mechanics can be used to make a prediction P for the value of some parameter (say, the position of a particle at a specified time) which is corroborated in the sense that the measured value of the parameter is found to be in some interval Δ around P, the interval Δ represents the limits of current experiment accuracy; relativistic mechanics predicts a value which is within the interval Δ. Second, there are cases in which the Newtonian prediction departs from the measured value by more than can be explained by reference to the limitations of our measuring techniques (i.e., bodies moving with speeds approaching that of the speed of light). In these cases relativistic mechanics predicts a value which is corroborated by a measurement approximating to the predicted value. If a pair of theories meet these two conditions I will say that the more successful theory *observationally nests* the less successful theory.

The third aspect of observational success relates to content. In my sense of content, two theories, one of which observationally nested the other, might have the same observational content. For any observational question answered by the one theory might be answered by the other theory. The nesting means that one theory is more successful in getting the right answer. The observational content of relativistic mechanics is greater than that of Newtonian mechanics, for there are observation questions answered by the former but not by the latter. For instance, Newtonian mechanics does not allow us to make any prediction about what will happen to a wave front expanding from a point in a cylindrical spacetime. Using a full theory of relativistic mechanics we can predict that the wave front will collapse on a point. I shall refer to this aspect of observation success as *content-increasing predictive power*. If a theory T_2 makes corroborated predictions on matters on which a theory T_1 is silent I shall say that T_2 displays *content-increasing predictive success*.

We define what it means to say that theory T_2 is observationally more successful than theory T_1 as follows:

(1) T_2 observationally nests T_1.

(2) T_2 displays content-increasing predictive success over T_1.

This definition does not give a linear ordering of theories in terms of observation success. We might find that both T_2 and T_3 were observationally more successful than T_1 but that T_2 was not better than T_3 nor was T_3 better than T_2. This is just the result we want, for we have no reason to assume that any arbitrary pair of theories are such that one is observationally more successful than another on the basis of the available evidence. In so far as our theory choice is guided by observational success we shall have to remain agnostic as to which of the theories T_2 and T_3 is the better in such a context. No doubt we shall endeavour to increase the available evidence and that may lead us to be able to determine which is the observationally more successful. Of course, we may find that before this issue is resolved some other theory T_4 is propounded, which is observationally more successful than both T_2 and T_3.

IX

SCIENTIFIC METHOD

1 THE QUEST FOR METHOD

There has been progress in science. This progress, I have argued, is best understood as an improvement in the verisimilitude of our theories. The explanation of the fact that science has been capturing more truth about the world is that we have evolved evidential or epistemic procedures of some success and that the development of science has by and large been determined by scientists acting on the basis of the outcome of the application of these procedures. Without assuming anything about the character of that procedure, not even that it can be given a verbal formulation, let us refer to it as scientific method, hereafter *SM*. Method, according to the *Oxford English Dictionary*, is 'a special form of procedure especially in a mental activity'. Is there anything special about *SM* that distinguishes it from other procedures for finding out about the world, procedures available to pre-scientific man and to the non-scientific man in the street? If so, is there any enlightening general verbal description of *SM*? These questions will be the focus of the discussion of this chapter. A full discussion of *SM* would have to cover a multitude of topics, including the design of experiments, the theory of measurement and the role of mathematics in science. My discussion will, for reasons of space, be largely restricted to the question of the possibility of giving an abstract characterization of the factors that ought to guide theory choice.

Suppose for the moment there is something special about *SM* which can be characterized. What benefit should we hope to achieve by describing *SM*? There is a long and venerable tradition ranging from Bacon through Mill and Whewell to the members of the Vienna Circle of assuming that the articulation of *SM* will, in Whewell's words, 'afford us some indication of the most promising mode of directing our future efforts to add to its [scientific knowledge's] extent and completeness'.[1] If this is so, the study of *SM* really would enhance our chances of making scientific progress, and methodology (the study of *SM*) ought to displace mathematics as the queen of the sciences. But this is the stuff of dreams. As we shall see, the study of *SM* will not produce a methodologist's stone capable of turning the dross of the laboratory into the gold of theoretical truth. This pessimism about the fruits of methodological studies should not deter us from proceeding. Even if it will not make us better scientists, it will give us a better understanding of the scientific enterprise. An analogy will help to bring this out.

There is an infinite set of finite sequences of words of English. Some of these are sentences of English and some are not. At a surprisingly young age children are able to distinguish with facility between those which are and those which are not sentences. This skill is exercised by the child on sequences of words which he or she has never heard after exposure to only a relatively small number of sentences of English. How is it that we are able to exercise this skill? There must be some finite number of rules which determine which sequences constitute sentences and which we implicitly internalized without having been explicitly taught these rules. Indeed, no one has been able as yet to give a fully satisfactory characterization of them. Yet we are convinced that they are there to be characterized. No one should suppose that having an explicit characterization will make us better able to make the practical discriminations needed in everyday discourse. We can already do this quite adequately. The project of articulating these rules is not intended to improve competency in the exercise of the skill which they explain. However, this project if successful will give us an understanding of the functioning of one aspect of language. It may be assumed that there is something special about *SM* which can be characterized. To do so will cast light on our understanding of the practice of science even if it will not make us more adept at that practice.

In introducing this analogy I am not presuming for the moment that there is something *SM*, which can be given an enlightening full verbal characterization. For there are skills which can be successfully exercised by individuals which elude any linguistic description. For instance, consider wine blending. Successful blenders judge the proportions of unpalatable wines to blend to produce a palatable wine. Different

209

blenders who agree on the correct proportions are notoriously unable to agree on a description of what it is about the taste of the wines that leads them to their judgments. For the moment the question as to whether the skill of the successful practitioner of *SM* is partially or entirely like that of the wine blender is to be left open.

My aim in this chapter is to build up a partial picture of *SM*. In the next section I consider and reject the view that *SM* is nothing more than a refinement of our common-sense, pre-scientific procedures for discovering facts about the world. A consideration of method in mathematics (Section 3), while it fails to provide a model of *SM*, does assist in bringing into focus certain aspects of *SM*. Following that we explore the possibility in Section 4 that formal work in the theories of probability and confirmation might provide an account of the aspect of *SM* which is of greatest interest for this work: namely, the matter of choice between rival theories. The theories of probability and confirmation cannot be used in this way. They have, none the less, a vital role to play within contemporary scientific practice (Section 5). Their ascendancy indicates one of the ways in which *SM*, has evolved. Another aspect of the evolution of *SM* is presented in Section 6. As we shall see, this fact of evolution in *SM* indicates that rationalist accounts of the scientific enterprise of the type advocated by Popper, Lakatos and Laudan are seriously deficient. In the following two sections an account is given of the factors that ought to guide theory choice. These verbal articulations are not the entire story. For *SM* involves an essential element of judgment, the role of which is discussed in Section 9. Finally, we consider the question all too frequently ignored in philosophical discussion of *SM* of the extent to which the relative costs of developing rival theories should be taken into account in making theory choices.

2 THE RUPTURE WITH REFINED COMMON SENSE

Some practising scientists have described *SM* as nothing more than refined common sense. In this section we shall first examine the grain of truth lying behind this characterization and then expose the grave distortion it involves. Pre-scientific common-sense procedures include the discovery of correlations between observables. At the most mundane level this can take the form of noticing, say, that fruits which look alike taste alike. Unless we possessed this faculty (which we share with the higher animals) the human race would never have survived to found the institution of science. Certainly the discovery of correlations between observables is an important part of scientific activity. The search for regularities involves a refinement of common sense both in the fact that the observables may be more precisely specified and in the fact that there will be a search for correlations that are not so evident and may have no connection with phenomena which concern us in everyday life. While science does involve this refinement of a primitive capacity, we shall see that the exercise of this capacity is not the end of science but the stage setting for science proper.

The procedures of common sense involve not only noting repeated conjunctions of observables but also conjecturing hypotheses on the basis of hunches and putting them to the test. Some primitive Popperian man noting that logs floated might have conjectured that a large log would support a man and in putting this to the test invented the boat. Obviously this is part of scientific method, a technique much refined in science through more precise specification of the conjectures about observables that are tested and through bringing about controlled circumstances in which to test the conjecture.

Notwithstanding the fact that one can see certain aspects of *SM* as involving a refinement of the procedures of common sense, *SM* as currently constituted is more aptly described as involving a rupture with the procedures of common sense. For the discovery of correlations between observables, far from being the end of science, is but its beginning. Science begins when, having noted correlations, we seek an explanation of why they obtain. Standardly this involves the postulation of other properties and items and correlations which explain the observed correlations. The primitive atomic theories of the Greeks, Galileo's postulation of mountains on the moon (to explain certain changing patterns as shadows cast by mountains), the postulation of quarks to explain hadronic jets: these are paradigms of scientific moves in that they go beyond the deliverances of a refined common sense by seeking to explain those deliverances. It is just because science involves the postulation of underlying explanatory mechanisms that scientific method is problematic. For once we move beyond investigating correlations between observables the question of what does or should guide our choice between alternative explanatory accounts becomes problematic.

The most profound change in science has been the development of theories introducing ever more theoretical items and properties for explanatory purposes. As this process develops the evidence for our

211

theories becomes ever more indirect and tenuous. No doubt the present concern with methodological questions in science arises in part from this very fact. The farther we delve into the inner constituents of matter and the farther we go in speculating about the extent and origins of the universe, the less sure we can be about our theories and consequently the more we are inclined to seek reassurance through articulating the factors which should guide us. This change in science is reflected in writings on science. Mill confidently characterized the methods of science, and to the extent that science is concerned with discovering correlations between observables his account provides reasonable guidance.[2] It is significant that nothing in Mill's discussion corresponds to what I called inference to the best explanation. Mill was concerned with hypotheses that would admit of fairly direct testing. The scientific hypotheses that capture the contemporary interest are not of this character. The theory of the quark is advocated on the grounds that it is the only explanatory account anyone has been able to come up with of certain phenomena, and it is part of that theory that it cannot be tested through isolating free quarks. Of course one can find abundant examples of hypotheses advanced on such indirect evidence in the early history of science, and that many writers realized this is shown in their endorsements of the hypothetical-deductive method in science. However, it was natural that Mill should have overlooked this because such highly theoretical theorizing did not have the extensive place in science that it now has.

3 METHOD IN MATHEMATICS

Whether there is in general progress in science towards greater verisimilitude is a matter of controversy. Even if my arguments have stemmed this sceptical tide, it will obviously remain a matter of controversy which of two rival theories we should select in trying to move towards truth. Mathematics provides an interesting and enlightening foil for our investigation of *SM* because in mathematics this sort of controversy is almost non-existent. Mathematics is undoubtedly progressive in that it is accumulative. Results, once established, remain in the repertoire of the mathematical community. Interest in certain results may wax and wane as a function of the interest in applications to which they can be put. But the results remain. The truths of projective geometry may no longer excite in the way that truths about the mathematics of Hilbert spaces do in view of their applicability to quantum mechanics. But the truths of projective geometry remain because in mathematics there is what we can aptly describe as a logic of justification, which is largely invariant through time and across the members of the mathematical community at any time (this needs qualifications given below).

Proofs in mathematics are just that — proofs. They are not conjecture about a possible result, they establish that result. Broadly speaking, in pure mathematics proofs fall into two classes. In one case one defines a class of structures through a set of axioms (i.e. group theory) and one proves something about all such structures or about specified sub-classes by showing that the result follows logically from the characterization given. In the other case one has something like number theory, where we have strong and well-developed intuitions about properties of the number system. In this case one offers axioms (i.e. Peano's axioms) which, one conjectures, capture all the previously accepted truths about numbers. One then seeks to prove further properties of the numbers by appeal to the axioms, and one conjectures that in so far as the properties of the number system can be systematically characterized they are done so by the axiom system. If someone comes up with something we are inclined to hold to be true about the number system which cannot be established from the axioms we would most likely add additional axioms. The hardness of the logic of justification in mathematics comes from the constraint that a proof must be representable in some acceptable formal logic where any putative proof can be checked for validity by an algorithm; that is, by a mechanical procedure that a suitable computer could carry out.

If by method in mathematics one has in mind the procedure for checking the acceptability of proofs, then that method is characterizable. I have over-stressed the extent to which there is general agreement on the characterization to be given and it will be instructive to see what is wrong with this stress. Setting aside for the moment contemporary intuitionist mathematicians, one would not have found at times in the past the agreement one finds to-day on the conditions a proof should meet. These conditions of logical rigour arose as a result of the inconsistencies Russell discovered in set-theory at the turn of the century. Thus method in mathematics has evolved. Indeed, some results once accepted but no longer accepted would not have been accepted in the past if these current constraints had operated.

Even in this limited sense of method, just what the method in mathematics should be is a matter of some controversy. For intuitionist mathematicians reject certain classical laws of logic (i.e., the Law of the Excluded Middle). The consequence of this is that within the confines of their weaker logic some results provable in classical logic do not appear to be provable. Intuitionists thus reject as unproved mathematical propositions accepted as proved by classical mathematicians. For our purposes this debate is of interest, for it reveals a mixture of *a priori* and *a posteriori* considerations. Perhaps the strongest intuitionist case is that of Dummett, in which it is argued in a philosophical manner, by appeal to general considerations about meaning and the nature of logic, that classical logic is too strong.[3] Thus we have an *a priori* critique of classical mathematical methods. On the other hand one finds classical mathematicians arguing as follows. Certain results (largely to do with the continuum) have great practical applicability. Their utility confirms that there is something in these results, therefore there must be something wrong with intuitionist methods if they cannot produce these results. Here we find an *a posteriori* argument in favour of a certain conception of mathematical method. The moral to be drawn for application to our subsequent discussion of *SM* is that one will expect to find that some aspects of method are open to *a priori* criticism and some to *a posteriori* criticism.

Obviously there is much more to mathematics than the checking of putative proofs. In some areas of mathematics not only do we have an algorithm for checking proffered for cogency, we have an algorithm for generating and proving results. For example, we can mechanically check that $234 + 123 = 357$ and mechanically generate a proof that this is so. And, more generally, in a complete mathematical theory (i.e., one in which for any sentence 'A' either 'A' is a theorem or 'not-A' is a theorem) there is a mechanical procedure for determining whether or not an arbitrary sentence 'A' of the language is a theorem which will give us a proof of 'A' if it is a theorem and a proof of 'not-A' if 'A' is not a theorem. These sorts of mechanical procedure have only limited applicability, and the heart of interesting mathematics involves thinking of interesting structures to investigate and thinking of lines of argument that will turn out to give valid proofs in systems that are not complete (i.e., for which there is no mechanical proof-generating procedure). Here there is nothing of general interest to be said. Unlike philosophers of science, no philosopher of mathematics has ever offered rules to be followed in thinking of what to investigate or in thinking of how to come up with proofs. Given the right kind of native wit an exposure to the right kind of experience can assist. Few mathematical results are produced by people who have not worked through the mathematical works of others. There may be room to investigate empirically which methods of exposing students to the corpus of mathematics is most likely to be productive. For instance, one finds it argued that better mathematicians are produced if in teaching mathematics exposure is given to the applications of mathematics and if students are kept away from the presentation of mathematics in axiomatic form. The importance of this for our consideration of *SM* is to provide illustration of the fact that we can acquire skills whose successful exercise is open to decisive checking even though we cannot give any rules or general characterization of how that skill is exercised. While elderly scientists of some repute are prone to write books with titles like *Advice to a Young Scientist*,[4] this phenomenon is almost unknown among successful mathematicians (excepting the occasional suggestion of interesting propositions for which a proof or disproof might be sought). But no advice is offered about how to achieve a result one way or another. Thus if mathematics, the results of which are largely accumulative, lacks such guiding principles we should not be surprised to find that the methods of science cannot be specified in an exhaustive set of guiding principles.

4 PROBABILITY AND CONFIRMATION

For the greater part of the time during which the institution of science has existed the goal was seen to be the discovery of necessary truths. In so far as this was how the goal was conceived, the method of science was taken to be demonstration. The scientist, like the mathematician, would imaginatively conjure a hypothesis and would seek to provide a proof. This conception of science lingered on and is, for instance, evident in Locke's lament that there will never be a science explaining the secondary qualities of bodies in terms of the primary qualities of their minute parts because no logical demonstration of the necessary connection between these is possible.[5] The development of the modern conception of science as a search for contingent, empirical explanatory theories was, interestingly, accompanied by the development of the quantitative concept of probability. If the basic hypotheses of science were not candidates for being proved demonstratively, but were to be supported by inductive arguments, it was natural to explore the possibility that the theory of probability could be invoked in representing the process of theory choice. For instance, given rival theories T_1 and T_2 and total available evidence E, one looks to see which theory E renders more probable. The fact that probabilities can in certain contexts be represented by numerical values led to the hope that one could assign values to the degree to which a body of evidence rendered a theory probable. We shall see that a quantitative concept of probability is of no use in representing the process of theory choice.

Probability is a Janus-faced concept. On the one hand it relates to matters of chance. For example, we say that the probability of getting a 2 on a toss of this die is 1/6 or that the probability of a man of 20 living to be 65 is 4/5. To say that the probability of some outcome will occur is m/n in some set-up or situation is best understood as ascribing a property to that set-up or situation. That the probability is m/n entails that for large N we can reasonably expect the number of times the outcome occurs to be $N.m/n$. For example, we can reasonably expect that in 1,200 tosses of the coin there will be around 600 heads. We can expect that something in a group of N twenty-year-olds, something in the region of $4/5\ N$ will live to be 65. Probability assignments in these chance set-ups are governed by the following axioms of the probability calculus:

(1) $0 \leqslant P(h,e) \leqslant 1$.
(2) $P(h,e) = 1 - P(\text{not-}p,e)$.
(3) $P(h \text{ or } h',e) = P(h,e) + P(h',e)$, (where h and h' are independent).

Probability is, on the other hand, in Bishop Butler's phrase, 'the guarded guide'.[6] If I say that it will probably rain tomorrow I am asserting that it will rain tomorrow but I am hedging by indicating that I have less than conclusive grounds for this assertion. If I wish to assign a measure of my confidence in propositions being true on a 0 to 1 scale, those assignments must obey the axioms given above. I will refer to the first aspect of probability as that of *objective chance* and the second as that of *guarded assertion*.

There is no possibility of using the first notion of probability in representing theory choice. For, as Peirce remarked:[7]

It is nonsense to talk of the probability of a law, as if we could pick universes out of a grab-bag and find in what proportion of them the law held good.

That is, probabilities in the sense of objective chances are related to proportions, and since we have but one universe, the stage is not set for the application of this notion. In any event, I have argued that since truth eludes our grasp at the level of theories we must employ instead the notion of being approximately true. And as the argument below shows, the notion of a theory's being probably approximately true does not obey the axioms of the probability calculus. This is very significant. For in spite of the fact that there is great controversy on the matter of the interpretation of the notion of probability, all parties are agreed that assignments of probabilities must obey the standard axioms.

We cannot assume that the operator 'It is probably true that –' obeys the same laws as the operator 'It is probably approximately true that –'. Indeed, we shall show that a function introduced to represent this new operator does not in fact obey the classical laws of probablity. Let 'P–' be the function representing the probability that '–' is true and let 'Pv–' be the function representing the probability that '–' is approximately true. Let N be a theory consisting of Newton's three laws of motion. Let N_1 be a theory consisting solely of the first law, and let N_2 be a theory consisting solely of the second and third laws. Clearly N_1 and N_2 are independent. The theory N has a much greater degree of approximation to the truth than either N_1 or N_2. If we have measured approximation to the truth on a scale from 0 to 1 and have selected, say, 0.9 as the point at which we wish to say that a theory is approximately true we can well imagine a world in which N reaches that degree of approximation, i.e. $Pv(N) = \frac{3}{4}$. N_1 and N_2 would both fall below that degree. Therefore we want to set the probability of N_1's being approximately true quite low, say, $\frac{1}{4}$. And similarly we set $Pv(N_2) = \frac{1}{4}$. But $Pv(N) = \frac{3}{4}$, say. In classical probability theory if N_1 and N_2 are independent (as they are in this case), $p(N_1 \& N_2) = P(N_1).P(N_2)$. If we assume that this constraint holds for Pv we obtain a contradiction. $N = N_1 \& N_2$. $Pv(N_1 \& N_2) = Pv(N) = \frac{3}{4}$. $Pv(N_1 \& N_2) = Pv(N_1) \& P(N_2) = \frac{1}{4}.\frac{1}{4} = 1/16 \neq \frac{3}{4}$. Thus, in so far as our concern is with approximation to the truth and not with truth, classical probability theory will be of no help in arriving at a rule guiding the choice between theories.

Probability construed as guarded assertion fares no better than probability construed as objective chance in representing theory choice. On this conception of probability, to assert that the probability that p is true is m/n is to assert that p is true and to indicate that one's confidence in the assertion of p is m/n. However, in the face of the pessimistic induction one can never assert with reason that a theory is true. That is, in a choice situation we would have to assign the same degree of confidence in the truth of T_1 and in the truth of T_2: namely, 0. Thus probability as guarded assertion can give us no guidance. In point of fact when we assert a theory we assert it as being to some degree approximately true. However, if we imagine ourselves trying to assign measures of our confidence that a theory has a certain degree of being approximately true on a 0 to 1 scale we face the problem articulated above. The probability calculus is invoked on the guarded assertion view to deal with the degree of confidence that the assertion is true. It is therefore not surprising that it fails to hold when we replace truth by being approximately true.

Other construals of probability besides the two considered above have been offered. Some have regarded the term 'probable' in some of its uses as expressing a logical relation between evidence and hypothesis. To assert that the probability of a hypothesis, h, being true on evidence e is m/n is, on this construal, to assert that the measure of the degree of support or confirmation given to h by e is m/n. To make such a probability judgment is not to assert h at all but merely to say how much h is supported by e. Carnap, for instance, thought that this concept of probability 'should supply an exact quantitative explication of a concept which is basic in the methodology of empirical science, i.e. the concept of the confirmation on an hypothesis with respect to a given body of evidence'.[8] Sometimes, as in the case of Carnap, this notion of probability is taken as an explication of the notion of support. Others define a notion of support in terms of probability. For instance, Swinburne takes it that the support given to a hypothesis h by evidence e with background evidence $P(h,e \& k)/P(h,k)$.[9]

For the purpose of my present argument these differences are irrelevant. For all those who seek to explicate a notion of support or confirmation in terms of probability assume that probability functions obey the classical probability calculus. However, in science we ought to be interested in support for claims that a theory is approximately true or is more approximately true than another theory, and not in support for claims that a theory is true. We have already seen that the probability calculus fails if we shift from a concern with truth to a concern with verisimilitude. This means that no notion of confirmation or support defined via a notion of probability which obeys the probability calculus can be of assistance. In any event this entire enterprise has an air of unreality about it. For suppose we set aside the thesis that the probability of any theory's being true is zero on any evidence (excepting evidence that entails the hypothesis). How are we to assign numerical values to the probability of a theory on the basis of evidence? This is what we must be able to do if we are to be assisted in theory choice by the evaluations of the relative degree of confirmation provided for rival theories by the available evidence. What probability should have been attached in 1905 to the claim that the Special Theory of Relativity is true? How much has that probability been raised by the evidence which has subsequently been obtained? Even to ask these questions in the expectation that quantitative answers will be forthcoming that ought to guide us in theory choice is to be misled into thinking that the numerical estimates of probability appropriate in chance set-ups can be carried over to epistemic contexts, contrary to Peirce's warning.

The fact that 'Pv' fails to satisfy the axioms of the probability calculus means that no definition of confirmation in terms of probability can assist us, given that we are trying to select the theory which on the evidence it is more reasonable to assume has the greater verisimilitude. However, some have argued that the notion of confirmation required is non-probabilistic. For instance, Cohen, having argued this, provides a theory of *support* (Cohen's term for confirmation).[10] It is easily seen that Cohen's theory of support will not do if we construe 'evidence e supports hypothesis h' more than it supports hypothesis h''' as meaning that given e it is more likely that h' is a better approximation to the truth than h''. This follows from the fact that Cohen's axioms for support entail the following theorem:

$$\text{If } s(h',e) \geqslant s(h'',e) \text{ then } s(h' \& h'',e) = s(h'',e).$$

Consider this theorem in the context of our previous example. It is easy to imagine that the available evidence, e, should give us good reason to say that N is approximately true. The same evidence might give us good reason to say that N_2 is a better approximation to the truth than N_1. In this case the putting N_2 for h$'$ and N_1 for h'' renders the antecedent of the theorem true and the consequent false.

It may be that someone will devise a probability function which is appropriate if our concern is not with the probability of truth but the probability of approximate truth. It may be that some non-probabilistic theory of support or confirmation can be devised to deal with support for claims of approximation to the truth. However, we have reasonable grounds for being sceptical of the utility of this approach. For the question will remain as to the grounds on which we would make assignments of degree of probability or support. As we shall see, the factors that are in fact relevant to theory choice in the face of evidence are such as to make the prospects of being able to make such quantitative assignments very unlikely.

There is of course nothing to preclude us using the concept of probability in the context of saying that one theory probably has a greater degree of verisimilitude than another theory; if, that is, we mean no more by this than that we have better reasons for thinking that the one theory has greater verisimilitude than the other theories. But this rather minimal use of the notion of probability will not be of help in theory choice. It is simply a way of recording the results of deliberations on the basis of reason as to which theory we should adopt. After outlining the legitimate role of probability within science in the next section, we shall turn in the following section to consider what constitutes a good reason for thinking that one theory is better than another.

5 STATISTICAL TESTING

To be sceptical of the utility of the mathematical theory of probability in the context of theory choice, is not to denigrate the role of probability within science. Without this theory and the associate theory of the testing of statistical hypotheses, modern science as we know it could not exist. Quantum Mechanics is an essentially probabilistic theory. Medicine and genetics are but two examples of sciences in which statistical hypotheses are all-important.

The primary use made of probability theory within science is in the choice between statistical hypotheses. For instance, suppose we are investigating a type of plant which sometimes possesses a characteristic, C. Let us suppose that we know that whether or not a given plant possess C is a matter of heredity and not environment. Suppose further that C is independent of other genetically transmitted characteristics. On our current theory, if C is a dominant characteristic, the probability that a given plant has C is 3/4. That is, if C is dominant we can expect the number of plants having C will be approximately 75 per cent in a large enough collection. If C is regressive, our theory tells us that the chances of a given plant having *C* will be 25 per cent. We can use probability theory to calculate on the hypothesis of dominance the chances that the proportions of plants in a collection of *n* plants having *C* will lie within some interval *D* of 3/4. Similarly we calculate the chances of finding the proportions of plants having *C* on the hypothesis that *C* is regressive to be within *D* of 1/4 in a collection of *n* plants. If we examine our collection of *n* plants and find that the proportion of those having *C* is 30 per cent, we shall opt for the hypothesis of regression, as that result is not nearly so unlikely on the hypothesis of regression as it would be on the hypothesis of dominance.

The design of tests to be used in choosing between statistical hypotheses is a complex and often controversial matter. It is of essential importance to contemporary science. I have drawn attention to this obvious fact in order to allay any suspicions that my dismissive attitude to the use of formal theories of probability and confirmation in the context of their choice betokens a hostility to all use of probability and statistics in science. In fact I would wish to stress the contrary. One of the most dramatic illustrations of the alteration in the methods of science is the addition to recent scientific procedures of this statistical technique. The point is that these procedures are usable when we are dealing with questions of the proportion of items in a collection that possess some characteristic. They are not usable in the context of theory choice for three reasons. First, as Peirce remarked, we do not have a collection of universes which we can examine to see in which proportion of them a given theory holds. Second, our concern in theory choice is not with truth but with approximate truth; and the probability calculus, designed as it was to deal with proportions (in its application to chance situations) and to deal with measures of degree of confidence (in its guarded guide mode), holds for truth but not for approximate truth. Third, there is no hope of assigning measures of the degree of confidence we should have in rival theories. This will become obvious in Sections 7 and 8 where we consider the factors relevant to theory choice.

6 THE EVOLUTION OF METHOD

It is all too frequently supposed that scientific method was discovered, and once discovered that was that. It was then there to be used, and change in science has resulted from the regular use of this tool which was finely honed at some point in the past. No one supposes it was discovered at an instant of time. Opinions differ as to the period of time during which it was discovered, but there is a tendency to assume that it was discovered and having been discovered it remained as it was. Nothing could be further from the truth. We continually make discoveries in science, and there is every reason to suppose that we make discoveries in the area of methodology as well. We have already cited one uncontroversial example of a change in scientific method. Given that those methods include statistical testing we can easily point to great science done before those tools were available, and to the science that only became possible through their evolution, which is still continuing, as any survey of the literature on statistical testing over the last decade will reveal. This uncontroversial case of a change in method might seem somewhat unexciting since it amounts to an addition to the repertoire. Nothing had to go out to make room for it. A more interesting sense in which the methods evolve will become apparent if we consider the case of Quantum Mechanics.

The vast majority of working scientists and philosophers of science regard Quantum Mechanics as essentially probabilistic. The best that we can hope for if we are studying a Quantum Mechanical system is to be able to make statistical predictions of the outcome of measurements done on the system. Prior to this century the natural response to such a situation would have been to suppose that we had left something out. If we knew more about the world we should discover variables, the determination of the values of which would enable us to make non-probabilistic predictions of the outcome of measurements. In the classical framework statistical laws represented the limits of current knowledge. God and the Laplacian super-scientists had no need of statistical laws. Knowing all that there was to know would be to know enough to make non-statistical predictions. Few cling as did Einstein to this view, hoping to find hidden variables which will turn Quantum Mechanics (hereafter cited as *QM*) into a deterministic theory. But there are powerful arguments against this, and we must take as the best assumption that the world is essentially probabilistic. A complete specification of the properties of, say, an electron together with the laws of *QM* only allows for the calculation of the probability of particular future states occurring.

Given that the goal of science is to achieve an understanding of the physical world through the production of explanations having predictive power, the probabilistic character of *QM* requires a shift in our conception of science. For it would have once been held to be a necessary feature of a good theory that it gave rise to non-statistical explanations. *QM* means that this feature cannot be satisfied. We have had to shift our conception of what constitutes a scientifically acceptable explanation to make way for statistical explanations as more than halfway houses in which the ignorant are forced to take temporary refuge. This does not mean that in areas in which we are at the moment possessed only of statistical laws (i.e. medicine) we should not seek variables hidden from our gaze that would generate deterministic theories. It does mean that an absolute requirement on any theory that it be deterministic has to be relaxed. One imagines that if a scientist in the nineteenth century had drawn up a list of the good-making features of theories that they should be deterministic would have seemed an obvious candidate for inclusion.

7 THE ULTIMATE TEST

One of our starting points in this work was the assumption that the goal of science is truth, an assumption that has had to be qualified in two ways. First, it is not just any old truth that interests us. If it were merely truth we sought we could achieve that by working out more and more logical truths or by simply cataloguing observable properties of the particular everyday objects that surround us. In fact, what we aim at in science is the discovery of explanatory truths. Second, we have had to recognize in the face of the pessimistic induction that this aim needs to be reconstrued in a more modest way. Explanatory power comes from theories; but since there is no hope of having grand theories that are strictly speaking true, we should see ourselves as aiming at theories which have an ever-increasing degree of verisimilitude. For a theory to have explanatory power it must latch on to something about the world. In the long run the ultimate test as to whether one theory has more successfully latched on to a facet of the world than another theory is their relative observational success. Observational success has two aspects. The most important aspect is the generation of novel predictions which are corroborated. It is this that explains our preference for contemporary physical theories over the animistic theories of primitive man. There is an affinity between these two types of theory in that both invoke unobservables in order to explain observed phenomena. However, we feel that if those animistic theories had latched on to something about the world they ought to have generated novel predictions. Latching on in part to the mechanisms in the world responsible for things we have observed ought to generate predictions about aspects of the world we have not examined.

Our notion of observational success should be broadened to include success in accounting for known observations. As we argued (cf. pp. 87–8) the explanation, for example, of the known rate of advance of the perihelion of Mercury must count in favour of the General Theory of Relativity. None the less we do tend to pay more attention to the successful generation of corroborated novel predictions than to the explanation of known facts, because given a finite set of known facts we could with ingenuity devise some theory (it might be very cumbersome and complex) from which we could derive those facts. Our primary guard against such *ad hoc* theories is the requirement that some corroborated novel predictions should be forthcoming.

It is to be remembered that the distinction between the observational and the theoretical is a matter of degree. While it is reasonable in giving a rational reconstruction of the development of the scientific enterprise to represent that process as initially providing theories to explain low-level relatively observational facts, science comes in time to provide deeper theories which explain those theories. In what follows, by a successful theory I shall mean one whose success includes not only observational success but theoretical success. Theoretical success is a matter both of the generation of novel predictions which themselves are theoretical and of the explanation of accepted theories. It remains the case that the success of these higher-level theories depends on their having observational success mediated through the lower-level theories that they generate.

In the long run, then, the ultimate test of the superiority of one theory over another is observational success. There can be no serious question but that relativistic mechanics has been established as observationally more successful than Newtonian mechanics in the run of time since 1905. But in 1905 no one knew and no one could have known how things would turn out. Hence this ultimate test is not one which can be employed by the working scientist faced with the choice between two rival theories. We need other factors to guide us which can serve as fallible indicators of likely long-term observational success. The articulation of such inductive factors is one aspect of the study of scientific methodology. The grounds for including any particular factor will be meta-inductive. If we can locate factors that have guided scientists in making theory choices which turned out to be correct on the ultimate test, we shall have inductive grounds for operating within the constraints of these particular inductive factors.

We must guard against setting our expectations too high. For these factors are inductively correlated with success. Even if in a given context they all point in the same direction, there is no guarantee that that is the right direction. Furthermore, it is likely that they will not all point in the same direction. For that reason each has to be read as containing a *ceteris paribus* clause. That is, these are rules of the form: all things being equal, prefer theory T_2 over T_1 if T_2 but not T_1 possesses feature φ. In the case of divergence there is no way of weighting the relative importance of the differing factors. And, in addition, there is the problem that it will not be clear whether one theory does possess the good-making feature to a better degree than the other.

This does not mean that the list of factors is devoid of content. The choice of theories is a social matter carried on in a dialectical fashion, and these features define the parameters of scientific debate. The proponents of one theory cannot ignore the criticism of their opponents if that criticism is based on appeal to one of these factors. An analogy will be instructive. We may debate endlessly as to whether someone is honest, courageous, just, charitable. But we know that this is what we should be debating if our goal is to decide whether he is a good or virtuous man. We may differ to some extent on the list of features we think are important in determining virtue or goodness of a man. We may differ about the relative importance of the various factors. And we may have more or less stringent requirements for someone to count as, say, courageous. However, we recognize that the debate is to be carried on in terms of these parameters. Someone who thought that these considerations were simply irrelevant would have failed to grasp our conception of a good man. Of course there is a disanalogy, for the factors relevant to the debate about whether a man is good or virtuous are constitutive of what it is to be good or virtuous. The factors relevant to theory choice in science are not constitutive of a good theory. The goodness of theories is constituted by their degree of verisimilitude. The factors are fallible inductive indicators of that. Still, the analogy is instructive in reminding us that a family of vague, hedged principles which may conflict can none the less have force by defining the parameters within which debate occurs.

Obviously these principles are not algorithms admitting of mechanical application and giving certain knowledge of the ultimate degree of success of a theory. In mathematics, once the putative proof is there we can (with the odd exception) definitely decide by the mechanical applications of the methods of mathematics whether it is or is not acceptable. In science we have to decide whether to accept the theory to work on at a stage in which no such definitive test is available. The guiding principles in science can point in different directions, and even if they point all in the same direction it may turn out to be the wrong direction. There is a further instructive contrast with mathematics. In mathematics there is a hard distinction between the context of justification (proof checking) and the context of the creative production of a proof. In science if we are dissatisfied with our current theory we do not simply creatively generate a new one and then apply the guiding principles to see which it is better to opt for. For those principles will guide us in deciding what theory to develop prior to any decision to work on it. Thus, unlike mathematics, there is no sharp contrast between a context of discovery and a context of theory justification. In what follows I enumerate the good-making features of theories, the features that ought to guide us before the final results are in.

8 THE GOOD-MAKING FEATURES OF THEORIES

(i) Observational nesting

A theory ought to preserve the observational successes of its predecessors. Given that the goal of science is the discovery of explanatory theories of ever greater verisimilitude, and given that increasing observational success is our primary indicator of increasing verisimilitude, it will count against a theory if it is unable to replicate the observational successes of the theory currently in the field. To the extent to which a theory fails in this regard we shall expect it to have dramatic observational successes in areas where the current theory is not successful. If a theory not only preserves observational success but improves it by increasing the accuracy of corroborated predictions and/or by increasing the area in which corroborated predictions are made, this obviously counts in its favour.

(ii) Fertility

A theory ought to have scope for future development. It should contain ideas to guide research. This is akin to but more nebulous than Lakatos's notion of a positive heuristic. This may come from a metaphorical component in the theory as in the early days of the ideal gas theory. Gases were thought to be like collections of small hard balls colliding in space. The metaphorical component suggests exploration of the similarities and dissimilarities with the phenomenon to which it has been likened. Fertility may also come from a novel idea as when, for example, Planck introduced the quantum of action in the course of explaining the distribution of radiation given off by a black body. This suggested the possibility of applying the idea of the quanta to other unexplained phenomena. The justification for including this factor comes from a well-supported meta-induction on past science. Theories are evolving historical entities which rarely spring into existence fully fleshed out. Those that have tended to be ultimately successful have as a matter of fact come with association ideas for further development. This factor, like the others to be advanced, are only fallible inductive indicators of ultimate success. A fertile theory may not in the end deliver the goods. Freud's theory of psychoanalysis certainly was fertile. It suggested a host of possible developments and applications. Cynics about psychoanalytic theories may well argue it is to be held against the theory that while apparently fertile it has not borne fruit.

(iii) Track record

In making judgments of a theory's degree of fertility we are being forward looking. The longer the theory is in the field, the more important its past track record becomes. Continuing observational success not only counts in itself for the theory, it is also an indicator of future fertility. The cynic concerned with psychoanalysis referred to above is likely to cite what he regards as the disappointing track record from the point of view of observation success in arguing against the theory.

(iv) Inter-theory support

It counts in favour of a theory that it supports a successful extant theory. This support may take the form of providing an explanation of the laws of one theory by the other. For instance, it counted in favour of statistical mechanics that it was able to explain the predictively successful laws of thermodynamics. It counts against a pair of theories if no matter how successful they are in their own domains they clash in the sense that they cannot be consistently worked together in domains of common application. For example, most scientists would agree that if, as seems to be the case, there is no way of integrating Quantum Mechanics and General Relativity, one or other of those theories cannot be correct as they stand. We have a metaphysical picture of a unified physical world and we consequently expect either to be able to unify diverse theories into a single all-encompassing theory or to have a family of mutually supporting theories. The ground for holding to this picture is simply the success we have had in operating under it.

(v) Smoothness

Nice theories have observation successes. However, as we noted in earlier chapters, any theory will also have its failures. The smoothness with which adjustments can be made in the face of failure is an important factor in theory evaluation. It is reasonable in the early stages of a theory (particularly if the theory lacks competitors) to ignore failures or to invoke auxiliary hypotheses to explain them away. Once there are alternatives, it is important to consider which theory can more smoothly cope with its failures. The smoother the theory the more its failures can be covered by a single auxiliary hypothesis. If a theory is smooth in this sense it means that there is something systematic about its failures. There is hope of discovering what it is that is wrong about the theory with a view to correcting it. In this case it looks as though the theory, while having an erroneous aspect, is in fact on to something. If it is not smooth and requires a diverse range of different unrelated auxiliary hypotheses to explain the failures, this suggests that the theory is not headed in the right direction. Newtonian mechanics is a smooth theory, for there is something systematic about its failures. For example, it fails for high speeds. That is why we regard the theory as being on to something, even though it will not do as it stands.

(vi) Internal consistency

A theory ought to be internally consistent. The grounds for including this factor are *a priori*. For given a realist construal of theories, our concern is with verisimilitude, and if a theory is inconsistent it will contain every sentence of the language, as the following simple argument shows. Let 'q' be an arbitrary sentence of the language and suppose that the theory is inconsistent. This means that we can derive the sentence 'p and not-p'. From this 'p' follows. And from 'p' it follows that 'p or q' (if 'p' is true then 'p or q' will be true no matter whether 'q' is true or not). Equally, it follows from 'p and not-p' that 'not-p'. But 'not-p' together with 'p or q' entails 'q'. Thus once we admit an inconsistency into our theory we have to admit everything. And no theory of verisimilitude would be acceptable that did not give the lowest degree of verisimilitude to a theory which continued each sentence of the theory's language and its negation. This does not mean that if we find an inconsistency in other theories we simply scrap it and return to the drafting board. Our first response ought to be to explore the possibility of modifying the theory perhaps by re-construing some of the terms in it to avoid the inconsistency.

(vii) Compatibility with well-grounded metaphysical beliefs

Theory construction and theory choice are guided by certain very general metaphysical beliefs. For instance, with one or two exceptions no theory that violates the principle of the acausality of time has ever been seriously propounded. This is the principle enunciated explicitly by Maxwell, Frege and others, precluding citing the mere time at which an event occurs as a causal factor in explaining why the event occurs. We reject the proposal that something in the physical world happened because the time was ripe for it to happen. We look to something happening in time to explain the event. I call this a metaphysical principle because it cannot be subject to any empirical test, even of the most indirect kind. One who held a relationist theory of time might seek to offer an *a priori* proof of the principle. However, as I have argued elsewhere, no form of relationism which has this consequence is tenable.[11] Our ground for holding this belief is simply the success we have had in operating under it. We employ it implicitly as a constraint on theory construction and theory choice because we do not want to throw away lightly that which has served us well in the past. Some of the planks of our ship must remain in place most of the time. If, however, things go badly wrong we may even have to replace the keel, but until they do we ought to tamper with the more accessible upper timbers. It is in the context of the discussion of such principles that we find *a priori* considerations deployed.

This principle, and the others enumerated above, are topic-neutral in the sense that they are applicable to all areas of all sciences. However, within the category of well-grounded metaphysical beliefs there should be included some with specific content. For instance, within physics there is a hostility to theories involving action at a distance. One may well query whether the reasons which were operative historically in generating a hostility to action at a distance were good reasons. The fact remains that we have had success in avoiding action at a distance and this provides a ground for continuing to impose this as a constraint unless things go badly wrong. Some may hesitate to include such factors in an account of principles of comparison or methodological principles in view of their specific content. How we describe such factors is not as important as recognizing that they do operate. Our picture of science will be distorted if we do not note this.

(viii) Simplicity

Many scientists and philosophers of science would include simplicity as a good-making feature of a theory. This is, however, problematic for a number of reasons. First, no one has produced a criterion of relative simplicity that successfully measures the simplicity of a theory as opposed to the language within which the theory is expressed. Nor do we even have a satisfactory way of assessing the relative simplicity of different linguistic formulations of the same theory. Relative simplicity to a large extent lies in the eyes of the theoretician and not in the theory. Second, we have been including factors on the ground that they are indicative of long-term observational success. It is not clear that apparent simplicity has been a good sign of long-term success. In so far as we have a grasp of the notion of relative simplicity, Quantum Mechanics looks more complicated than classical mechanics and general relativity looks more complicated than Newtonian gravitational theory. It may be objected that in these cases the other relevant factors pointed in the other direction. A case might be advanced for saying that simplicity does operate on the grounds, for example, that we prefer inverse square laws such as

$$G = g\frac{m_1 m_2}{r^2}$$

to one in which *r* is raised to some power, say, 2.0000000001 where no test will allow us to choose between these two values. Let us grant that it is simpler to take the value 2. However, the fact that it is simpler provides no reason to think that it is more likely to be true that this is the correct value. At best we are entitled to say that the value is approximately 2. For a theory with the value 2.0000000001 will have equal observational success. Consequently no case for simplicity in this sort of context can be developed by reference to past successes. The fact that we can point to examples of successful theories in which such choices were made does not help, for we could have developed equally successful alternative theories in which the computationally more complex choice had been made. This does not mean that we should not continue to opt for simplicity given the choice in contexts in which the notion has hard content. The case for simplicity is pragmatic. It simply is easier to calculate with simpler theories. But there is no reason to see greater relative simplicity of this sort as an indicator of greater verisimilitude.

Any model of the factors relevant to theory choice must include a feedback mechanism. Assumptions about which factors ought to guide us need to be assessed in the light of long-term success as measured by the ultimate test. This is most obviously so in the case of what I called general metaphysical beliefs. If making choices under these constraints continues to give success, this reinforces the grounds for acting on those assumptions. Should progress prove illusive, we would seek (as the case of Quantum Mechanics illustrates) to revise those constraints. And as we noted in our discussion of Feyerabend, it is rational for the scientific community to support some heretics who are attempting to develop theories which are at odds with the normal constraints even when progress is occurring. *SM* in so far as it involves theory choice evolves under the regulation of the feedback mechanism of the ultimate test. This feature of *SM* is entirely missing from the accounts of Popper and Lakatos. Consequently when we move in the final chapter to the characterization of a tempered rationalist model of science, that model will have to be a dynamical one in which the principles of comparison are allowed to alter through time.

McMullin[12] has astutely remarked that the real difference between rival methodologists lies not in the advice they give to the scientist, but in the account they offer of why the methodology works as it does. This is to a large measure correct. Lakatos's stress on the importance of generating novel predictions has affinities with what I called the ultimate test. And my list of factors given above is an extension of Kuhn's five ways (which he regards as being but a partial list of relevant factors). However, I have argued that we are justified in regarding these factors as being by and large epistemic. The fact that there has been progress towards greater verisimilitude gives reason to think that the factors which have been guiding theory choice are fallible indicators of verisimilitude. Thus my view of the status of these factors is at odds with how Kuhn regards his five ways. For, as we noted in Chapter V, Kuhn holds that they merely represent general agreement among the members of the scientific community and no justification can be given for treating them as evidential indicators of verisimilitude. Lakatos certainly regards the greater power of one research programme to generate novel predictions over another as a sign that that programme embodies theories of greater verisimilitude. However (see Chapter IV), his hesitation about admitting inductive arguments precludes him from providing any reason for this claim. Thus what distinguishes my position from that of Kuhn and Lakatos is not so much in the advice given (though there are differences) but in the fact I have argued that these factors work by being corrigible signs of increasing verisimilitude.

9 THE ROLE OF JUDGMENT

There is more to scientific decision making than can be encompassed within the sphere of judgments justified by appeal to rules specifying the good-making features of theories. A practising scientist is continually making judgments for which he can provide no justification beyond saying that that is how things strike him. This should come as no surprise in a post-Wittgensteinian era. Wittgenstein repeatedly drew attention to the fact that we cannot specify usable, logically necessary and sufficient conditions for the application of many commonly employed predicates. Any specification of the conditions under which an object is, say, a table will admit of cases which the rules do not cover, cases where we simply have to make up our minds. In such cases we have to decide the matter, and prior to our making the decision there is nothing to be right or wrong about. It may be that in the long run some decisions turn out to be better than others. To take that favourite example of the whale: suppose that prior to the discovery of whales we thought of mammals as animals that live on the land and suckle their young. Fish live in water and do not suckle their young. We think that we might have decided in the face of the lack of help given by the rules that the whale was a fish. Later we would have found that this decision made life complicated. For our general theories about fish would require more caveats excluding whales than our general theories about mammals would require if the whale were counted as a mammal.

This sort of situation represents but one of the sorts of case in which scientists have to make decisions on the basis of their own sense of things, where the factors that might justify the decision come much later in the evolution of the science. Even in mathematics this is the case, as Lakatos has demonstrated with regard to the concept of a polyhedron.[13] Judgment also enters in at an even more humble level. Many predicates we ascribe to objects are predicates the ascription of which cannot be justified. There is nothing much for me to say if you challenge my assertion that the pillar box is red. I can only say that that is how it looks to me and that there is no reason to assume that normal conditions for the perception of colours do not obtain. The scientist cannot escape this sort of reliance on his own judgment. Thus there is something radically wrong with the prevalent picture of the scientist as one who does get away from a reliance on judgments that he cannot explicitly ground. This erroneous picture arises in part from the fact that the scientist may develop theories by appeal to which he grounds judgments made without explicit grounds in ordinary life. By appeal, for example, to a theory of light he measures the wave lengths emitted from the pillar box and appears to add justified confidence to the judgment that it really is red. But his grounding of the judgment in this way depends on a host of ungrounded judgments about, for example, the readings of his meter. Indeed, one might even wish to turn this picture on its head. For the scientist has a richer repertoire of concepts which he applies on the basis of experience without giving explicit grounds than the man on the Clapham omnibus (at least the man who is not on his way to his laboratory). When he applies the notion 'pair-production' on looking at a plate taken of a cloud chamber, he has no more grounds for the application than simply that that is what it looks like. Just as our success in dealing with the world in everyday life reinforces justifiably our faith in our perceptual judgments, the scientist's success gives him justified grounds for relying on his judgment.

This faculty of judgment, of making decisions without being able to provide an explicit justification at the time, is exercised not only in the lowly way noted above. The good experimenter (sadly ignored by philosophers of science in favour of the great theoretician) makes countless such decisions in the design and execution of his experiments. He acquires a skill the exercise of which is essential to science, and there is no reason to assume that that skill can be exhaustively described in some explicit theory. The fact that it cannot is no reason for denying that a genuine skill is being exercised. Our desire to find some magical algorithm that would create and justify theories has left its legacy in our inclination to suppose that there is a partial algorithm playing the role of an invisible hand in science, if only we could learn to describe its operations. The time has come to model at least some aspects of the scientific enterprise not on the multiplication tables but on the exercise of the skills of, say, the master chef who produces new dishes, or the wine blender who does deliver the goods but who is notoriously unable to give a usable description of how it is that he does select the particular proportions of the wines that add up taste-wise to more than the sum of their parts.

On the account given of theory choice there is an even grander role to be played by judgment in science. For even if we do our best to pay attention to the relevant features, no clear verdict may be forthcoming. Reasonable men may be expected to have reasonable disagreements about what to do in the circumstances. There is no knock-down proof of superiority at the time the choice has to be made. Two scientists may find there is nothing to appeal to in justifying their differing choices. It is a tie, let us suppose, a tie agreed to be a tie; and what remains is a feeling on each side that one choice represents the more plausible, the more reasonable way of proceeding. This is not to say with Feyerabend that at this point we should put the matter out to the populus for a democratic vote. For we have every reason to suppose that becoming a successful scientist involves an improvement in the powers of judgment that are called upon. Scientists do proceed on hunches and guesses. Some have great success. One of the occupational hazards of being a successful scientist is the tendency to have an overly developed sense of the importance of one's intuitive judgments. Planck, as a young man, was disappointed in his career. The powers that be thought that there was nothing in his approach. Bitterly he complained that new theories triumphed only through the death of old theoreticians,[14] a lesson he forgot in practice in arguing against Einstein in his Nobel lecture[15] on the basis of nothing more than his own sense of where the truth lay. Reliance on judgment at this level, like any high-gain strategy, is a high-risk strategy, and happily we are rarely in the situation in which we have nothing to do but to follow our intuitions. But on occasion we have to, and one who ignores this will have a distorted picture of the scientific enterprise.

10 COUNTING THE COSTS

Suppose I want to achieve some goal G, and suppose that there are no certain steps that I can take which will lead to the goal. There are different courses of action that may bring success. If I am being rational in my decision making I shall try to arrive at an assessment of the relative probabilities of each course of actions leading to the goal. One may have a 1 in 4 chance, another a 1 in 2 chance of success. Rationality requires to consider more than this. There may be costs involved which differ with the courses of action. The courses of action may, even if successful, give me a different degree of realization of the goal. Suppose, for example, I want to earn more money and that I have ten working years left. If I stay in my current job, a course of action which costs me nothing, I have a 1 in 4 chance of a promotion which will increase my salary by £1000, making me £10,000 better off if the promotion comes off. If we multiply the chances of the benefit by the probability of getting it we have what is called the *expected utility* of that course of action. In this case it is £2500. Intuitively we can think of this as representing the average gain in a ten-year period if I was to live through an indefinite number of such ten-year periods. Suppose I have the alternative of taking a once-and-for-all chance of a job with another company, which will involve relocation at a cost of £3000. In this new job I have a 1 in 2 chance of a promotion that will give me an extra £1000 per annum with a total gain then of £10,000. The expected utility is £5000. But once I take into account the cost of relocation I am probably better off staying where I am. If on the other hand the chance was 1 in 2 of earning £2000 per annum more, giving an expected utility of £10,000, even taking into account the relocation costs, I should probably be better off moving.

Should decision making in science take into account costs and expected utilities? Might we not face a choice between two theories where the indications are that T_2 is more likely to be approximately true than T_1? Absurd as it is to do so, let us assign a probability of 1/3 to T_1 being approximately true and 2/3 to T_2's being approximately true. In that case, letting the pay off in both be 90 units the expected utility of T_2 is 60 and of T_1 30. But suppose the cost of developing T_2 is going to be 85 units and that of T_1 only 25 units. Surely we should opt for the theory that seems less likely to be the better? In the circumstances I have specified it is obviously right, and this serves to remind us of what is often overlooked in discussions of the rationality of science: namely, costs and expected utilities. However, this is a theoretical reminder and not practical advice. For, unlike my example given above, we should be in no position to quantify costs and utilities and probabilities if we were, say, comparing the programmes of Einstein and Lorentz in 1905.

The situation is not so absurd if we imagine ourselves in a position to decide how a limited budget should be spent on research. Given that we attach much greater utility to, say, a successful theory about the cause of cancer (one allowing for a cure), we may prefer to spend more money on the search for that theory although the probabilities of success are lower than they would be for coming up with a successful theory about the composition of the atmosphere of Uranus. Even without being able to quantify the costs and probabilities and expected utilities, we may be able to come to a reasoned judgment of the balance of expected utilities and we should be guided by that. While a full exploration of this sort of rational decision making falls outside the scope of this present work, it is, in practical terms, a much more important issue once one turns to a wider social context of science than the questions of the rationality of theory choice of a scientist choosing between theories within science.

X

STRONG PROGRAMMES

1 THE RATIONALIST PROGRAMME AND THE EXPLANATION OF SCIENTIFIC CHANGE

The rational model of Popper, Lakatos and Laudan of the scientific enterprise embodies a normative account of the factors that ought to govern theory choice. While these rationalists offer considerably different accounts, they are united by a belief in the importance of articulating how one ought to decide which of a number of rival theories is most likely to be the best relative to a given body of evidence. First, like Whewell, they take it that such an account will assist us in making progress in science. Second, the model is intended not only to provide guidance in our decisions about which theories to adopt, but also to explain (at least for the main part) the particular changes of allegiance that have occurred within the history of science. In giving such an explanation the rationalist appeals to his model, which specifies both the goal of the scientific enterprise and principles of theory comparison. A transition from a theory T_1 to a theory T_2 'is explained' by showing that relative to the evidence at the time T_2 was a better theory than T_1.

Rationalists hold that theory transition in the case of mature sciences like physics is by and large change from the decent to the even better. A rationalist concedes that there may be occasions on which the change was not progressive as judged by his latter-day lights. It is on those occasions and only on those occasions that a sociological or psychological explanation of the change is appropriate. External non-scientific factors are to be brought into play when and only when we have deviations from the norms implicit in the rational model. As was noted in Chapter I, an appropriate analogy is Newtonian mechanics. Only deviations from uniform motion are explained (by appeal to forces). Uniform motion is a natural state not amenable to explanation within the theory. Similarly, rational change is taken to be a natural state for the cognitive sociology of science; only deviations from this are explained by social causation. It is conceded that some aspects of a transition which basically fits the rational model will require reference to external factors. For instance, such factors may play a role in determining the rate at which a new theory gains acceptance. However, internal factors play the main explanatory role in most transitions. To put the point bluntly, sociology is only for deviants.

The scope which Laudan allows to cognitive sociology of knowledge (i.e., sociological investigations of belief as opposed to investigations, say, of scientific societies, or laboratories) includes problems which arise[1]

> whenever, for instance, a scientist *accepts* a research tradition which is less adequate than a rival, whenever a scientist *pursues* a theory which is non-progressive, whenever a scientist gives greater or lesser *weight* to a problem or an anomaly than it cognitively deserves, whenever a scientist chooses between two equally adequate or equally progressive research traditions.

In addition sociological investigations would include[2]

> an exploration of the *social determinants of problem weighting*, since that phenomenon — probably more than the others — seems intuitively to be subject to the pressures of class, nationality, finance and other social influences.

However:[3]

> *When a thinker does what it is rational to do, we need inquire no further into the causes of his action*; whereas, when he does what is in fact irrational — even if he believes it to be rational — we require some further explanation.

Lakatos, who would demarcate a field for the sociologists of scientific knowledge along the above lines, has striven at the same time to minimize the need for them:[4]

> An 'impressive', 'sweeping', 'far-reaching' external explanation is usually the hallmark of . . . a relatively weak internal history (in

terms of which most actual history is either inexplicable or anomalous) is that it leaves too much to be explained by external history. When a better rationality theory is produced, internal history may expand and reclaim ground from external history.

In this chapter we explore the extent to which a rational model can be used for explanatory purposes. Given that a rationalist has vindicated his claim that his model provides a viable account of what makes one theory better than another, he still has the task of displaying that it can be used to explain scientific change. A host of contentious theoretical issues must be settled before it would be fruitful to begin to look at actual scientific practice in relation to particular rational models. My aim is to make progress on the theoretical front, leaving this other task for another occasion. Consequently, the discussion will take place at a level of considerable abstraction, and as such it does not depend on the details of any particular rational model. The central theoretical controversy is between the rationalists and the adherents of the so-called strong programme in the sociology of scientific knowledge, who attack the whole notion of the rational explanation of scientific change. The rationalist programme involves the differential assessment of belief. For the rationalist turns over to the sociologist transitions that he regards as unjustified. The central claim of the proponents of the strong programme is that explanation should be symmetrical. That is, the same type of explanation is to be given of all transitions whether or not we regard them as rational.

On this approach the cognitive sociologist would not restrict himself to dealing merely with the deviations from the norms of rational transitions. The entire field of scientific change would be his legitimate province. At a superficial level this dispute can appear simply as a territorial fight. On the other hand, the philosopher of science *cum* historian of science, versed as he is in the business of representing the content of theories and evaluating the degree of support for rival theories, seems to be trying to capture for himself all the good moments in the history of science. In a rather demeaning way he hands over to the sociologist the few bad episodes when falsehood and/or irrationality flourished. On the other hand, the sociologist, concerned with the social determinants of belief and often largely ignorant of, or uninterested in, the logical evaluation of scientific theories, seems to be trying to capture the entire field for himself. At a less superficial level we can see the sociologist advancing the following *prima facie* reasonable

239

case. What should our judgments now about who was right, who was wrong, who was being reasonable, who unreasonable during some past scientific controversy have to do with the explanation of why things turned out as they did? To make our explanations depend on judgments of this sort is to project our own current beliefs (prejudices) in an illegitimate way. Surely a scientific account of past scientific transitions should not depend on our personal preferences. But, the rationalist counters, in normal everyday explanations of behaviour once we have shown the behaviour to be rational we let the matter rest. We bring in psychologists only in the face of the irrational. Why should it be any different when we come to account for past scientific change?

In this chapter it will be argued that both the strong programme in the sociology of knowledge (a detailed characterization of which is given in Section 4) and the strong programmes in the rationality of science (the programmes of Lakatos and Laudan) are both seriously mistaken. I have selected for discussion the views of extremists as a heuristic device to aid in articulating a number of issues which would arise even if one were to consider more moderate versions of these basic positions. The primary issue concerns the question of the role of our current normative assessment of the activities of past scientists. It will be argued that sociologists have been right in objecting to the role that rationalists accord to such assessment in the explanation of scientific change. However, the sort of explanation that can be used without this normative appraisal is not of the type advocated by the adherents of the strong programme in the sociology of knowledge. That programme, I will argue, is incoherent as it stands. Even if it is modified so as to avoid obvious inconsistency it cannot account for something which needs explaining and that is the phenomenon of scientific progress, which, unlike the explanation of mere change, does require normative assessment of the efforts of previous scientists.

2 HOW TO EXPLAIN THINGS THE RATIONAL WAY

This debate, while overlaid with a tangle of confusions, raises important and difficult questions about explanation, rationality and the connection between them. In trying to come to an understanding of what would be involved in giving a rational explanation of scientific change it will be instructive to begin by reminding ourselves of some of the features of the rational explanation of actions. To this end, imagine the following hypothetical situation. An interested, diligent and successful philosophy student abandons the study of philosophy in favour of Chinese. Worried perhaps that the philosophy department is failing, we ask why. It turns out that the student's long-term goal in life is to have an academic career and that having such a career is more important to him than having the chance to study as an undergraduate the subject he most enjoys. It turns out that he has come to believe that in the current job market there will be no employment for him in teaching philosophy. He believes, however, that there is a reasonable chance in Chinese studies. These factors, together with his belief in his own ability to reach the required standard in Chinese, explain the action. For in the story as told they display the action of taking up the study of Chinese in place of philosophy as the means most likely to realize his goal, given his beliefs. To generalize, to explain an action as an action is to show that it is rational. This involves showing that on the basis of the goals and beliefs of the person concerned the action was the means he believed to be most likely to achieve his goal.

In this sense of rationality, which is sometimes called *instrumental rationality*, the success of an explanation does not depend on the reasonableness of the goal. Neither does it depend on the truth or falsity of the beliefs in question, nor on their reasonableness or unreasonableness. Our explanation of the student's change to Chinese studies would not be undermined if it were shown that the goal of having an academic career is unreasonable. It does not matter for the explanation whether the belief that he has a chance of a job in Chinese studies but not in philosophy is true or false. Nor does it matter whether on the basis of the evidence available to him it was reasonable to hold such a belief. The explanation works by displaying the action as being what he believed to be the best means to the goal (or the means most likely to realize the goal). Any such explanation of an action which does not include a normative assessment of the goal or an evaluation of the truth or falsity, reasonableness or unreasonableness of the beliefs will be called a *minimal rational account* or, for short, a *minirat account.*

The vast majority of our actions can be subsumed under a minirat account. It may be very difficult to discover what the goals and beliefs are, and in some cases they may strike us as bizarre. But we expect that there are goals and beliefs which will generate a minirat account of virtually all actions. For if an action is not rational in this instrumental sense the agent has not done what he himself believes is the best thing to do in the circumstances. It is because we find it so hard to understand why someone would act against his own best judgment that we assume that actions by and large can be given a minirat account. No doubt there are actions that cannot be so explained. It is arguable that if we are to find explanations for such irrational actions we have to turn to psychoanalytic theories.

The typical form of such explanatory accounts of action is the following: A did X because . . . In completing the account in a given case we do not give both a full specification of the goals and a complete list of the relevant beliefs. We single out on the basis of the context of the action and the context of the explanation what seems most informative. For instance, I might say that Icabod left the conversation to go to the kitchen because he was thirsty. I do not bother to say that he believes that he will find there water to drink. I take it that this is common knowledge, and that my audience is perhaps interested to learn whether he just wanted to avoid the conversation. This is a general feature of the pragmatics of explanation and can be illustrated in the case of a causal explanation, when, for example, the insurance inspector says that the fire was caused by a short circuit without making explicit mention of the presence of oxygen and combustible material. It should also be noted that what we choose to explain will be determined by features of the context. We are more likely to be interested in explaining the unexpected than the expected, although, irrational action excepted, all action is capable of a rational explanation.

The multifarious term 'rational' applies not only to actions but also to beliefs. In a minirat account of an action the success of the explanation does not depend on the truth or falsity, reasonableness or unreasonableness of the beliefs involved. But it is very much in our interest to act on true beliefs. If I generally act on false beliefs the chances of realizing my goals will be adversely affected (though it is easy to imagine particular cases where it could be in my interest to act on a false belief). To achieve the goal of having true beliefs it is in my interest to take reasonable steps to acquire evidence and to assess that evidence shrewdly. In condemning a belief as not rational we are claiming that the believer did not take reasonable steps to acquire the relevant evidence and/or that he did not assess the evidence satisfactorily. In addition to applying the term 'rational' to beliefs we also apply it to goals. To assess a goal as to rationality is to assess the balance of reasons for and against someone's adopting the goal. Most often this takes the form of relating one goal to another. It may be said, for example, that it is not rational for me to pursue the goal of satisfying my craving for butter on the grounds that the satisfaction of this goal will interfere with my more important long-term goal of maintaining good health. Whether one can assess a goal except in relation to other goals is a matter of major controversy within moral philosophy; while this is important it is not of particular relevance to our present concerns. In the next section of this chapter we shall consider the explanation of action, deferring a consideration of the explanation of belief until Section 5.

3 MINIRAT ACCOUNTS OF SCIENTIFIC CHANGE

To give a minirat account of an individual scientist's action in abandoning one research programme for another would be to show that that action was most likely to be the best means to his goal, given his beliefs, without evaluating the reasonableness of either his goal or his beliefs. His goal might be to work on what he thinks is the best scientific theory or it might be to improve his career prospects. His beliefs may or may not be scientifically respectable. Rationalists are obviously not making the minimal claim that most scientist's actions can be given minirat accounts. Their claim is that a certain normative model of the scientific enterprise can be used to explain by and large most individual actions of the majority of individual scientists and most collective actions by the scientific community. One of my central contentions is that rationalists have a confused conception of what they are trying to do. Consequently, I consider first what it would mean to claim that a given rational model could be used to explain a particular scientific change, in full awareness that this is not what the rationalists see themselves as doing. That having been done, I shall consider how they see the situation.

A rational model specifies a goal for the scientific enterprise and a family of principles to be used in deciding between rival theories or research programmes. To use such a model to explain the action of a given scientist would be to show that he had the goal in question and that he believed in the principles, and that the action in question was the best thing for him to do given his goal and these beliefs. Of course, the complete account of his action would require reference to a host of other beliefs. But there is nothing wrong in talking about the model as providing an explanation if we mean to draw attention to what we take to be the most important general beliefs determining his action. To establish that such a model could be used to explain the collective action of the scientific community in, say, abandoning the aether drift theory for the Special Theory of Relativity would require showing the following. First, the majority of the members of the community had the goal specified in the model. Second, they were united by and large in their belief in the principles of comparison specified in the model. Third, given this goal and these general methodological beliefs together with other beliefs (i.e., concerning the outcome of experiments) this action was the most appropriate and was perceived by them as such.

A rational model will encapsulate our current beliefs about the goal of science and the factors that ought to govern theory choice. If we are able to show that a past transition is the right one relative to this model we shall not have explained that transition unless the scientists involved shared these beliefs. To assume that to display a fit between the actual decision and the guidance our model gives us to explain the transition would be to treat rationality (as determined by our model) as a sort of invisible hand determining outcomes even though unnoticed by those concerned. It is for this reason that I built into the characterization of the use of a rational model in the explanation of scientific change in Chapter I the three factors cited above. However, Lakatos assumes that it is enough to show that an episode fits his model without regard to whether it was the model of those concerned. But to show that past scientists made what we regard as the right choice in no way explains why they made the choice. For that we need to know what their goals and beliefs were.

It will be an empirical question whether any given model can be used to explain some or all episodes in the history of science. In using a model in this way to generate minirat accounts one need not regard them as capable of objective justification. Thus the use of models for the explanation of change is not the exclusive prerogative of the rationalist. Kuhn, for example, has a model of science which makes the goal problem solving and in which the principles of comparison are the five ways. What makes Kuhn a non-rationalist is his thesis that these cannot be given an objective justification. This in no way precludes his using his model in generating minirat accounts, a good example of which is found in his recent study of Planck. In this work, in which, interestingly, Kuhn does not make any use of his own theoretical framework of gestalt shifts between incommensurable paradigms, he explains why Planck opted for his distribution law for the radiation given off by a black body through a reconstruction of Planck's beliefs and reasoning processes. One example of a general methodological belief one would cite as explaining the scientific community's acceptance of Planck's theory is the belief.in the importance of theoretical unification. This, in part, motivated the community to prefer to use Planck's single formula which covers all temperatures instead of using Wien's formula for low temperatures and the Rayleigh-Jeans law for high temperatures. Whether we endorse that principle or not is irrelevant to the success of the explanation. What matters is that the community whose activities we are seeking to explain held that it was an important *desideratum*. This means that a rational representation of science should consist not of a single model but of an evolving series of models. Scientific change at any time would be explained in so far as it can be rationally explained by reference to the model which articulates the beliefs of the scientists of the time concerning what makes a good theory a good one. We can expect this sequence of models to be itself progressive, representing an improvement in our ways of learning about the world.

Lakatos and Laudan wish to keep the sociologist at bay by defining a particular province within which he is to operate, a province they see as small and unappetizing. Obviously there is one possible type of case that has to be handed over to someone. This is the case of irrational behaviour, where an individual scientist has performed an action which is one he himself thinks is not the optimal one given his goals and beliefs, whatever these may be. This is presumably a case for treatment by psychoanalysis. It is no doubt a rare phenomenon and not one that arises simply because the action fails to fit our model of science. It is a case in which the action was not optimal given his conscious goals and beliefs. In any event, this is not the sort of case Lakatos and Laudan are concerned to hand to a sociologist. In what follows I shall assume that sociology is not concerned with the production of minirat accounts of action. I am not interested in defending this assumption. Indeed, given the pre-paradigmatic state of sociological theorizing it is hard to see how one would even set about investigating it. I state this merely as my understanding of how Lakatos and Laudan see sociology. They see it as concerned with social causation, so that any cognitive sociology of knowledge would give causal explanations of actions and changes in beliefs by reference to social structures. I further assume that we have articulated a sequence of evolving models which by and large allows us to explain the evolution of science. The question is: are there any special classes of failures that really ought to be turned over to sociology?

Consider the situation cited by Laudan (see above p. 238) in which a scientist pursues a research programme which is non-progressive. If 'non-progressive' means 'non-progressive as judged by our current conception of what makes one research programme better than another', we do not necessarily have a case for sociological treatment. We obviously have to allow that there can be reasonable disagreements about the proper goals and methods of science. In addition, as we noted, the goals and/or methods alter through time. Thus it may be that relative to the transgressor's conception of the proper goals and methods of science, the programme he worked on was in fact progressive. In this case his goals and/or methods are recognizably scientific even if we think they are in some respects mistaken. And so we can give a minirat explanation of his actions *qua* scientist. That is, while the episode does not fit our current model it will be given a minirat account in terms of internal factors, factors relating to a conception of the goal of science which is sufficiently close to ours as to be legitimately seen as a conception of a goal for science, and factors relating to the relative merits of rival programmes which are sufficiently like the factors we take to be relevant for theory choice to be seen as scientific reasons for theory choice.

A more interesting case of failure to fit with the model is one in which the goal of the transgressor is one that is not scientific on either his conception of science or on our conception of science. We can well imagine a scientist in an earlier era who seeks high office in the church being influenced by that goal to opt to work on the theory most pleasing to the church authorities (or a contemporary young scientist who seeks tenure selecting the programme advocated by the head of his department even though in his heart of hearts he believes it to be the scientifically inferior programme). In this case we can give a minirat account of his actions, but it will not be one that operates in terms of internal scientific factors. We do not explain his behaviour *qua* scientist, we explain it by reference to his non-scientific goals and related beliefs. This sort of failure raises interesting questions of a sociological/psychological sort concerning what it is about the social institutions and the particular individual that has produced in him this particular goal. But this type of failure of fit does not define a particular province for the sociologist/psychologist. For precisely the same question arises with regard to the actions of scientists that fit the model. What is it about our situation that leads to the development of an institution of science with the goals it has? What is it that leads some individuals to make these goals their goals? Sociological/psychological explanations can be given in supplementation of a minirat account both when the individual's goal is to work on the best theory and when it is some other goal.

There remains the possibility that the failure of fit arises because the individual whose activities are being studied holds beliefs about what makes one theory better than another which strike us as totally unreasonable. That is, the principles of comparison which he appears to be employing are so different from those specified in our model that we cannot regard this as a simple difference of opinion. Does the fact that we would judge the general beliefs to be unreasonable (scientifically speaking) mean that this is a case for sociological treatment? While we can give a minirat account of his actions under these beliefs, the question arises as to whether such accounts need sociological supplementation when and only when the beliefs in question are held by us to be unreasonable. This will be discussed after we have developed in the next two sections an account of what is involved in the explanation of belief.

4 THE STRONG PROGRAMME

I have accused some rationalists, in particular Lakatos, of being under a serious misconception of what it is to explain a transition in science. What matters is not whether a given transition fits his normative model of current science, but what the beliefs and goals were of those involved. There is, however, something, namely progress as opposed to mere change, which requires more than a minirat account, and which I will consider in Section 6 after having discussed the strong programme in the sociology of knowledge. The crucial tenet of the strong programme (hereafter cited as *SP*) is that in explaining why someone or some group held a particular belief or in explaining why a belief transition took place, it is not relevant to consider whether the beliefs in question are true or false; have high or low truth-content; are reasonable or not. Bloor articulates the programme as involving the following four tenets:[5]

1 *Causality*: It would be causal, that is, concerned with the conditions which bring about belief or states of knowledge. Naturally there will be other types of causes apart from social ones which will co-operate in bringing about belief.

2 *Impartiality*: It would be impartial with respect to truth and falsity, rationality or irrationality, success or failure. Both sides of these dichotomies will require explanation.

3 *Symmetry*: It would be symmetrical in its style of explanation. The same types of cause would explain, say, true and false beliefs.

4 *Reflexivity*: It would be reflexive. In principle its patterns of explanation would have to be applicable to sociology itself. Like the requirement of symmetry this is a response to the need to seek for general explanations. It is an obvious requirement of principle because otherwise sociology would be a standing refutation of its own theories.

The background assumption against which Bloor and Barnes develop their *SP* is what they call the naturalist assumption that belief is just one natural phenomenon among others which is to be given a causal explanation.[6] It is clear from their case studies that they are seeking covering law explanations which link belief and belief transition to social factors. We are simply to take beliefs and belief transitions as they come without inquiring as sociologists into their truth or falsity, reasonableness or unreasonableness, and get on with explaining why they are held or changed. In the abstract this seems a most attractive project. For we are to set aside the tricky business of differential assessment and focus on developing interesting generalizations which account for the changing of beliefs. Bloor and Barnes subscribe to this general thesis of symmetry together with a particular thesis about the type of explanation (covering laws linking the cognitive and social worlds) which is to be deployed. The general thesis which could be held in conjunction with different views of the type of explanation to be used will be discussed first without particular reference to the latter, which will be considered in Section 7.

One defence of the symmetry thesis which is to be found in the writings of Bloor and Barnes involves an attack on the very notions of true and false, reasonable and unreasonable. If these distinctions were somehow bogus one could not even articulate the non-symmetry thesis. This line of defence involves maintaining that there is something wrong with our picture of our beliefs as being true or false as the case may be, in virtue of something independent of ourselves and with the picture of the rational assessment of belief on which it is supposed that there are contexts in which things can be cited as reasons for holding the beliefs in question which are reasons for anyone, regardless of his own inclinations, social position, ideology and so on, for holding the belief to be true or more likely to have more truth-content than its negation.

It is somewhat paradoxical to advance arguments in support of a programme according to which there is no real distinction between propaganda and rational argument. The Edinburgh school, like other academics, are prepared to spend hours arguing their case. But if the very concepts of truth and rationality are to be jettisoned, there is no reason for them not to attempt simply to bribe us into agreement. In point of fact they have responded to this objection by biting the bullet and maintaining that it is simply a brute sociological fact that the best way to persuade academics to accept your position is to manipulate the rhetoric of argumentation. Barnes regards the differential assessment of belief as akin to an addiction to a bad habit. After noting the relativistic consequences of the *SP* he writes:[7]

> What matters is that we recognize the *sociological* equivalence of different knowledge claims. We will doubtless continue to evaluate beliefs differentially ourselves, but such evaluations must be recognized as having no relevance to the task of sociological explanation; as a methodological principle we must not allow the evaluation of beliefs to determine what form of sociological account we put forward to explain them.

But if the differential assessment of beliefs is illegitimate or a sort of weakness of the will, the sociology of knowledge deprives itself of a subject matter. It is supposed to be about beliefs. If it is to have a subject matter it must be possible to identify the beliefs of an individual or community. As we argued in Section 4 of Chapter 2, we cannot determine what someone's beliefs are independently of assessing to some extent the truth or falsity of the beliefs. If we adopt some self-denying ordinance not to indulge in differential assessment we shall have no route into the belief systems of others. It is not simply that we shall, through custom and habit, continue to assess beliefs differentially. Unless such assessment is allowed as legitimate in the determination of beliefs, the sociology of knowledge, which purports to be a scientific activity, has no subject matter. The practitioners of this programme not surprisingly do not live up to their own methodological assumption. For they take it that there are the beliefs of an individual and that these can be determined. Anything goes in the strong programme except with regard to the ascription of beliefs. But if such ascriptions, which are after all low-level bits of theory, are true/false, rational/non-rational, should other theories or bits of theories be different?

This strong line is definitely to be found in the writings of the Edinburgh school. Barnes claims that the realist account of scientific theories is untenable and cites Kuhn in support. He concludes that 'our present theories should stand symmetrically with earlier scientific theories'.[8] The consequential relativism is something, he claims, that one has to live with. However, the legitimacy of the scientific enterprise is dependent on the legitimacy of the concepts of truth and rationality. If there is to be a scientific sociology of knowledge its practitioners will have to learn to live with this fact. Unless these concepts are legitimate and unless the sociologist of knowledge invokes them in relation to his own theory (i.e., in the claiming that it can be shown to have more truth-content than its rivals) there is no reason to take him seriously. To claim as he does that his theory is more scientifically respectable just is to invoke implicitly these notions in an effort to represent his theory in a favourable light.

If we are to have a scientific sociology of scientific knowledge we are committed to using the categories true/false and reasonable/unreasonable. The notion of truth required is one which makes our hypotheses true or false in virtue of how things are in the world (including the social world). The notion of reasonableness required is an objective one. Whether in a given context with given evidence it is more reasonable to believe a hypothesis than either to disbelieve it or to suspend belief is not something that is up to us. In response to criticisms of the sort I have offered, Bloor has weakened his symmetry thesis to what he calls a *thesis of methodological symmetry* which is the requirement that:[9]

> The investigator should not assess the beliefs he studies so as to use that assessment in deciding what kind of explanation to offer, e.g., offering a causal account of beliefs he rejects and treating beliefs he accepts as self-explanatory, self-evident, or generally unproblematic. The requirement is not that the investigator should refrain from evaluating the beliefs he studies. Nor does it deny that he will use theories which imply an evaluation of the beliefs studied. The requirement is that the same set of explanatory resources; the same theory; the same factors; should be used to explain both the beliefs you agree with and those you don't. So, of course, endorsing is asymmetrical. The question is: should the mode of explanation *vary* with these endorsements? I say no.

The thesis of methodological symmetry does not presuppose that the categories of truth/falsity, reasonable/unreasonable are bogus. The claim is rather that it is methodologically undesirable to make use of the differential assessment of belief in developing a naturalistic account of belief transition. Bloor does not offer any arguments in favour of this position over and above the arguments for the stronger thesis which we have rejected. But this is perhaps not unreasonable. For *qua* a methodological programme it is to be evaluated in terms of its fruits. But these are few and far between (as we will note later) and, furthermore, the general thesis as applied to the explanation of belief will be shown to be false.

Any explanation of scientific change must involve the explanation both of actions and of beliefs. It will be seen that while these are intimately inter-related there are significant differences in their form. It is unfortunate that neither Bloor, Barnes nor Lakatos respects this distinction in his treatment of the scientific enterprise. Before developing in the next section an account of the explanation of belief, it will be fruitful to review the discussion of the explanation of action through a consideration of Bloor's impartiality and symmetry conditions. Clearly Bloor is correct in insisting that any action, whether rational or not, requires an explanation. An action is displayed as rational by providing a correct minirat account of it which explains it. If no such account can be provided we shall have to seek a different sort of explanation which is likely to involve a psychoanalytic approach. Thus the symmetry thesis fails. It must, however, be noted that very few actions by scientists will fail to be rational in the instrumental sense. It may well be that in more cases than some champions of science would admit the scientist while acting rationally is not acting rationally *qua* scientist. That is, his goals and/or beliefs may not be scientifically respectable. I will refer to such actions as rational actions that are not scientifically rational. Lakatos and Laudan regard such actions as cases for external treatment. If this means 'explain the actions by reference to psychological or sociological factors', Lakatos and Laudan have erred, for we have seen that such actions can be explained by minirat accounts. Of course we shall be interested in looking at the psychological and sociological factors that lead a scientist to have adopted on some occasion a non-scientific goal. But equally we can and should investigate the factors of this type that lead individuals to have scientifically respectable goals. This means that we can grant Bloor and Barnes one of their primary points. We should investigate the role of socio-economic factors in determining the interests people have. We should do this in the case of all actions by scientists be they scientifically rational or not. Thus while symmetry fails, strictly speaking, Bloor and Barnes are correct to seek in all cases further, deeper explanations of action by looking at the factors which determine goals. It is likely that such explanations will be causal and will depend on biological and socio-economic factors.

5 THE EXPLANATION OF BELIEF

According to Bloor and Barnes the truth or falsity and the reasonableness or unreasonableness of a belief are not relevant to the question of the type of explanation to be given of why the belief is held. However, if we consider the following mundane example the symmetry thesis applied to belief will be seen to be implausible. Isabel, whose perceptual faculties are operating normally, is sitting on a chair and believes that she is. Icabod is sitting on the floor but believes he is sitting on a chair. He talks about the chair, attempts to swing his legs as if he were sitting on a chair. For the sake of the example we assume that he is not lying but sincerely believes he is sitting on a chair. The fact that Isabel's belief is true whereas Icabod's is false makes a great difference to the answer we give to the question as to why they have the belief in question. In Isabel's case the explanation is simply that she is sitting on a chair and that her perceptual faculties are operating normally. The chair is causing the appropriate visual and tactile experiences which lead her to hold the belief. In Icabod's case the matter is not straightforward. It may be that he has been taking a hallucinogen or that he has a history of psychiatric disorders with attendant perceptual problems. Given that we adopt, as we should, a causal theory of perception, the difference between these explanations is not that in one case it is causal and in the other not. Thus we can agree with Bloor and Barnes that the explanation of perceptual belief should be causal whether the belief is true or false.

The difference between these cases amounts to the following. In the case of Isabel, the state of affairs that gives her belief its truth-value (the presence of the chair making it true) is to be cited in the explanation of why she holds that belief. The state that makes the belief true is a cause of her holding the belief. In Icabod's case the state of affairs that gives the belief its truth-value (the absence of a chair making it false) is not to be cited in explanation of why he holds the belief. The state of affairs that makes the belief false is not a cause of his having the belief. It is clear then that in the case of beliefs which purport to be beliefs of a simple kind about objects given in perception, we cannot begin to decide what kind of explanation is appropriate until we know whether or not the belief is true. Thus symmetry fails as a general thesis. The explanation in both cases is causal. In the case of a veridical perceptual belief the causal chain involved runs through the state of affairs that gives the belief its truth-value. With non-veridical perceptual beliefs the causal chain may have nothing to do with the state of affairs that gives the belief its truth-value.

It may be that Bloor and Barnes would be willing to concede that symmetry fails for such low-level cases of perceptual belief; that is, for cases in which, if the belief is true, that it is believed is to be explained by reference to the causal mechanisms of normal perception. Cases in which it is false are to be explained by some causal interference with normal perceptual mechanisms. That they might concede this is suggested by their willingness to rest part of the explanation of someone's holding the beliefs they do hold on the state of their physical environment. If we turn from simple beliefs about objects given in perception to, say, general and theoretical beliefs it might seem that a symmetry thesis could be defended. For the distinction I have drawn will not be applicable. In the case of such a general belief, even if it is true there is no object whose state makes the belief true and to which I am in a perceptual causal relation. Furthermore, it may well be that I cannot determine whether the belief in question is true or false, and so if I am to explain why it is held, my explanation cannot turn on whether it is true or false.

In many cases, if I am asked to explain why I hold some general belief that p, I answer by giving my justification for the claim that p is true. I may explain, for example, why I believe Pythagoras's theorem by producing a sound proof and showing that I understand it. I might explain why I believe a certain scientific hypothesis by citing experiences I have had and relevant general beliefs. What I offer may amount to a justification of the claim that p. However, it may not. An account which fails to justify the belief does not necessarily fail to explain it. For instance, one can imagine someone in a pre-Copernican era justifying his belief that there are seven planets by appeal to the belief that there are seven virtues. Even if I could be persuaded that there are exactly seven virtues I would not take this as justifyiing the hypothesis that there are exactly seven planets. Indeed, I may not at first glance be able to understand how he could see the one belief as a reason for the other. However, it may turn out that in the context of his overall belief system and his experiences this does provide a reason. For instance, it may stem from a general belief in the existence of a God who created a world of harmony in which man and the cosmos mirror one another. It does not matter whether I think the belief in p to be reasonable; nor does it matter whether I regard what he regards as a reason for believing p as really being a reason for believing p. What matters is whether in the context of his experiences and his web of beliefs the justification he offers provides him with a better reason to believe p than to disbelieve p or to suspend judgment concerning p.

My thesis is that in many cases one explains why someone, A, believes something, that p, by discovering what A's reasons were for believing p and showing that in the context those reasons justified a belief in p rather than disbelief or the suspension of judgment. Neither an evaluation of the reasonableness of my here and now believing in p, nor an evaluation of whether here and now what was taken by A as justifying the belief in p would give me a reason to believe in p, is relevant to the explanation. Such explanations of belief will be called *minirat accounts*. It is to be noted that the minirat approach involves not a subjective notion of reason but a contextual one. It is contextualist because whether something is a reason for something else depends on the overall web of belief. That there are seven virtues in some contexts gives a reason for believing in seven planets, and not in others. It is not subjectivist, for once the context is fully specified we face the question: did was what was cited as a reason really support the belief?

When what someone would offer as his reason for believing p does indeed provide reason for believing that p, I will say that he is following the *dictates of reason*. If someone is following the dictates of reason, then showing that this is so, that is, giving a minirat account, explains his belief. If he is not following the dictates of reason we shall, *ex hypothesi*, have to give a different type of explanation for his believing what he does. Failures to follow the dictates of reason can be divided into those that are rationalizations and those that are not. The latter would include cases of carelessness, lack of intelligence, lack of interest, and cases in which the person in question is acting on a hunch and cannot provide any further reason.

More interesting cases of failure to follow the dictates of reason arise in the case of rationalization. It may be that what is offered as a justification for the belief is nothing more than a rationalization. Consider, for example, a slave owner who in the course of justifying slavery appeals to his belief that blacks are less intelligent than whites. Let us suppose that the evidence he adduces to support this belief is much weaker than the evidence he himself would require before agreeing, say, that one breed of horse was less intelligent than another. Let us suppose further that there is a tension between this belief and his religious beliefs about God creating all men equal in potential. The story could easily be elaborated more fully to the point where we want to say that the reasons he gives for his belief do not explain why he believes it. It would not be outlandish to suppose that the real explanation is that this belief serves his interest as the owner of cheap labour and that that is in part why he believes it. He is not following the dictates of reason, and we explain his reasons for believing in terms of factors that he would no doubt reject.

This means that symmetry fails at the level of general beliefs. If A, in believing that p, is following the dictates of reason, then to explain why A believes that p is simply to display that in the context of his experience and web of belief, p is the reasonable thing for him to believe. If he is not following the dictates of reason we seek a different sort of explanation, different in that what we give as an explanation of his reason for believing is not what he would say in justification of the belief but, say, an account of how holding that belief served his interests.

Sociologists in general, and not only the proponents of the strong programme, have been puzzled by philosophers who claim that to show that the dictates of reason have been followed is somehow self-explanatory, and that we should only have recourse to, say, interests in the case of deviations from the norms of reason. In this puzzlement they are correct. For some explanation is required of the fact that we tend to rest content once it has been shown that A in believing that p has followed the dictates of reason. The reason why an explanation of this has been overlooked is that it is too obvious. It is simply that we have an interest in following the dictates of reason. To have a belief system at all we have to be doing this at least to some extent. If we fail to adjust our web of belief on the basis of experience, using the dictates of reason, we should not survive for long. This takes us back to our discussion of the explanation of action. The best means of realizing our goal of survival involves following to some extent the dictates of reason. It is because we have this general standing interest that we require no further explanation of why someone believes something when he is doing this as a result of following these dictates.

This interest in following the dictates of reason is a general and standing interest, and in many cases other particular interests conflict with it. The asymmetrical treatment of belief arises from the fact that in cases where someone is not following this general interest we want an account of the particular other interests that are leading him to adopt beliefs contrary to the dictates of reason. Thus, while we have to reject the symmetry thesis of Bloor and Barnes, we ought to be sympathetic to two features of their position that led them to this thesis. First, in explaining why someone believes something general and theoretical, the question as to whether we endorse the belief or not is irrelevant, as Bloor rightly remarks. Bloor fails to see that setting this aside as irrelevant does not mean setting aside the question as to whether the person in question was following the dictates of reason, given his experiences and general web of belief. Second, we can share their interest in investigating the effects of interest on judgment. But a general interest in following the dictates of reason is enough to explain why it is that people do this. Showing that they do so is not somehow self-explanatory. It is explained by a general standing interest. Because there is this general interest, we want to know what particular other interest has intervened when someone is not following the interest in being rational.

Our central question concerns the use of rational models in the explanation of belief and belief transition in science. We have seen that we explain nothing by showing merely that a particular belief held by a past scientist is a belief which we would hold to be reasonable, given our current normative model of the methodology of science. We have to assess the reasonableness of the belief relative to the particular scientist's conception of methodology. This means that we should bring to bear on the history of science an evolving sequence of models displaying the changing conceptions of scientific methodology. We have given a scientifically rational explanation of a belief if we have shown both that the believer in coming to have that belief was following the dictates of reason, and that his reasoning was scientifically respectable relative to the state of scientific methodology at the time.

A belief which fails to be scientifically rational may none the less be rational in the sense that the believer has been following the dictates of reason. Displaying that this is so explains why the belief was held. We do not (*pace* Lakatos and Laudan) have something requiring sociological or psychological treatment just because it is not scientifically rational. Such treatment is most likely to be called for in the case in which the believer in question has been operating contrary to the dictates of reason. As we noted before, this is not because following the dictates of reason is self-explanatory. It is simply that we recognize a standing interest in following the dictates of reason, which explains why we do it; and we want to know what other interest has competed successfully with this interest when someone has acted contrary to the dictates of reason.

With regard to belief as with regard to action, Bloor's impartiality constraint holds. True and reasonable belief requires explanation just as false and unreasonable belief does. However, symmetry fails. For example, in the case of low-level perceptual beliefs, the truth or falsity of the belief makes a difference to the explanation. And in the case of general, theoretical belief, a belief that is reasonable in the context is explained by displaying the reasoning process of the believer whereas a belief which is unreasonable, which runs contrary to the dictates of reason, *may* be explained in terms of interests which run contrary to the general interest in reason. While symmetry fails, it does not fail in the manner the rationalist supposes. It is not the case that a belief is to be explained in psychological or sociological terms just because it is not scientifically rational. Furthermore, a minirat approach to belief goes a long way towards avoiding the sort of differential assessment of belief so decried by Bloor and Barnes. For our concern is not with our own judgments of the reasonableness of the belief but with our judgments of the reasonableness in the context of the belief. In addition it gives room for interesting sociology of knowledge. For interests play a role in the formulation of all beliefs. In the case in which someone is acting contrary to the dictates of reason we want an account of the interests that have been in competition, and this will no doubt bring in the sort of socio-economic factor that interests Bloor and Barnes. Of course in the case of belief which arises from following the dictates of reason the role of interest seems too obvious to mention. For the brute fact is the simple one that we have an interest in survival which brings with it an interest in following the dictates of reason.

6 THE FUNCTION OF THE MAXIRAT ACCOUNTS

To summarize the position thus far: I have been distinguishing between the explanation of action and the explanation of belief. I have argued that actions can be explained by developing minirat accounts. Such accounts of action meet a condition of impartiality and symmetry in the sense that our judgment about the desirability of the goal or the reasonableness of the belief is irrelevant to the acceptability of the explanation. I have argued that one form of explanation, a minirat account, of why someone holds the belief he does works by displaying that in the context the belief was reasonable in the sense that he had better reasons for believing it than believing in its negation or for suspending belief. If the belief is incompatible with the dictates of reason in the context, we should look for a further explanation, which may be given in terms of the distorting effect on his judgment of special interests. This means that in a sense symmetry is not satisfied. That is not because reasonable belief is somehow self-explanatory. It is that we have a standing interest in following the dictates of reason. That interest explains why we do this when we do. In not following the dictates of reason we are not following that interest and hence we require an account specifying the interests that are affecting our judgment.

In explaining why someone holds a general belief by giving an account of his reasons for that belief we have to decide whether the belief was reasonable for him to hold in the context. We do not have to decide whether we in our context find the belief reasonable. Strong rationalists display an interest in deciding whether the beliefs of past scientists in methodological principles are in fact reasonable. For theirs is a normative model of science with principles of comparison which they argue are correct. I shall refer to any explanation of an action which involves a positive endorsement of the goal and/or beliefs cited as a *maxirat account*. This same label will be used of any explanation of why a belief is held that involves a positive endorsement of the content of a belief. I have argued that maxirat accounts are not needed in the explanation of scientific action nor in the explanation of why scientific beliefs of a theoretical character are held. However, there is something the explanation of which does require a maxirat account, and to that I turn.

The rationalist is impressed, indeed, one might say overly impressed, with the successes of contemporary science, particularly physics. Popper, Lakatos and Laudan, unlike Bloor, see the historically generated sequence of theories as progressive. Each has his own conception of progress and each has his own theory about the marks of progress, but progress there is indeed, or so they would claim. For Popper and Lakatos this is not so much argued for as taken as a basic datum to be accounted for. Lakatos holds that there is growth of scientific knowledge and that agreement can be expected on certain spectacular cases of growth. The problem is to understand what gives rise to growth. They are too sanguine about this but, as I argued in Chapter IX, we can supplement their conviction with argument. For it is undeniable that the contemporary scientist is better able to predict and manipulate the world, and this fact is to be explained by reference to the increasing verisimilitude of theories. Not even Kuhn and Feyerabend deny the data which form a premise of this argument for progress, though Feyerabend is wont to remind us of the fact that past theories had some successes not replicated by current theories, and that there are other fun things to do besides predicting and manipulating the world. This phenomenon calls out for explanation, and an adequate explanation will involve the differential assessment of beliefs.

Differential assessment is, of course, involved in the recognition of the phenomenon to be explained. In setting up what is to be explained we are characterizing the contemporary scientists' belief system as containing more truth than that of their predecessors. We are not simply saying that they believe that they are better, we are concurring in this judgment and are asking how is it that they have managed it. The rationalist's answer is that there are certain general truths about what makes one theory likely to be better than another which the scientific community has discovered and on which it by and large acts. Bloor and Barnes fail to see the need to develop such an explanatory account because they fail to appreciate that there has been genuine progress and not mere change, as is evident in the following quotations from Barnes:[10]

> Progressive realism is one of the ideal accounts of scientific knowledge which has it moving towards something, in this case a description of the real existing mechanisms in the world. There are now several independent strands of work which imply that such theories are misconceived, and that all knowledge generation and cultural growth should be regarded as endlessly dynamic and susceptible to alteration just as is human activity itself, with every actual change or advance a matter of agreement and not necessity.

> The upshot of all this is that our current scientific models and mechanisms are likely to be seen at some future time as part of what is an endlessly unfolding chain of such mechanisms, constructed and eventually abandoned (or stripped of their ontological standing) as the activity of knowledge generation proceeds. Clearly

then our present theories should stand symmetrically with earlier scientific theories, and for that matter with any other.

Of course, the history of science is a history of flux. Of course, our current theories are doomed. Of course, in so far as truth (strictly speaking) is concerned all theories stand together. For they are all false. But admitting that the historical scene is a flux does not mean that nothing is preserved or that there is no progress. There is progress through flux, and it is this phenomenon which the rationalists wish to account for, and for the explanation of which we need differential assessment. The Einsteinians have captured more truth than the Newtonians, who had more truth than their predecessors. The only possible explanation of this fact is that they both held methodological beliefs of some truth-content and made their decisions on the basis of these beliefs and not because of sociological or psychological factors. Once we focus on the march towards truth this march seems a total mystery if either the scientists made their decisions on the basis of external factors (i.e., in the hope of pleasing the church) or if their belief systems (particularly as regards methodology) were entirely wrong-headed. You can explain why someone changed his mind by reconstructing his thought processes without assessing his beliefs. If, however, you want to explain why there was progress you cannot do so simply by appeal to belief. It will not do to say there was progress because they had certain beliefs. Those beliefs will explain progress only if it is shown that those beliefs were true or at least had some truth in them.

Bloor and Barnes advocate symmetry because they eschew differential assessment. Once one admits the importance of differential assessment, symmetry fails. To see this, suppose we have an historically generated sequence of theories which we see as progressive. In that case we shall look to their beliefs, expecting to find that these included beliefs about methodology which we can endorse as capturing something of the truth. No doubt we shall also look to sociology. For the full story will have to include an account of the growth of institutions in which these beliefs could be developed and put to work. However, part of the story, an essential and fundamental part, is the truth or approximate truth of certain of their beliefs. If on the other hand we see the series as not being progressive – let us suppose we see it as being monstrously regressive – then there are at least two possibilities. Either on examination it seems to us that their methodological beliefs are false, in which case the explanation of failure turns crucially on the falsity of the beliefs. It is not simply that they held these beliefs. It is that these beliefs are false that makes the explanation work. Or, if it turns out that the beliefs seem to us to be basically correct, sociology will come into its own. For in this case we shall expect to learn that, perhaps, the requisite social institutions did not grow up or some external factors distorted the decision-making processes. Perhaps they set aside their better judgments to please the church.

The rationalist has been confused. His primary interest is in explaining progress. To that end he needs to develop a normative model of theory appraisal (normative in the sense that he claims it embodies an account of what makes a theory good) and to show that the community of scientists made their decisions within frameworks that approximate it to some extent. He has failed to see that in explaining action and belief we do not need to indulge in differential assessment from our current perspective. This false belief leads him to hand over to the sociologist transitions which can be explained on minirat accounts of belief and action. Bloor and Barnes on the other hand, while aware that differential assessment is not required in the explanation of belief transition, fail to recognize that the explanation of progress requires a maxirat account. They fail to recognize the progressive character of scientific evolution and the fact that its explanation requires differential assessment; and consequently that there is a significant difference in the character of the explanation of progress and of mere change.

I have argued that if we wish to explain past scientific transitions we can do so by giving minirat accounts of the beliefs and actions of those involved. If both the goals and the general beliefs about what makes one theory better than another which were operative in determining the outcome were recognizably scientific, they were acting reasonably as scientists. Such explanations do not require us to endorse their comception of the goals and methods of science. However, if we want to explain why there was progress and not merely change we shall be led to attribute some degree of truth to their beliefs about the goals and methods of science. This latter activity involves us in positive endorsement in a way that the former does not. Unfortunately, in describing scientific transitions as rational there has been a tendency to run these two activities confusedly together. This conflation arises naturally from the fact that in talking of beliefs and actions as rational we sometimes mean that they were reasonable in the context and sometimes mean that they are what we would ourselves in our context regard as reasonable. This evaluative interest is irrelevant to the mere explanation of the belief or action. It is not irrelevant if our interest is in explaining how what we regard as success or progress has been achieved.

7 CAUSATION IN EDINBURGH

It has been argued that if we wish to explain the evolution of a belief system this can be done (at one level at least) through reconstructing the internal reasoning processes of the believers in question. So long as we wish to explain why they changed their minds and not why they were more successful after having changed their minds we can avoid differential assessment. Bloor and Barnes are not going to be happy with my style of explanation of beliefs and actions. For they wish to have explanations of this phenomenon in terms of causal laws linking the social and cognitive worlds. Bloor[11] talks of theories 'connecting public, objective forms of knowledge with social structure'. By knowledge, Bloor, the non-cognitivist that he is, means simply beliefs generally accepted within a social group. This is an interim state. The end goal is to obtain theories which would lead to corroborated predictions about the particular beliefs of particular individuals. When he poses the question: 'Why was there a methodological revolution in mathematics in the 1840s?' he is not looking for an answer that might run through the reasoning processes of the mathematicians of the time. Instead we are told this was a causal consequence of 'the introduction of centralized, bureaucratic appointments criteria' in Germany at the time.[12]

There are many problematic aspects to this programme concerning which Bloor and Barnes are cavalier. First, their notion of causality is Humean, at least to the extent that they take it that causes and effects must be separately identifiable. But can one identify social groups and social structures independently of identifying their belief systems? It is in many cases part of being a member of a social group that one shares or represents oneself as sharing a common set of beliefs. Specifying the structure of a group may require specifying certain of the group's defining beliefs. To be a member of a political party or church may, in part at least, involve accepting certain beliefs. In some cases, however, it might seem that we can identify the group either without reference to their beliefs or using only beliefs that we are not trying to explain. For instance, one might specify a group as the group of those who hold teaching and/or research posts and concern themselves with the study of bees. Even here the sort of question of interest to the sociologists of science generally requires a finer distinction of groups through reference to shared belief. For instance, for many years it has been the received opinion of those who do in fact study bees that they do little dances the role of which, it is said, is to indicate to other bees the location and volume of nectar. Recently this has been challenged by a group who believes that the bees either do not dance or that their dancing has nothing to do with the gathering of nectar. A description of this conflict requires a division between the establishment group and the dissident group, and this can only be specified in terms of their beliefs. I am not at this stage endeavouring to develop an *a priori* objection to the *SP*. My point is only that its supporters erroneously assume that the separate identification of social group and the belief system of the group is an unproblematic matter. In addition they assume without argument that all interesting causal relations operate from social conditions to belief system and not vice versa.

The response of Bloor and Barnes to these and related objections is to remind us of the dangers of laying down *a priori* the form of any legitimate scientific explanation. Not unreasonably, they wish to be given the opportunity to display the merits of their programme through its fruit. Unfortunately, sociology of knowledge is more often talked about than done. Bloor and Barnes have not come up with any precisely specified and testable putative covering laws linking the social and the cognitive. The stage they see as preliminary to this is to establish some general laws (not exceptionless) linking types of social pressure with types of intellectual strategy. So, for example, one might hope to discover a generalization of the form: in conditions C there will be a tendency for a paradigm change to take place.

Accepting this sort of causal generalization is no threat to a rationalist who seeks to explain scientific change by giving a minirat account in terms of internal factors. For he can easily concede that social factors having nothing to do with science can prompt members of the scientific community to reassess their current theoretical commitments. Perhaps if I see my social or political world falling apart, my confidence in everything including my theories may be eroded. Who knows? Why not? The rationalist can make this concession and thus open the way for an interesting sociology of knowledge, while maintaining that the explanation of the outcome of the process once set in motion is to be given by an internal account of the reasoning processes.

This sort of generalization, far from displacing the rationalist's internal accounts, merely heightens the significance of those accounts. For what we want explained is why the crisis in confidence issued in the particular paradigm it did and not another one. Let us suppose that Feuer[13] is right that no one would have been interested in listening to radically new ideas about space and time around 1905 if they had not become accustomed to radical new political ideas. That does not explain why it was Einstein's theory that triumphed. The explanation of that requires reference to the methodological principles upheld by the scientific community. There is always a space of possible theories, and a law of the form we are considering predicts only that there will be a change and not what the particular change will be. Thus we need to supplement it with an explanation of why one theory rather than another was selected from the space of theories (or rather why one of the publicly available theories was selected: i.e. why Einstein rather than Lorentz or Poincaré). This space of possible theories means that we need a rationalist waiting in the wings to take over from Bloor and Barnes once they have explained why there was to be some change or other.

Bloor and Barnes aspire to be Laplacian super-sociologists of knowledge in that they talk of finding causal predictive accounts of the generation of particular beliefs in particular individuals. The only way that this could be done would involve discovering correlations between types of social circumstance and types of theory where the types in question were so finely specified that when taken together with a specification of initial conditions (social and physical) they would entail that a particular theory would come to be believed. If we had such a theory, the deliberations of the actors might just be a sort of *epi-phenomenon* playing no real determining role in the outcome. But this possibility represents such an outlandish speculation that the rationalist can, for the moment, sleep easily at night. It is not going to happen in our time. One must bear in mind that the tighter the specification of the type of social conditions and the tighter the specification of the type of theory that will issue from those circumstances, the less possibility there will be of gaining evidence for the covering law through the discovery of confirming instantiations of the generalizations. The degree of precision required is such that we are most likely to have only one-off correlations, in which case there would be no reasons to think that these are causal rather than accidental. Note that if we had such laws we should have produced the ultimate theory-generating machine. For we could use them to articulate the details of theories by plugging in different initial conditions and deriving different theories. That this can be done is the sort of groundless metaphysical posturing that the naturalistic Edinburgh school so fiercely deride in their writings.

We do not have and are unlikely to have a general theory for the explanation of scientific change. The reason for this is quite simply that we do not possess any general theory for the explanation of human action (including belief). There is no successful theory for the human domain that can be applied to all action as, say, Newtonian mechanics can be applied to all systems of particles in a Newtonian world. Furthermore, there is nothing so special about transition in scientific activity or belief systems that suggests we could more easily develop a limited theoretical framework for the explanation of these as an easy special case of action and belief. If one wished to give programmatic advice to sociologists in view of the current state of human ignorance it would be to investigate those general conditions that assist and those that hinder the development of scientific theorizing. This more modest project is much more likely to bear some fruit than that of seeking covering laws linking the social and cognitive worlds so as to give real predictive power. One would not like to discourage investigations of why it is that we have certain general beliefs which are used in the evaluation of particular beliefs. But such an endeavour, one might reasonably conjecture, would take us outside the scope of either philosophy or sociology. Take, for instance, the question as to why we believe that collecting instances of generalization increases the probability that a generalization is true. A philosopher may explain this as a conceptual consequence of some general concept of what it is to have evidence. But that only prompts the question: why do we possess that concept rather than another? In the end it is probably only to be accounted for within some evolutionary framework in which the development and longevity of concepts is in part explained by reference to their utility in preserving our species.[14]

XI

TEMPERATE RATIONALISM

1 THE RATIONAL MODEL

How has the rationalist fared? Blooded, somewhat bowed and beaten into a form he himself may not easily recognize, he has none the less survived. From our discussions a viable perspective on the scientific enterprise has emerged. This, to be called *temperate rationalism*, is characterized in what follows. The original schematic characterization of a rational model involved the specification of two ingredients: a goal for the scientific enterprise and an account of the principles of comparison (a methodology) to be used to give guidance in making choices between rival theories. The rationalist, it was said, hoped to use his model to account for scientific change by showing that in the case of most scientific transitions from a theory T_1 to a theory T_2 the following conditions were satisfied. The scientific community had as its goal the goal specified in the model. Relative to the principles of comparison, T_2 was superior to T_1, given the evidence available at the time. The scientific community perceived this superiority, and that perception together with the goal was the motivating factor in bringing about the change of allegiance. Consequently, the rationalist regards the history of science as constituting, by and large, progress towards the goal. The main explanatory role is accorded to internal factors. External factors such as the social conditions of the times or the psychology of the individuals involved come in only when there is a deviation from the norms implicit in the rational model.

A would-be rationalist such as Popper, Lakatos or Laudan has to meet the following five challenges in order to vindicate his model. First, he has to solve the problem of incommensurability. That is, he has to meet the arguments of Kuhn and Feyerabend which purport to show that in the case of major theoretical change theories simply cannot be compared due to radical meaning variance of the terms in the theories. Second, the rationalist has to vindicate his claim about the goal of science. Having vindicated his goal he has to show, third, that the principles of comparison are in fact a means to that goal. Fourth, given his view of science as progressive, the rationalist has to establish not only that following his methodology will in the future bring progress but also that there has been progress in the past. Finally, the rationalist has to display that there has been an appropriate fit between the actual history of science and the reconstruction of history generated using his model. This means showing that progress came about because the choices were made with the guidance of the posited methodology, and that sociological or psychological factors played for the most part only an ancillary role.

2 TEMPERATE RATIONALISM

It was shown in Chapter VII that the alleged argument for incommensurability poses no threat to a rationalist account of science. These arguments presuppose an untenable holistic conception of the meaning of scientific terms. In addition an undue attention has been placed on questions of meaning to the exclusion of questions of reference and truth. By reversing this tendency and by vindicating a non-holistic causal-realist theory of meaning we were able to show how theories can be brought into comparison even across paradigm shifts.

The more minimal one makes the goal of science, the easier it is to vindicate the claim that there has been progress in science. For instance, if the goal were nothing more than the improvement of the predicative power of theories, as the instrumentalist would have us believe, it would be uncontentious to claim that there had been progress. For all parties to the rationality debate agree that there has been a dramatic improvement at the level of observational success. However, as was argued in Chapter II, the fact that we want not only to predict but also to explain means that our goal in science is truth-related. It cannot be truth *per se* if science is rational. For the pessimistic induction gives us good reason to think that we shall never hit upon powerful theories that are strictly speaking true. The solution to this problem is to recognize with Popper and Lakatos that we aim at theories of ever-increasing verisimilitude. It has to be conceded that no fully satisfactory analysis of the notion of verisimilitude has yet been provided. Even if one finds the preliminary sketch of a theory of verisimilitude offered in Chapter VIII totally wrong-headed, one should not conclude that that notion has no legitimate place to play in a theory of science. This would be as absurd as arguing that logicians ought not to have used the concept of truth in their theories of logic prior to Tarski. We should, in fact, adopt the hypothesis that there has been progress towards greater verisimilitude in science because that hypothesis provides the best explanation of the increase in predictive and manipulative powers provided by science. This conclusion was reinforced by exposing the deficiencies in Laudan's attempt to make the goal of science that of increasing problem-solving capacity. It was seen that his model is totally untenable unless the notions of truth and verisimilitude are introduced. And, interestingly, the crucial problem in the analysis of verisimilitude was found to recur in the analysis of the notion of problem-solving capacity. Thus we should conclude that the prospects are dim for a successful account of science which does not make the goal that of increasing verisimilitude. A rationalist who takes this as the goal meets the third challenge outlined above by showing the explanatory power of the hypothesis that there has been an increase in verisimilitude.

I have discussed the thesis that there is progress in science without as yet having considered the question of the vindication of the principles of comparison, even though I placed this question before that of progress in my listing of challenges to the would-be rationalist. The reason for doing so reveals an important difference between my position and that of Popper and Lakatos. They articulate their methodology and then raise the question of progress. As we saw in Chapters III and IV, Popper with his total rejection of induction and Lakatos with his reluctance to employ induction are unable to forge a link between their methodologies and the goal they posit for science. They provide us with no reason to think that following the method as they articulate it is a means likely to take us towards the goal. A much more promising approach is to argue from progress to the viability of a methodology. Scientists in choosing between theories do not act capriciously. They deliberate and in a dialectical process of discussion they offer reasons for their choice. Given that there has been progress, we have reason to think that the procedures they follow are by and large evidential. That is, in general at least, the considerations that motivate them in selecting theories are fallible indicators of verisimilitude. Consequently the vindication of a methodology should be sought by displaying that that methodology has been operative in bringing about progress. In practice Lakatos does operate in this way, though he never provides a satisfactory rationale for so doing. And it is unlikely he would have accepted my rationale, involving as it does very high-level inductivist argumentation.

The answer to those who, like Feyerabend, deny the existence of scientific method (*SM*) is quite simply that the special fruits of science (the production of which he himself acknowledges) indicate that there is something special about *SM*. If you want to make scientific progress you cannot do just anything. To put this point starkly: lazing in the sun reading astrology is highly unlikely to lead to the invention of a predictively powerful theory about the constituents of the quark. Even if one did hit upon such a theory in this pleasant manner (the sun at least, if not the astrology, giving pleasure), one certainly could not come to know that one had done so. To discover this one has to do the sort of thing that scientists standardly do (i.e., leave the beach for the laboratory). In saying that there is something special about *SM* one is not implying that there is some verbally specifiable exhaustive set of binding algorithmic rules the application of which is bound to bring success. I focused on just one aspect of *SM*: namely, the factors relevant to theory choice. Those listed in Chapter IX, which are abstracted from successful scientific practice, provide nothing more than loose general guiding maxims. But that is not to say (*pace* Feyerabend) that they are without content. For the temperate rationalist they have force because they define the current parameters of scientific debate.

The notion of a rational model as characterized in Chapter I represents the methodology of science as static. This is in keeping with the views of Popper, Lakatos and Laudan, none of whom does justice to the fact that methodology, like science itself, evolves. The change in methodology to which attention was drawn in Chapter IX means that our rational model of science must be dynamic. Instead of a single model we require a sequence of models each of which represents the principles of comparison operative during a period of time. A further element of dynamism would come in if one thought, as I do not, that there has been an evolution in the goals of science. If method changes we need a model which represents that process. The framework for such a model was provided by the distinction between the ultimate test for the superiority of one theory over another and the factors which govern theory choice before the results of that test are in. The ultimate test in terms of long-range predictive success controls the evolution of the other factors through a feed-back mechanism. Long-range success in science is rightly taken as reinforcing our faith in the factors. Failure to make progress leads us not just to try different theories, but also to investigate the effects of altering the list of controlling factors. In the long run we can hope, not unreasonably, to improve our beliefs about the world by improving the ways we come to decide between theories. Temperate rationalism represents this process by offering a dynamic theory of science.

The introduction of a dynamical factor into our theory of science is not the only difference between temperate rationalism and the rationalism of Popper, Lakatos and Laudan. In their accounts no reference is made to the role of judgment. No doubt they feel that to include this element would introduce, in some objectionable sense, a subjective element. However, as we saw in Chapter IX, *SM* cannot be exhaustively specified in some articulated system of rules, if for no other reason but that there are cases in which the rules conflict. Consequently, the scientist has to exercise judgment concerning the relative weight to be attached to the conflicting rules. The success of a wine blender gives us reason to have faith in his judgment. So too the success of the institution of science gives us reason to have faith in the faculty of judgment, the exercise of which lies at the very heart of *SM*. That something is a matter of judgment in this sense has as a consequence the fact that there can be disagreements without a technique being available at the time to resolve them. If our wine blenders disagree we have to wait and see whose blend matures into the better wine. If scientists disagree in matters of judgment similarly we have to play a waiting game. Unless we recognize this point (rightly stressed by Kuhn) we shall be unable to explain the existence and longevity of controversies between scientists who had the same evidence available. Thus a temperate rationalism accords an important role to judgment in its account of *SM*.

3 THE TEMPERATE RATIONALIST AT WORK

The rationalist approach to the explanation of scientific change has been found to be seriously deficient. In characterizing the temperate rationalist's position it will be helpful to review briefly some aspects of our general discussion of rationality. To give a rational explanation of an action $\emptyset$ done by A is to show that on the basis of A's beliefs A did what he thought was most likely to realize his goals. In this minimal sense of rationality, the vast majority of human actions are rational. In talking of scientific rationality we are using a more restricted notion of rationality which requires for an action to be rational that, first, the goal in question be scientific. For instance, if a scientist chooses to work on one theory rather than another because that will please the Vatican he is not reaching the standards of scientific rationality. Second, given that a scientist's goal is to work on the best theory available, scientific rationality requires that he have good, scientifically respectable reasons for thinking that the theory for which he opts is the better theory. He has failed to live up to this aspect of rationality if he believes the theory to be the best because mother told him so after asking her Ouija board. To claim that a particular rational model can be used to explain a particular transition in the history of science is to claim that by and large the members of the community had as their goal the goal posited by the model, and that they made their judgments as to which theory was the best by reference to the principles of comparison specified in the model. It is not enough to show merely that the transition fits the model in the sense that relative to the model the best theory triumphed. We have to show that the model encapsulates the goals and methodology of those concerned in the transition.

Given that there is evolution in method, we cannot necessarily use our current normative account of the facts that now govern scientific practice in explaining past transitions. We shall have to uncover, for each period of history, the conception of the good-making features of theories which were then operative. A temperate rationalist will thus work with an evolving series of models in giving rational accounts of scientific activity. Consequently, unlike Lakatos and Laudan, he will not turn over for sociological treatment a past episode in the history of science just because it fails to fit an evaluation made on the basis of our current conception of methodology. In fact, he will not demarcate *a priori* any particular province for the sociologist of science. If an individual scientist or a scientific community is found to be acting on non-scientific motives, he will seek a sociological account of why this should have happened. But equally he will require a sociological account of why it is that there are individuals and communities which adopt as one of their goals, the goal of science. If the temperate rationalist finds that the real reason why a scientist believes that one theory is better than another is not that he has good reasons (on his own terms), but that believing this serves some non-scientific interest, he will seek a sociological explanation. But, equally, if he finds that scientists are following the dictates of reason in formulating their beliefs, he will seek an explanation in terms of interests as to why they follow the dictates of reason. As was suggested in Chapter X, this may be accounted for simply in terms of the fact that we have a general interest in following the dictates of reason because it is an evolutionarily successful strategy.

A temperate rationalist, then, does not turn over an episode for external treatment by the cognitive sociologist of science just because it is not 'rational' as judged by our current conception of *SM*. Whether episodes are properly described as being scientifically rational depends on the conception of *SM* operative at the time. Even if an episode is rational in this sense, sociological explanation is not ruled out. For we require an account in terms of external factors as to why a conception of *SM* should have arisen and why individuals or groups had an interest in acting under that conception.

Rationalists such as Lakatos and Laudan have been keen to appraise the activities of past scientists by reference to their (Lakatos's and Laudan's) static model of *SM*. But, as we have seen, judgments of the rightness or wrongness of past scientists made from our contemporary vantage point are irrelevant to the explanation of their activities and to the question of whether they were being scientifically rational. However, such assessment has a role to play if we are interested in the question of progress as opposed to mere change. For instance, there was progress in physics in the nineteenth century. We should therefore expect to find that the conception of *SM* then operative had some truth in it. Consequently, it is of interest to appraise it normatively in terms of our current conceptions. If we were to find that relative to our current conception of how to do science, their conception was totally wrongheaded, we should be faced with a major puzzle. Unless we are able to explain how it is that they made progress while operating under what we regard as a mistaken conception of method, we ought to re-examine the description we have made of the current state of *SM*. The temperate rationalist allows for an evolution in *SM*. He sees science as progressively capturing more truth about the world, a process accompanied by an enriched and improved conception of *SM*. Consequently, he expects a normative assessment of past conceptions of *SM*, judged by our current lights, to reveal this. Normative appraisal is of interest to him not because it is part and parcel of the explanation of scientific change, but because of its relevance to his general picture of progress both in theories and in methodology.

A distinction was drawn in Chapter I between exciting and boring attacks on the rationalist perspective on the scientific enterprise. Exciting attacks purport to show that rationalism is flawed at the very core on the grounds, for example, that theories are incommensurable. Boring attacks have the more modest goal of showing that the institution of science fails, more often than its practitioners would like to think, to live up to its own standards of rationality. If my defence of temperate rationalism has been successful, the exciting attacks have failed. The success of the boring attacks should be conceded without further ado. We know enough about the complexity of human motivation to reject any picture of the scientific community as a collection of disembodied Cartesian egos freed of any motive except the pursuit of truth, and equipped for that with the divine light of *SM*, which they apply without the distorting effects of other interests. Boring attacks become interesting when they provide the fine detail of how particular non-scientific interests had distorted particular scientific activities. The temperate rationalist looks with interest on such studies. However, he holds that the marked progress in science indicates that there is a sufficiently strong interest in the rational pursuit of the goals of science to keep such distortions the exception rather than the rule. But, unlike the rationalist, he is interested in explaining in terms of non-scientific interests why the rational pursuit of science should have become a human interest.

Oscar Wilde has a character respond to the demand for the truth 'pure and simple': 'The truth is rarely pure and never simple.' Popper ('conjecture and refute') and Feyerabend ('anything goes') have the charm of simplicity if not purity. But the truth about the nature of science is not simple and scientists are not purely rational nor purely non-rational. Still, if one wants a slogan: realism is the truth and temperate rationalism the way.

NOTES

I THE RATIONAL IMAGE

1 Popper (1963), p. 216.
2 Reichenbach (1959), p. vii.
3 *Ibid.*, p. 305.
4 Feyerabend (1975), p. 307.
5 For a discussion of this particular controversy from a rationalist persective see J. Worrall's 'Thomas Young and the "refutation" of Newtonian optics: a case study in the interaction of philosophy of science and history of science', in Howson (1976).
6 Zahar (1973).
7 Feuer (1974), Ch. 1.
8 Feyerabend (1975), p. 55 and (1978), p. 70.
9 Kuhn (1970), p. 102.
10 *Ibid.*, p. 150.
11 Feyerabend (1975), p. 55 and (1978), p. 70.
12 See in this regard Suppe (1977), Ch. I-VI and Afterword.
13 See in this regard Feyerabend (1978), p. 67.
14 See Laudan (1977), *passim.*

II OBSERVATION, THEORY AND TRUTH

1 Carnap in Feigl and Brodbeck (1953), pp. 63–4.
2 Hempel (1965), p. 179.
3 For an example of such a version of correspondence theory of truth see Davidson (1969).
4 Rosen (1959), pp. 24–5.
5 Hesse, in Edwards (1967), p. 407.
6 Quinton (1973), p. 288.
7 Pap (1963), p. 355.

8 Hesse, in Edwards (1967), p. 407.
9 See Newton-Smith (1980) for a critical discussion of this treatment of instants.
10 Newton-Smith (1978).
11 *Ibid.*

III POPPER – THE IRRATIONAL RATIONALIST

1 Popper (1972), p. 319.
2 *Ibid.*, p. 40.
3 *Ibid.*, p. 191.
4 Schlipp (1974), p. 1105.
5 Popper (1963), p. 387.
6 *Ibid.*, p. 388.
7 Popper (1968), Appendix vii.
8 Hesse (1974), ch. 8.
9 *Ibid.*, ch. 8.
10 See A. Shimony, 'Scientific Inference', in Colodny (1970).
11 Popper (1963), p. 54.
12 *Ibid.*, pp. 54–5.
13 Popper (1972), p. 319.
14 *Ibid.*, p. 52.
15 Miller (1974), pp. 170–2.
16 Tichy (1974), pp. 156–7.
17 Popper (1972), p. 18.
18 *Ibid.*, pp. 18–19.
19 Popper (1968), pp. 108–9.
20 *Ibid.*, p. 111.
21 Schlipp (1974), p. 1111.
22 Feyerabend and Maxwell (1966), pp. 343–53.
23 Popper (1972), p. 53.
24 Schlipp (1974), pp. 1192–3.
25 Popper (1972), p. 103.
26 Schlipp (1974), p. 32.
27 *Ibid.*, p. 986.
28 Popper (1963), p. 38, n. 3.

IV IN SEARCH OF THE METHODOLOGIST'S STONE

1 I am extremely grateful to John Worrall for helpful and detailed comments on an earlier version of this chapter.
2 Hacking (1979), passim.
3 Lakatos (1978a), p. 31.
4 *Ibid.*, p. 32.
5 On this non-standard usage McMullin has commented that 'one wonders whether the term "falsification" is used other than as a

gesture of piety to the [Popperian] tradition';Cohen (1976),p. 412.
6   Lakatos (1978a), p. 48.
7   *Ibid.*, p. 50.
8   *Ibid.*, p. 50.
9   *Ibid.*, p. 168.
10 *Ibid.*, p. 112.
11 *Ibid.*, p. 48.
12 *Ibid.*, p. 48.
13 *Ibid.*, p. 110.
14 Popper (1968), p. 109.
15 Lakatos (1978a), p. 110.
16 Everett (1976).
17 Lakatos (1978a), p. 88.
18 *Ibid.*, pp. 110–11.
19 Howson (1976), pp. 238–9.
20 *Ibid.*, pp. 110–11.
21 Newton-Smith (1980), ch. 2.
22 Lakatos (1978a), p. 77, n. 2.
23 *Ibid.*, p. 50.
24 *Ibid.*, p. 51.
25 *Ibid.*, p. 110.
26 Zahar (1973), pp. 101–4.
27 Lakatos (1978a), p. 185.
28 *Ibid.*, p. 5.
29 *Ibid.*, p. 88.
30 *Ibid.*, p. 1.
31 *Ibid.*, pp. 89–90.
32 *Ibid.*, p. 117.
33 *Ibid.*, p. 117. See also Clarke in Howson (1976), pp. 43–4.
34 *Ibid.*, p. 102.
35 *Ibid.*, p. 122.
36 *Ibid.*, p. 133.
37 *Ibid.*, p. 133.
38 Howson (1976), p. 167.
39 *Ibid.*, pp. 164–5.
40 Lakatos (1978b), p. 191.
41 *Ibid.*, p. 187.
42 Hacking (1979).
43 *Ibid.*, p. 386.
44 Lakatos (1978a), p. 100.
45 Lakatos (1978a), p. 113.

V T. S. KUHN: FROM REVOLUTIONARY TO SOCIAL DEMOCRAT

1   Masterman in Lakatos and Musgrave (1970), pp. 59–90.
2   Shapere (1964), pp. 3–16.
3   Kuhn (1970), p. 182.

4 See Kuhn (1970) and (1977), and his papers in Lakatos and Musgrave (1970) and in Suppe (1974).
5 Kuhn (1977), p. 297.
6 *Ibid.*, p. 299.
7 Kuhn (1970), p. 184.
8 Kuhn in Suppe (1974), p. 482.
9 *Ibid.*, p. 482.
10 *Ibid.*, p. 517.
11 Kuhn (1970), p. 43.
12 Kuhn (1978).
13 Lakatos and Musgrave (1970), p. 5.
14 Kuhn (1970), p. 94.
15 *Ibid.*, p. 102.
16 *Ibid.*, pp. 198–9.
17 *Ibid.*, p. 104.
18 *Ibid.*, p. 105.
19 *Ibid.*, p. 110.
20 Kuhn (1977), pp. 321–22.
21 *Ibid.*, p. 322.
22 *Ibid.*, p. 324.
23 Kuhn (1970), p. 152.
24 Kuhn (1977), p. 335.
25 *Ibid.*, p. 335.
26 See in this regard Newton-Smith (1978).
27 Kuhn (1970), p. 170.
28 Lakatos in Lakatos and Musgrave (1970), p. 178.
29 Kuhn (1977), pp. 330–1.
30 Kuhn (1970), ch. 10.
31 See in this regard Eddington in Gardner (1957), pp. 243–62.
32 Kuhn (1970), p. 110.
33 *Ibid.*, p. 115.
34 *Ibid.*, pp. 115–16.
35 *Ibid.*, p. 110.
36 *Ibid.*, p. 150.
37 See in this regard Suppe (1977), p. 473, n. 18.
38 Kuhn (1970), p. 150.
39 Laudan (1977), *passim*.
40 Kuhn (1970), p. 171.
41 *Ibid.*, p. 206. See also Kuhn in Lakatos and Musgrave (1970), p. 265.
42 Kuhn in Lakatos and Musgrave (1970), p. 21.
43 Kuhn (1970), p. 69.
44 Kuhn in Lakatos and Musgrave (1970), p. 235.
45 Kuhn (1970), p. 206.
46 Kuhn in Lakatos and Musgrave (1970), p. 20.
47 Kuhn (1977), pp. 324–5.

VI FEYERABEND, THE PASSIONATE LIBERAL

1 Feyerabend (1975). The position advanced there is developed and clarified in Feyerabend (1978).
2 Feigl (1970), p. 4.
3 Feyerabend (1975), p. 23.
4 Feyerabend (1978), p. 128.
5 *Ibid.*, pp. 67–8.
6 *Ibid.*, p. 68.
7 *Ibid.*, p. 69.
8 Feyerabend (1975), p. 295.
9 Feyerabend (1978), pp. 210–11.
10 Feyerabend (1975), p. 23.
11 Russell (1959), p. 63.
12 Feyerabend (1975), p. 29.
13 *Ibid.*, p. 35.
14 *Ibid.*, p. 36.
15 Everett (1976).
16 Feyerabend (1975), p. 38.
17 *Ibid.*, p. 38.
18 *Ibid.*, p. 46.
19 Mill (1972), ch. 2, passim.
20 *Ibid.*, p. 96.
21 *Ibid.*, p. 111.
22 *Ibid.*, p. 82.
23 Feyerabend notes that a defence of his position is found in Mill. See Feyerabend (1975), p. 48, n. 2; (1975), p. 53; (1978), p. 86.
24 Feyerabend (1978), p. 145.
25 Feyerabend (1975), p. 155.
26 *Ibid.*, p. 27.
27 *Ibid.*, pp. 30–1.
28 *Ibid.*, p. 67.
29 Mill (1972), p. 82.
30 Feyerabend (1975), p. 68.
31 *Ibid.*, p. 67.
32 *Ibid.*, p. 69.
33 *Ibid.*, p. 83.
34 *Ibid.*, p. 99.
35 Feyerabend (1978), p. 65.
36 Feyerabend (1975), p. 284.
37 *Ibid.*, p. 269.
38 *Ibid.*, p. 270.
39 *Ibid.*, p. 271.
40 *Ibid.*, p. 284.
41 *Ibid.*, p. 284–5.
42 Feyerabend (1978), p. 9.
43 Feyerabend (1975), p. 302.
44 Feyerabend (1978), p. 101.

45 *Ibid.*, p. 100.
46 *Ibid.*, p. 102.
47 *Ibid.*, p. 102.
48 *Ibid.*, p. 105.
49 Feyerabend (1975), p. 21, n.

VII THEORIES ARE INCOMMENSURABLE?

1   Kuhn (1970), p. 103.
2   *Ibid.*, pp. 199–200.
3   Kordig (1971), ch. 2.
4   Hempel (1965), p. 183.
5   See in this regard Przelecki (1969), ch. 7.
6   For instance, see Przelecki (1969). Carnap, noting that his 'reduction pair' sentences were not analytic, modified them to achieve analyticity. See English (1978), p. 60.
7   Quine (1961), pp. 20–46.
8   Carnap (1956), pp. 50–1.
9   For a detailed comparison of Kuhn and Carnap on meaning change, see English (1978).
10 Schlipp (1964), pp. 964–5.
11 Quine (1970).
12 Kuhn (1970), p. 198.
13 Kordig (1971), ch. 3.
14 *Ibid.*, p. 58.
15 Kuhn (1970), p. 102.
16 Davidson (1973), p. 324.
17 Hesse (1974), p. 60.
18 Putnam (1975b), p. 200.
19 Quoted in Achinstein (1968), p. 107.
20 *Ibid.*, p. 108.
21 Halliday and Resnick (1960), p. 556.
22 Putnam (1975b), p. 231.
23 Fine (1975).
24 Mach (1960), p. 589.
25 Kitcher (1978).
26 Field (1973), p. 477.
27 Earman and Fine (1977), pp. 535–8.
28 Field (1973), p. 477.
29 Quine (1969), ch. 1.
30 Quine (1975).
31 *Ibid.*, pp. 327–8.

VIII THE THESIS OF VERISIMILITUDE

1   Laudan (1977), p. 125.
2   Laudan talks of 'weakening our notions of rationality and progress' so that we can 'decide whether science is rational and progressive', Laudan (1977), p. 127.
3   Lenin (1938), vol. 13, p. 137.
4   Feyerabend (1975), p. 230.
5   *Ibid.*, p. 180.
6   Laudan (1977), p. 127.
7   *Ibid.*, p. 25.
8   *Ibid.*, p. 68.
9   *Ibid.*, p. 16.
10 *Ibid.*, p. 49.
11 *Ibid.*, p. 126.
12 *Ibid.*, p. 16.
13 This caveat would be required if one adopted, for instance, the account of counter-factuals favoured by J. Mackie in his 'Conditionals' (Mackie, 1973).
14 Laudan (1977), p. 16.
15 *Ibid.*, p. 15.
16 *Ibid.*, p. 14.
17 *Ibid.*, p. 109.
18 *Ibid.*, p. 68.
19 See Newton-Smith (1978).
20 In reply to an earlier version of this argument presented at the University of Aarhus, Denmark, in August 1978.
21 Sklar (1974), *passim*.
22 Harman (1973), pp. 130–5.
23 This argument is in the wind. One finds hints of it in Popper's notorious 'whiff of induction' footnote, and Putnam attributes a version of it to Boyd. See Putnam (1978), p. 21.
24 Laudan (1977), pp. 125–6.

IX SCIENTIFIC METHOD

1   Whewell (1857), p. 4.
2   Mill (1868), vol. 3 and vol. 4.
3   Dummett (1977).
4   Medawar (1980).
5   Locke (1961), vol.II, pp. 151–2.
6   Butler (1856), pp. 4–5.
7   Peirce (1932), p. 500.
8   Carnap (1950).
9   Swinburne (1973), p. 4.
10 Cohen (1970), ch. 1.
11 Newton-Smith (1980).

12 McMullin in conversation. See also his 'Philosophy of Science and its Rational Reconstructions' in Radnitzky and Andersson (1978).
13 Lakatos (1976).
14 Planck (1949).
15 Planck (1922).

X STRONG PROGRAMMES

1   Laudan (1977), p. 222.
2   *Ibid.*, p. 222.
3   *Ibid.*, pp. 188-9.
4   Lakatos (1978a), p. 134.
5   Bloor (1976), pp. 4-5.
6   Barnes (1974), p. 154; Bloor (1976), pp. 2-3.
7   Barnes (1977), p. 25.
8   *Ibid.*, p. 23.
9   Bloor (1979), p. 2.
10 Barnes (1977), p. 24.
11 Bloor (1978), p. 261.
12 *Ibid.*, p. 264.
13 Feuer (1974).
14 I am grateful to Dr Per Strømholm for suggesting the labels 'minirat' and 'maxirat'.

BIBLIOGRAPHY

Achinstein, P. (1968), *Concepts of Science* (Baltimore: Johns Hopkins University Press).

Ackermann, R. J. (1976), *The Philosophy of Karl Popper* (Amherst: University of Massachusetts Press).

Barnes, B. (1974), *Scientific Knowledge and Sociological Theory* (London: Routledge & Kegan Paul).

Barnes, B. (1977), *Interests and the Growth of Knowledge* (London: Routledge & Kegan Paul).

Benn, S. I. and Mortimore, G. W. (1976), *Rationality and the Social Sciences* (London: Routledge & Kegan Paul).

Bernstein, R. J. (1976), *The Restructuring of Social and Political Theory* (University of Philadelphia Press).

Bloor, D. (1976), *Knowledge and Social Imagery* (London: Routledge & Kegan Paul).

Bloor, D. (1978), 'Polyhedra and the Abominations of Leviticus', *British Journal for the History of Science* 39, pp. 245–72.

Bloor, D. (1979), 'Notes on Martin Hollis's paper "The Social Destruction of Reality" ' (unpublished paper).

Bloor, D. (1981), 'Durkheim and Mauss Revisited: Classification and the Sociology of Knowledge', in *The Language of Sociology* (forthcoming), ed. J. Law.

Boolos, G. S. and Jeffrey, R. C. (1974), *Computability and Logic* (Cambridge University Press).

Burian, R. M. (1977), 'More than a Marriage of Convenience: On the Inextricability of History and Philosophy of Science', *Philosophy of Science* 44, pp. 1–42.

Butler, J. (1856), *The Analogy of Religion* (London: The Religious Tract Society).

Carnap, R. (1950), *Logical Foundations of Probability* (University of Chicago Press).

Bibliography

Carnap, R. (1953), 'Testability and Meaning', in *Readings in the Philosophy of Science* (New York: Appleton-Century-Crofts) ed. H. Feigl and M. Brodbeck, pp. 47–92.

Carnap, R. (1956), 'The Methodological Character of Theoretical Concepts', in *Minnesota Studies in the Philosophy of Science*, vol. 1 (Minneapolis: University of Minnesota Press), pp. 38–76, ed. H. Feigl and M. Scriven.

Churchland, P. M. (1979), *Scientific Realism and the Plasticity of Mind* (Cambridge University Press).

Clark, R. W. (1973), *Einstein* (London: Hodder and Stoughton).

Cohen, L. J. (1970), *The Implications of Induction* (London: Methuen).

Cohen, R. S. et al. (eds) (1976), *Essays in the Memory of Imre Lakatos* (Dordrecht: Reidel).

Colodny, R. G. (ed.) (1970), *The Nature and Function of Scientific Theories* (University of Pittsburgh Press).

Davidson, D. (1969), 'True to the Facts', *Journal of Philosophy* 66, pp. 748–64.

Davidson, D. (1973), 'Radical Interpretation', *Dialectica*, pp. 27, 313–27.

Dummett, M. (1977), *Elements of Intuitionism* (London: Oxford University Press).

Earman, J. and Fine, A. (1977), 'Against Indeterminacy', *Journal of Philosophy* LXXIV, pp. 535–8.

Edwards, P. (ed.) (1967), *The Encyclopaedia of Philosophy* (New York: The Macmillan Company and The Free Press).

Enderton, H. B. (1972), *A Mathematical Introduction to Logic* (New York: Academic Press).

English, J. (1978), 'Meaning and Partial Interpretation', *Journal of Philosophy* LXXV, pp. 57–76.

Everett, A. E. (1976), 'Tachyous, broken Lorentz invariance, and a penetrable light barrier', *Physical Review* 13, pp. 785–94.

Feigl, H. (1970), 'The Orthodox View of Theories', in *Analyses of Theories and Methods of Physics and Psychology* (Minneapolis: University of Minnesota Press), ed. M. Radner and S. Winokur, pp. 000–000.

Feigl, H. and Brodbeck, M. (eds) (1953), *Readings in the Philosophy of Science* (New York: Appleton-Century-Crofts).

Feuer, L. S. (1974), *Einstein and the Generations of Science* (New York: Basic Books).

Feyerabend, P. K. (1962), 'Explanation, Reduction and Empiricism', in *Minnesota Studies in the Philosophy of Science*, vol. III (Minneapolis: University of Minnesota Press), ed. H. Feigl and G. Maxwell, pp. 28–97.

Feyerabend, P. K. (1975), *Against Method* (London: New Left Books).

Feyerabend, P. K. (1977), 'Changing Patterns of Reconstruction: review of W. Stegmüller: Theorienstrukturen und Theoriendynamik', *British Journal for the Philosophy of Science* 28, pp. 351–69.

Feyerabend, P. K. (1978), *Science in a Free Society* (London: New Left Books).

Feyerabend, P. K. and Maxwell, G. (eds) (1966), *Mind, Matter and Method: Essays in Philosophy and Science in Honour of Herbert Feigl* (Oxford University Press).

Field, H. (1973), 'Theory Change and the Indeterminacy of Reference', *Journal of Philosophy* 70, pp. 462–81.

Fine, A. (1975), 'How to Compare Theories: Reference and Change', *Nous* 9, pp. 17–32.

Friedman, M. (1979), 'Truth and Confirmation', *Journal of Philosophy* 76, pp. 361–81.

Gardner, M. (ed.) (1957), *Great Essays in Science* (New York: Pocket Books).

Gardner, M. R. (1979), 'Realism and Instrumentalism in the 19th Century Atomism', *Philosophy of Science* 46, pp. 1–34.

Grünbaum, A. (1976a), 'Is the Method of Bold Conjecture and Attempted Refutations Justifiably the Method of Science?' *British Journal for the Philosophy of Science* 27, pp. 105–36.

Grünbaum, A. (1976b), 'Ad Hoc Auxiliary Hypotheses and Falsificationism', *British Journal for the Philosophy of Science* 27, pp. 329–62.

Hacking, I. (1975), *The Emergence of Probability* (Cambridge University Press).

Hacking, I. (1979), 'Imre Lakatos's Philosophy of Science', *British Journal for the Philosophy of Science* 30, pp. 381–402.

Halliday, D. and Resnick, R. (1960), *Physics* (New York: J. Wiley and Sons).

Harman, G. (1973), *Thought* (Princeton University Press).

Harré, R. (1970), *The Principles of Scientific Thinking* (London: Macmillan).

Hempel, C. G. (1965), *Aspects of Scientific Explanation* (New York: Macmillan).

Hesse, M. (1974), *The Structures of Scientific Inference* (London: Macmillan).

Hookway, C. and Pettit, P. (1978), *Action and Interpretation* (Cambridge University Press).

Horton, R. (1970), 'African Traditional Thought and Western Science', in *Rationality* (Oxford: Blackwell), ed. B. Wilson, pp. 131–71.

Howson, C. (ed.) (1976), *Method and Appraisal in the Physical Sciences* (Cambridge University Press).

Hunter, G. (1971), *Metalogic* (London: Macmillan).

Jeffery, R. C. (1965) *The Logic of Decision* (New York: McGraw-Hill).

Kitcher, P. (1978), 'Theories, Theorists and Theoretical Change', *Philosophical Review* LXXXVII, pp. 519–47.

Kordig, C. R. (1971), *The Justification of Scientific Change* (Dordrecht: Reidel).

Kuhn, T. S. (1970), *The Structure of Scientific Revolutions*, 2nd ed. (Chicago University Press).

Kuhn, T. S. (1977), *The Essential Tension* (Chicago University Press).

Kuhn, T. S. (1978), *Black-Body Theory and the Quantum Discontinuity* (Oxford University Press).

Kyburg, H. E. (1970), *Probability and Inductive Logic* (London: Collier-Macmillan).

Lakatos, I. (1976), *Proofs and Refutations* (Cambridge University Press), ed. J. Worrall and E. Zahar.

Lakatos, I. (1978a), *The Methodology of Scientific Research Programmes* (Cambridge University Press), ed. J. Worrall and G. Currie.

Lakatos, I. (1978b), *Mathematics, Science and Epistemology* (Cambridge University Press), ed. J. Worrall and G. Currie.

Lakatos, I. and Musgrave, A. (eds) (1970), *Criticism and the Growth of Knowledge* (Cambridge University Press).

Laudan, L. (1977), *Progress and its Problems* (Berkeley: University of California Press).

Lenin, V. I. (1938), *Collected Works*, vol. 13 (London: Martin Lawrence).

Locke, J. (1961), *An Essay Concerning Human Understanding* (London: J. M. Dent), vols I and II, ed. J. W. Yolton.

Mach, E. (1960), *The Science of Mechanics* (La Salle, Illinois: Open Court), trans., T. J. McCormick.

Mackie, J. (1973), *Truth, Probability and Paradox* (Oxford University Press).

Maxwell, G. (1962), 'The Ontological Status of Theoretical Entities', in *Minnesota Studies in the Philosophy of Science*, v. III (Minneapolis: University of Minnesota Press), ed. H. Feigl and G. Maxwell.

McMullin, E. (1978), 'Structural Explanation', *American Philosophical Quarterly* 15, pp. 139–47.

McMullin, E. (1980), 'How do scientific controversies end?' unpublished manuscripts.

Medawar, P. B. (1980), *Advice to a Young Scientist* (New York: Harper & Row).

Mill, J. S. (1868), *A System of Logic* (London: Longmans, Green, Reader & Dyer), vols I and II.

Mill, J. S. (1972), *Utilitarianism, On Liberty and Considerations on Representative Government* (London: J. M. Dent), ed. H. B. Acton.

Miller, D. (1974), 'Popper's Qualitative Theory of Verisimilitude', *British Journal for the Philosophy of Science* 25, pp. 178–88.

Nagel, E. (1961), *The Structure of Science* (London: Routledge & Kegan Paul).

Newton-Smith, W. H. (1978), 'The Underdetermination of Theory by Data', *Aristotelian Society* Supplementary Volume LII, pp. 71–91.

Newton-Smith, W. H. (1980), *The Structure of Time* (London: Routledge & Kegan Paul).

O'Hear, A. (1980), *Karl Popper* (London: Routledge & Kegan Paul).

Pap, A. (1963), *An Introduction to Philosophy of Science* (London: Eyre & Spottiswoode).

285

Bibliography

Peirce, C. S. (1932), *Collected Papers of Charles Sanders Peirce* vol. II (Cambridge, Mass.: Harvard University Press), ed. C. Hartshorne and P. Weiss.

Peirce, C. S. (1958), *Collected Papers of Charles Sanders Peirce*, vol. VII (Cambridge, Mass: Harvard University Press), ed. A. W. Burks.

Peirce, C. S. (1960), *Collected Papers of Charles Sanders Peirce*, vols V and VI (Cambridge, Mass.: Harvard University Press) ed. C. Hartshorne and P. Weiss.

Planck, M. K. (1922), *The Origin and Development of the Quantum Theory* (London: Oxford University Press).

Planck, M. K. (1949), *Scientific Autobiography and Other Papers* (New York: Philosophical Library), trans. F. Gaynor.

Popper, K. R. (1963), *Conjectures and Refutations* (London: Routledge & Kegan Paul).

Popper, K. R. (1966), 'A Theorem on Truth-Content', in *Mind, Matter and Method* (Minneapolis: University of Minnesota Press), ed. P. K. Feyerabend and G. Maxwell, pp. 343–53.

Popper, K. R. (1968), *The Logic of Scientific Discovery* (London: Hutchinson).

Popper, K. R. (1972), *Objective Knowledge* (London: Oxford University Press).

Przelecki, M. (1969), *The Logic of Empirical Theories* (London: Routledge & Kegan Paul).

Putnam, H. (1975a), *Mathematics, Matter and Method* (Cambridge University Press).

Putnam, H. (1975b), *Mind, Language and Reality* (Cambridge University Press).

Putnam, H. (1978) *Meaning and the Moral Sciences* (London: Routledge & Kegan Paul).

Quine, W. V. O. (1961), *From a Logical Point of View* (Cambridge, Mass.: Harvard University Press).

Quine, W. V. O. (1969), *Ontological Relativity and Other Essays* (New York: Columbia University Press).

Quine, W. V. O. (1970), 'On the Reasons for the Indeterminacy of Translation', *Journal of Philosophy* LXVII, pp. 178–83.

Quine, W. V. O. (1975), 'On Empirically Equivalent Systems of the World', *Erkenntnis* 9, pp. 313–28.

Quinton, A. (1973), *The Nature of Things* (London: Routledge & Kegan Paul).

Radnitzky, G. and Andersson, G. (eds) (1978), *Progress and Rationality in Science* (Dordrecht: Reidel).

Ramsey, F. P. (1931), *The Foundations of Mathematics* (London: Routledge & Kegan Paul; new edn 1978), ed. R. B. Braithwaite.

Reichenbach, H. (1959), *The Rise of Scientific Philosophy* (Berkeley: University of California Press).

Rescher, N. (1978), *Scientific Progress* (Oxford: Blackwell).

Rorty, R. (1980), *Philosophy and the Mirror of Nature* (Princeton University Press).

Rosen, E. (ed.) (1959), *Three Copernican Treatises* (New York: Dover).

Russell, B. (1959), *Problems of Philosophy* (New York: Oxford University Press).

Schaffner, K. F. (1970), 'A Logic of Comparative Theory Evaluation' in *Minnesota Studies in the Philosophy of Science* vol. V (Minneapolis: University of Minnesota Press) ed. R. Stuewer, pp. 311–53.

Schlipp, P. A. (ed.) (1964), *The Philosophy of Rudolf Carnap* (La Salle, Illinois: Open Court).

Schlipp, P. A. (ed.) (1974), *The Philosophy of Karl Popper*, Book I and Book II (La Salle, Illinois: Open Court).

Shapere, D. (1964), 'The Structure of Scientific Revolutions', *Philosophical Review* LXXIII, pp. 383–94.

Sklar, L. (1974), *Space, Time and Spacetime* (Berkeley: University of California Press).

Sneed, J. D. (1971), *The Logical Structure of Mathematical Physics* (Dordrecht: Reidel).

Suppe, F. (ed.) (1974), *The Structure of Scientific Theories* (Chicago: University of Illinois Press).

Swinburne, R. (1973), *An Introduction to Confirmation Theory* (London: Methuen).

Tichy, P. (1974), 'On Popper's Definition of Verisimilitude', *British Journal for the Philosophy of Science* 25, pp. 155–60.

Toulmin, S. (1972), *Human Understanding* (London: Oxford University Press).

Whewell, W. (1847), *The Philosophy of the Inductive Sciences* (London: John W. Parker).

Whewell, W. (1857), *History of the Inductive Sciences* (London: John W. Parker).

Wilson, B. R. (ed.) (1974), *Rationality* (Oxford: Blackwell).

Zahar, E. G. (1973), 'Why did Einstein's Programme Supersede Lorentz's?', *British Journal for the Philosophy of Science* 24, pp. 95–123 and pp. 233–62.

INDEX

289

Index